T0202851

Lecture Notes in Computer Science　13482

More information about this series at https://link.springer.com/bookseries/558

Regina Bernhaupt · Carmelo Ardito ·
Stefan Sauer (Eds.)

Human-Centered Software Engineering

9th IFIP WG 13.2 International Working Conference, HCSE 2022
Eindhoven, The Netherlands, August 24–26, 2022
Proceedings

 Springer

Editors
Regina Bernhaupt 🆔
Eindhoven University of Technology
Eindhoven, The Netherlands

Carmelo Ardito 🆔
Polytechnic University of Bari
Bari, Italy

Stefan Sauer 🆔
Paderborn University
Paderborn, Germany

ISSN 0302-9743 ISSN 1611-3349 (electronic)
Lecture Notes in Computer Science
ISBN 978-3-031-14784-5 ISBN 978-3-031-14785-2 (eBook)
https://doi.org/10.1007/978-3-031-14785-2

This Springer imprint is published by the registered company Springer Nature Switzerland AG
The registered company address is: Gewerbestrasse 11, 6330 Cham, Switzerland

Preface

The 9th International Working Conference on Human-Centered Software Engineering, HCSE 2022, was held physically at the Eindhoven University of Technology, The Netherlands. This marks a change after the COVID-19 pandemic and will allow conference attendees and Working Group members to meet in person after a long time of virtual and hybrid meetings. HCSE is a biannual, single-track, working conference organized by the IFIP Working Group 13.2 on Methodology for User-Centred System Design which aims at bringing together researchers and practitioners interested in strengthening the scientific foundations of user interface design, examining the relationship between software engineering and human–computer interaction, and strengthening human-centered design as an essential part of software engineering processes. Previous events were held in Salamanca, Spain (2007); Pisa, Italy (2008); Reykjavik, Iceland (2010); Toulouse, France (2012); Paderborn, Germany (2014); Stockholm, Sweden (2016); Sophia Antipolis, France (2018); virtually (2020); and now Eindhoven (2022).

The organization of the HCSE 2022 conference reflected how research has changed during the pandemic, with some of the scientific contributions focusing on such changes. We have also seen a trend in novel forms of conference organization, including events that are held in a hybrid mode and intertwine with everyday research activities and work duties. We chose to be bold and hold the conference in person only, allowing participants to concentrate only on the conference.

HCSE 2022 took a broad view of the multi-properties in the software engineering process. It looked at how software engineering is changing perspective when it comes to the focus on users, and the impact of the pandemic on research was evident with more contributions relating to office life and health in general.

The HCSE 2022 program included contributions from Austria, Belgium, France, Finland, Germany, Iceland, and The Netherlands, to name a few. All contributions received at least three peer reviews. The Program Committee consisted of 21 experts (including the General Chairs) from 12 different countries who were supported by four additional reviewers. In total, HCSE 2022 accepted seven full research papers and four late-breaking results papers, with an acceptance rate of 39%. One poster and a demo were also accepted for inclusion in the conference program. Our sincere gratitude goes to the members of our Program Committee who devoted countless hours to providing valuable feedback to authors and ensuring the high quality of HCSE 2022's technical program.

The program was organized in five technical sessions, including the demonstration and poster presentations, and completed by keynotes and panel discussions. The conference program is available at https://www.hcse-conference.org/.

HCSE 2022 was supported by the Eindhoven University of Technology, the Software Innovation Campus Paderborn (SICP) at Paderborn University, Springer, and IFIP's Technical Committee on Human–Computer Interaction (IFIP TC13) whose generous support was essential for making HCSE 2022 successful! Finally, our thanks go to all the authors who undertook the research work and especially to the presenters who sparked inspiring discussions with all the participants at HCSE 2022.

For further information about past and future events organized by IFIP WG 13.2, its members, and activities, please visit the website at http://ifip-tc13.org/working-groups/working-group-13-2/.

We thank all contributors and participants for making HCSE 2022 a special and fruitful conference!

Stay safe and healthy,

July 2022

Regina Bernhaupt
Carmelo Ardito
Stefan Sauer

IFIP TC13 – http://ifip-tc13.org/

Established in 1989, the Technical Committee on Human–Computer Interaction (IFIP TC13) of the International Federation for Information Processing (IFIP) is an international committee of 34 national societies and 10 Working Groups, representing specialists of the various disciplines contributing to the field of human–computer interaction. This includes (among others) human factors, ergonomics, cognitive science, and multiple areas of computer science and design.

IFIP TC13 aims to develop the science, technology, and societal aspects of human–computer interaction (HCI) by

- encouraging empirical, applied, and theoretical research;
- promoting the use of knowledge and methods from both human sciences and computer sciences in design, development, evaluation, and exploitation of computing systems;
- promoting the production of new knowledge in the area of interactive computing systems engineering;
- promoting better understanding of the relation between formal design methods and system usability, user experience, accessibility, and acceptability;
- developing guidelines, models, and methods by which designers may provide better human-oriented computing systems; and
- cooperating with other groups, inside and outside IFIP, to promote user-orientation and humanization in system design.

Thus, TC13 seeks to improve interactions between people and computing systems, to encourage the growth of HCI research and its practice in industry and to disseminate these benefits worldwide.

The main orientation is to place the users at the center of the development process. Areas of study include

- the problems people face when interacting with computing devices;
- the impact of technology deployment on people in individual and organizational contexts;
- the determinants of utility, usability, acceptability, accessibility, privacy, user experience …;
- the appropriate allocation of tasks between computing systems and users, especially in the case of automation;
- engineering user interfaces, interactions, and interactive computing systems;
- modeling the users, their tasks, and the interactive system to aid better system design; and
- harmonizing the computing system to user characteristics and needs.

While the scope is thus set wide, with a tendency toward general principles rather than particular systems, it is recognized that progress will only be achieved through both general studies to advance theoretical understanding and specific studies on practical issues (e.g., interface design standards, software system resilience, documentation, training material, appropriateness of alternative interaction technologies, guidelines, integrating computing systems to match user needs and organizational practices, etc.).

IFIP TC13 stimulates working events and activities through its Working Groups (WGs). Working Groups consist of HCI experts from multiple countries, who seek to expand knowledge and find solutions to HCI issues and concerns within a specific domain. New Working Groups are formed as areas of significance in HCI arise.

Further information is available at the IFIP TC13 website: http://ifip-tc13.org/.

WG 13.2 on Methodology for User-Centred System Design aims to foster research, dissemination of information, and good practice in the methodical application of HCI to software engineering. Further information about the Working Group can be found at http://ifip-tc13.org/working-groups/working-group-13-2.

IFIP WG 13.2 Members

Officers

Chair

Regina Bernhaupt   Eindhoven University of Technology, The Netherlands

Vice-chair

Carmelo Ardito   Politecnico di Bari, Italy

Secretary

Stefan Sauer   Paderborn University, Germany

Members

Balbir Barn	Middlesex University London, UK
Cristian Bogdan	KTH Royal Institute of Technology, Sweden
Birgit Bomsdorf	Fulda University of Applied Sciences, Germany
Jan Borchers	RWTH Aachen University, Germany
John Carroll	Pennsylvania State University, USA
Bertrand David	École Centrale de Lyon, France
Anke Dittmar	University of Rostock, Germany
Xavier Ferre	Universidad Politécnica de Madrid, Spain
Holger Fischer	Atruvia AG, Karlsruhe, Germany
Peter Forbrig	University of Rostock, Germany
Tom Gross	University of Bamberg, Germany
Jan Gulliksen	KTH Royal Institute of Technology, Sweden
Anirudha Joshi	IIT Bombay, India
Kati Kuusinen	Technical University of Denmark, Denmark
Rosa Lanzilotti	University of Bari Aldo Moro, Italy
Marta Lárusdóttir	Reykjavik University, Iceland
Célia Martinie	Paul Sabatier University, France
Syed Bilal Naqvi	Lappeenranta University of Technology, Finland
Philippe Palanque	Paul Sabatier University, France
Fabio Paternò	ISTI-CNR, Italy
Antonio Piccinno	University of Bari Aldo Moro, Italy
Ahmed Seffah	Lappeenranta University of Technology, Finland
José Luís Silva	Instituto Universitário de Lisboa, Portugal
Jan Hårvard Skjetne	SINTEF Digital, Norway
Alistair Sutcliffe	University of Manchester, UK

Ricardo Tesoriero	University of Castilla-La Mancha, Spain
Jan Van den Bergh	Hasselt University, Belgium
Janet Wesson	Nelson Mandela University, South Africa
Marco Winckler	Université Côte d'Azur, France
Enes Yigitbas	Paderborn University, Germany

Observers

Kai Biermeier	Paderborn University, Germany
Selem Charfi	HD Technology, France
Shamal Faily	Bournemouth University, UK
Jil Klünder	Leibniz University Hannover, Germany
Jonathan Tolle	Maltem, Canada

Organization

General Conference Chairs

Regina Bernhaupt   Eindhoven University of Technology, The Netherlands
Carmelo Ardito   Politecnico di Bari, Italy
Stefan Sauer   Paderborn University, Germany

Demos and Posters Chairs

Jil Klünder   Leibniz University Hannover, Germany
Enes Yigitbas   Paderborn University, Germany

Program Committee

Balbir Barn   Middlesex University London, UK
John Carroll   Pennsylvania State University, USA
Bertrand David   École Centrale de Lyon, France
Anke Dittmar   University of Rostock, Germany
Jil Klünder   Leibniz University Hannover, Germany
Rosa Lanzilotti   University of Bari Aldo Moro, Italy
Marta Lárusdóttir   Reykjavik University, Iceland
Célia Martinie   Paul Sabatier University, France
Syed Bilal Naqvi   Lappeenranta University of Technology, Finland
Philippe Palanque   Paul Sabatier University, France
Fabio Paternò   ISTI-CNR, Italy
Antonio Piccinno   University of Bari Aldo Moro, Italy
José Luís Silva   Instituto Universitário de Lisboa, Portugal
Alistair Sutcliffe   University of Manchester, UK
Ricardo Tesoriero   University of Castilla-La Mancha, Spain
Jan Van den Bergh   Hasselt University, Belgium
Janet Wesson   Nelson Mandela University, South Africa
Enes Yigitbas   Paderborn University, Germany

Additional Reviewers

Vita Santa Barletta   University of Bari Aldo Moro, Italy
Jean-Bernard Martens   Eindhoven University of Technology, The Netherlands
Lukas Nagel   Leibniz University Hannover, Germany
Marco Saltarella   University of Bari Aldo Moro, Italy

Local Organizing Committee

Melanie Berger	Eindhoven University of Technology, The Netherlands
Jonas Kamps	Eindhoven University of Technology, The Netherlands
Daisy O'Neill	Eindhoven University of Technology, The Netherlands

Web and Publicity Team

David Potanin	Paderborn University, Germany
Stefan Sauer	Paderborn University, Germany

Supporters

Partners

International Federation for Information Processing

Contents

Posters and Demos

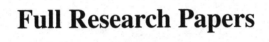

Full Research Papers

Meeting Strangers Online: Feature Models for Trustworthiness Assessment

Angela Borchert[1]([✉]) [iD], Nicolás E. Díaz Ferreyra[2] [iD], and Maritta Heisel[1]

[1] University of Duisburg-Essen, Forsthausweg 2, 47057 Duisburg, Germany
{angela.borchert,maritta.heisel}@uni-due.de
[2] Hamburg University of Technology, Am Schwarzenberg-Campus 1, 21073 Hamburg, Germany
nicolas.diaz-ferreyra@tuhh.de

Abstract. Getting to know new people online to later meet them offline for neighbourhood help, carpooling, or online dating has never been as easy as nowadays by social media performing computer-mediated introductions (CMIs). Unfortunately, interacting with strangers poses high risks such as unfulfilled expectations, fraud, or assaults. People most often tolerate risks if they believe others are trustworthy. However, conducting an online trustworthiness assessment usually is a challenge. Online cues differ from offline ones and people are either lacking awareness for the assessment's relevance or find it too complicated. On these grounds, this work aims to aid software engineers to develop CMI that supports users in their online trustworthiness assessment. We focus on trust-related software features and nudges to i) increase user awareness, ii) trigger the trustworthiness assessment and iii) enable the assessment online. For that reason, we extend feature models to provide software engineers the possibility to create and document software features or nudges for trustworthiness assessment. The extended feature models for trustworthiness assessments can serve as reusable catalogues for validating features in terms of their impact on the trustworthiness assessment and for configuring CMI software product lines. Moreover, this work provides an example of how the extended feature models can be applied to catfishing protection in online dating.

Keywords: Feature models · Trustworthiness · Nudging · Social media · User-centred design

1 Introduction

The use of online services as a common practice is characteristic of today's digital age. Many activities that were carried out offline in the early 2000s have partly shifted to the online sphere. These include activities such as offering or seeking carpooling, neighbourhood help, a place to sleep, or even friendship or romance. For individuals, it is often necessary to go beyond their own peer group to succeed in these endeavours.

© IFIP International Federation for Information Processing 2022
Published by Springer Nature Switzerland AG 2022
R. Bernhaupt et al. (Eds.): HCSE 2022, LNCS 13482, pp. 3–22, 2022.
https://doi.org/10.1007/978-3-031-14785-2_1

Social media platforms that offer so-called *computer-mediated introductions*, short CMI, provide users with the service of introducing them to strangers who potentially match their needs [1]. Examples of CMI are the Sharing Economy and online dating. While Sharing Economy connects unknown private individuals for a (monetary) exchange of goods or services, online dating tries to bring together people with compatible interests in terms of social relationships [1]. Apart from realising one's purposes, the benefits of CMI lie in the large number of options being proposed to the user independent of time and space. CMI eases interaction with strangers, which would not necessarily be possible offline because of missing social contact points. At the same time, strangers pose a high risk. Due to a lack of prior knowledge, it is difficult for individuals to assess the intentions of strangers and predict their behaviour. Therefore, CMI usage involves risks related to both online and offline interaction. Regarding Sharing Economy, risks are for example poor service or products, being underpaid by other users, or robbery [2,3]. In terms of online dating, risks involve among others damaged self-esteem, romance scam, sexually transmitted diseases, or sexual assault [4]. Furthermore, risks not only originate from users but also from service providers and the used software application. Companies may violate their users' privacy by misusing personal data [5]. Software applications pose security risks [6].

However, risks are tolerated if individuals perceive the party with whom they interact as trustworthy [7]. They then believe that the other party is willing and able to behave according to their positive expectations [8]. Perceived trustworthiness further impacts the decision-making process whether to start or continue an interaction [9]. Hence, not only private commerce and dating have shifted to the online sphere but also related psychological behaviours like assessing the trustworthiness of others.

Yet, it is a challenge for individuals to perform a trustworthiness assessment. Most often, it is an unconscious process in which individuals follow their gut feeling [10]. Furthermore, cues for evaluating properties of trustworthiness are different online than offline. They are hard to grasp and susceptible to manipulation [11]. Therefore, many CMI users perceive it as difficult to assess trustworthiness online. Instead, they wait for a real-world encounter to check on the other person [4]. Despite the relevance of trustworthiness assessments for safe CMI usage, CMI users perform them insufficiently, either because they are not sufficiently aware of them or because they consider them as complex.

Against this background, we ask ourselves, firstly, how CMI users can be prompted to perform a trustworthiness assessment and, secondly, how they can assess the trustworthiness of other parties online in the best possible way. As the CMI application is the main user interface, it mediates the trustworthiness assessment of other users, the respective service provider and itself as a technology [12]. Therefore, software engineers need to develop CMI applications that support their users in the assessment process. This can be achieved by integrating properties of trustworthiness into software development and the design of the graphical user interface [13].

Therefore, our research objective is to provide a method for software engineers to design, build and assess interactive applications that i) increase users' awareness of the trustworthiness assessment, ii) trigger the trustworthiness assessment and iii) enable the assessment online. We aim for a model-based approach by using extended feature models in a no-code development paradigm. Established feature models contribute to reusable, scenario-specific catalogues on which basis software product lines can be configured.

2   Theoretical Background

In this work, we adapt extended feature models to the context of trustworthiness and introduce software engineers how to use them to build user-centered, interactive CMI applications. This section provides a brief theoretical background of relevant research in trustworthiness assessment and how it can be considered in software development, software features and nudges, and feature models.

2.1   Trustworthiness Assessment

A trustworthiness assessment is a procedure on which basis an individual evaluates whether another party is trustworthy, and, thus, can be trusted [12]. In the past, various definitions for trust and trustworthiness arose.

Trust involves positive expectations regarding the actions of others [8]. Based on positive expectations, trust is the willingness to be vulnerable to another party and to depend on them [14]. Other researchers define trust as an individual's belief that another party possesses suitable properties necessary to perform as expected in a specific scenario [15]. This is in accordance with the definition of trustworthiness by Mayer et al. [16]. They identify ability, benevolence and integrity as the factors that capture the concept of trustworthiness in the context of interpersonal trust. Since then, these three properties have been applied to various other trust contexts, as for example trust in organizations and technology [15,17]. A multitude of other properties have been additionally related to the trustworthiness of *individuals, organizations* and *technology* by former research, as for example honesty, predictability and reputation [18]. Borchert & Heisel provide an overview of these properties that are unified under the term *trustworthiness facets*. Trustworthiness facets cover desirable properties that can be attributed to at least one of the three before-mentioned parties and positively impact their trustworthiness [19]. If facets are perceived as available, perceived trustworthiness increases. In the context of social media like CMI, trustworthiness facets affect people's trust in other CMI users (*computer-mediated interpersonal trust*), the service provider (*brand trust*), and the technical platform (*system trust*) [12]. CMI users evaluate trustworthiness facets in their trustworthiness assessment via the CMI platform. Assessing trustworthiness facets impact their decision with what service provider, application and other users they want to interact [19].

2.2   Identifying Trustworthiness Facets for Software Development

On these grounds, considering trustworthiness facets during software development is necessary to support CMI users in their trustworthiness assessment as good as possible [13]. Borchert & Heisel have conducted a literature review to provide an overview of trustworthiness facets [19]. Furthermore, they introduced a guideline for software engineers how to select appropriate facets for software development. Trustworthiness facets are determined in dependence on a specific problem. They can be derived by either analysing problematic characteristics or desired characteristics of a problem. Problematic characteristics are inherent to the problem context leading to trust issues. Desired characteristics resolve the trust issues of the problem. After obtaining such knowledge of the problem space, trustworthiness facets can be targeted by software features to address the problem in the solution space later in the software development process. Due to space constraints, we refer to Borchert & Heisel for the detailed procedure of the guideline [19].

2.3   Software Features and Nudges

Software features can be defined as user-accessible, useful concepts within software that realize both functional and non-functional requirements [20]. While functional requirements "describe the behavioral aspects of a system" [21], non-functional requirements are not directly related to system functionality [22]. They are rather a quality of a system functionality, such as performance or usability [21,22]. Overviews of software features have been collected in catalogues, such as the User Interface Design Pattern Library [23] or Welie.com - Patterns in Interaction Design [24].

Complying with the definition of software features, digital nudges can be categorized as features that are user-accessible and persuasive [25]. Digital nudges are user-interface design elements, more specifically "information and interaction elements to guide user behaviours in digital environments, without restricting the individual's freedom of choice" [26]. They can be characterized as soft paternalistic interventions and persuasive technologies [26]. Soft paternalistic interventions use information and guidance to point out safer and better choices for users' decisions without constraining their actions [27]. They can be used to increase user awareness concerning a specific issue [27]. Persuasive technologies try to change attitudes, behaviour or both [28]. In doing so, these technologies do not use any coercion or deception. In the context of persuasive technologies, the Fogg Behavioural Model names three requirements, which need to be considered simultaneously within the system for facilitating behaviour change of a target audience [28]. These are i) to encourage users' motivation, ii) to consider their ability to perform the targeted behaviour, and iii) to provide an effective trigger to show the targeted behaviour. Additionally, nudges may explain behaviour patterns of users and provide solutions for unfavourable behaviour [29]. Nudges can also be realized by presenting certain forms of content or information [26]. In order to create nudges, software engineers rely on nudge catalogues like the model for the design of nudges (DINU model) [26] or follow nudging design principles as from Sunstein [30].

2.4 Feature Models

Feature Models can be traced back to the Feature-Oriented Domain Analysis by Kang et al. [31] and to Czarnecki and Eisenecker [32]. They can be allocated to Software Product Line Engineering, which encompasses methodological approaches to develop software based on the reusability and variability of software features [33]. By feature models, software requirements are expressed on the abstract level of software features. Requirements are predefined by the software engineer and not part of the model. Based on the represented software features, feature models can be used for the development, configuration, and validation of software systems [34]. An example of a feature model is presented in Fig. 4 on page 14.

Feature models structure software features in a hierarchical tree. Software features are represented by single terms as nodes. At the root is the so-called concept feature, which represents a whole class of solutions. With increasing tree layers, the abstraction level of software features becomes more and more concrete. Features can be refined and become parent features by adding descriptive, related, more detailed child features in the next layer. These are called sub-features. Leaf elements of a tree are the ones that are most concrete and are called properties.

Based on the relationship of parent and child features, software product lines can be configured. This means that the software engineer can decide which features to include in a product. Relationships are modelled by the links between the features. They are depicted in Fig. 1. Links can mark single features as mandatory (simple line or line with filled bullet connected to feature) or optional (line with empty bullet next to feature). OR- or XOR-links can express the optionality of a set of sub-features. They are modelled by a semi-circle covering emanating links from a parent feature. The OR-link is modelled by a filled semi-circle. It means that at least one sub-feature must be included in an instance of the software product line. The XOR-alternative-link is modelled by an empty semi-circle. Only one sub-feature shall be selected for the software product while the others are consequently excluded. In addition to relationships between parent and child feature, there are cross-tree constraints. A dashed arrow is a requires-link. It denotes that a software feature implies another feature to be included

Legend

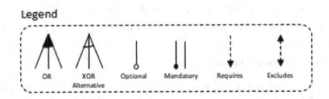

Fig. 1. Relationship links for feature models.

in the system. A double-sided dashed arrow expresses an excluded-link. Two features cannot be part in a software product line at the same time.

In the past, the basic feature model has been further extended. Extensions like the one of Benavides et al. have added additional information in form of so-called attributes to software features [35]. Attributes are any characteristic of a feature that are measurable. They are modeled next to the related feature in own boxes connected by a dotted link. Attributes may include a value that can either be continuous or discrete or mathematical relations between one or more attributes of a feature. These can be used for the validation of features [35].

3 Trust-Related Software Features

In this work, we aim to establish feature models whose features support the online trustworthiness assessment performed by CMI users. In order to contribute to the trustworthiness assessment, software features need to be trust-related. This means that they relate to at least one trustworthiness facet. Trustworthiness facets can be regarded as non-functional requirements of software features.

As we have mentioned in Sect. 1, trustworthiness assessments are a challenge for users. They are either not aware of the assessment itself or its relevance, or they perceive it as too difficult to execute online. On these grounds, we identify three categories of trust-related software features based on their purpose to support the trustworthiness assessment. **Awareness features** increase the user awareness of the trustworthiness assessment. They tend to make users realize the relevance of the assessment. **Trigger features** nudge users to perform the trustworthiness assessment. **Empowerment features** enable the user to perform the trustworthiness assessment. Most often, they provide information or interaction elements necessary for performing the trustworthiness assessment.

All three categories can additionally meet the definition of digital nudges, if they are designed to convince users to perform a trustworthiness assessment or if they shall raise user awareness [27,29]. Only empowerment features do not necessarily need to be realized in form of nudges. Instead, they may be "regular" software features.

4 Feature Models for Online Trustworthiness Assessments

Feature models are a useful approach to design software that supports its users in their online trustworthiness assessment. In the following, we introduce how we adapted the notation of the models for that purpose. Moreover, we explain how feature models for online trustworthiness assessments can be created.

4.1 Adaption of Feature Models

In order to support users in their trustworthiness assessment, we aim to cover all three software features types introduced in Sect. 3 within a model. For that reason, software features shall be labelled according to their type. Depending on the feature type, the labels are $<<awareness>>$, $<<trigger>>$ or $<<empower>>$. Labelling shall be performed on the first layer underneath the concept feature.

In addition, we follow the approach of extended feature models like Benavides et al. [35] and include trustworthiness facets as attributes to software features. Trustworthiness facets that are related to software features shall be considered in their design to reflect the trustworthiness of at least on of the three parties end-user, service provider or application. Thereby, software engineers can model whether computer-mediated interpersonal trust, system trust, or brand trust is impacted by a software feature. In order to distinguish the three different kinds of trustworthiness facets in the notation, they shall be framed in different colours. Facets for computer-mediated interpersonal trust that represent the trustworthiness of other users shall be framed green. Facets for system trust reflecting the trustworthiness of the software application shall be framed orange. Facets for brand trust depicting the trustworthiness of the service provider shall be framed purple.

4.2 Feature Model Creation

Feature models are created for a specific problem to provide solution approaches in form of software features. As an application is usually confronted with multiple problems, sets of feature models need to be created for the software development of the application. Feature model creation consists of two phases: Building the model on a feature level and the facet attribution process. Latter can be subdivided into allocation phase and propagation phase.

Building the Model and Refining Features. As a first step, the problem to be addressed needs to be determined. Based on the problem, the concept feature, which represents an abstract solution approach to the problem, can be derived. Building the feature model follows the same procedure described in Sect. 2.4. Software features shall be refined in the following layers of the model in more concrete information, interaction or design elements. The elements shall correspond to the purpose of the three software feature types of Sect. 3. For modelling, engineers may rely on their creativity and expertise. External catalogues for software features and nudges may provide additional input. In doing so, engineers may consider the brand image by design. Furthermore, feature models can be created to match the business strategies of the service provider and to convey the brand message.

Facet Attribution Process. After identifying possible software features as solution approaches, trustworthiness facets are attributed to them in the facet attribution process. It is subdivded in the allocation phase and propagation phase. In the *allocation phase*, trustworthiness facets are related to each software feature of a feature model and added as their attributes. For facet identification, the guideline of Borchert & Heisel [19] can be used.

The facet allocation phase starts at the layer beneath the concept feature and continues feature-wise layer by layer. Working down the tree structure of the model, it might happen that differences emerge between the trustworthiness facets of parent and child features. Such differences can be explained by the principle that the whole is greater than the sum of its parts [36]. A parent feature might evoke other trustworthiness facets by the combination of its sub-features than a sub-feature alone. An example is presented in Sect. 6, Fig. 4. The parent feature "identity verification" as a whole shows the legal compliance of the service provider, whereas its parts in form of sub-features are not associated with this facet.

Furthermore, a feature involves facets based on the configuration of its sub-features. Depending on the configuration, different facets can be involved. For example, a warning message formulated in natural language and displayed in certain colours may reflect different facets depending on the actual wording of the message and the colour chosen to convey the message. It may be perceived as either caring or patronising. At that point, the software engineer points out a design direction how software features shall be perceived by determining trustworthiness facets. This means that by further processing with the facet allocation for features at a lower layer, new facets may be derived impacting parent features.

On these grounds, the *propagation phase* is important to realise the inheritance principle so that parent features are associated with the trustworthiness facets of their child features. Starting from the leaves of a model, the software engineer needs to check whether there are facets of features that are not yet allocated to their parent feature. If this is the case, respective facets shall be added to the parent feature above. This process is repeated until the concept feature of a model is reached. It is usual that the number of trustworthiness facets associated with a concept feature is so large that it undermines the clarity of a feature model. Therefore, all facets of a model shall be documented in a list instead of linking them as attributes to the concept feature. The list of trustworthiness facets shall be created in the end of the propagation phase. When creating the list of trustworthiness facets, descriptive information about the frequency of occurrence for each facet can be added. This information supports software engineers in evaluating the impact of a concept feature on the trustworthiness assessment. It is a first step to feature model validation.

5   Method for Using Feature Models for Supporting Online Trustworthiness Assessments

In the following, we introduce a method on how feature models for online trustworthiness assessment can be efficiently used for software development. We explain necessary input for and useful output of the feature models. These are valuable for the three steps of the method, which are feature model creation (Step 1), feature validation (Step 2) and software product line engineering (Step 3). The method is depicted in Fig. 2.

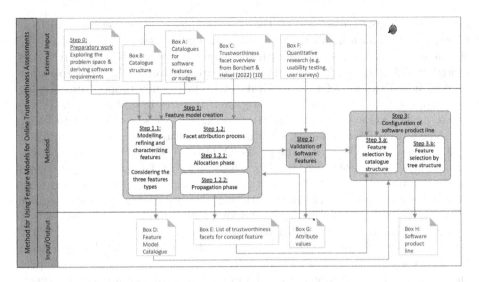

Fig. 2. Method for using feature models for online trustworthiness assessments.

5.1   Step 1: Feature Model Creation

Feature model creation can be divided into modelling software features (Step 1.1) and the facet attribution process (Step 1.2). The facet attribution process can be in turn divided into the allocation phase (Step 1.2.1) and the propagation phase (1.2.2). For the facet attribution process, the overview of trustworthiness facets and the guideline for facet selection by Borchert & Heisel serves as important input (Box C). The exact procedure for feature model creation is explained in Sect. 4.

In order to create feature models, preparatory work (Step 0) needs to be done first. Knowledge about the problem space, like user needs or software goals, as well as determining software requirements serve as input for creating feature models. Thereby, software features can be modelled that propose solution approaches to the problem. External catalogues of software features or nudges (Box A) like the User Interface Design Pattern Library [23] or the DINU model [26] may support the software engineer in this process. By creating feature models for a multitude of problems that a CMI application faces, a set of feature models tailored to the application is established, which can be regarded as a feature model catalogue (Box D). To be of use late for the configuration of software product lines, all software features of a feature model shall provide consistent information. Thus, software features shall be characterized according to the catalogue structure (Box B). The catalogue is introduced in Sect. 5.4.

5.2   Step 2: Feature Model Validation

The validation of feature models describes the process of testing the impact software features have on the online trustworthiness assessment and trust building. Since features are related to the trustworthiness assessment due to their facets, the validation involves testing to what extent users really associate the allocated trustworthiness facets with the software features. The feature model validation takes place after model creation (Step 2, Fig. 2). In order to realize validation testing, we refer to Arnowitz et al. [37]. They propose prototyping as an approach to let people experience single features in usability tests. Afterwards, participants can rate related trustworthiness facets on appropriate scales. For some trustworthiness facets, scientific scales already exist, as for example for ability, benevolence, integrity, and predictability [17]. Future work needs to support usability testing of those facets for which no scientific scales exist yet. Based on the answers of user ratings, quantitative attribute values can be calculated by which the impact of the features through the various facets is comparable (Box G). The attribute values shall be added within the feature model.

For validation reasons, additional attributes are useful for measuring the success rate of software features according to their feature type. For awareness features, *user awareness* is a suitable attribute to measure the feature's impact on how aware users are about the relevance of the trustworthiness assessment. Regarding trigger features, the *conversion rate* for trustworthiness assessments is interesting to know. It represents whether users really performed a trustworthiness assessment after interacting with the trigger feature. Thereby, it can be tested to what extent a trigger feature is convincing. For empowerment features, their *usefulness* to actually assess the trustworthiness of others is an indicator how well the system supports the online trustworthiness assessment.

5.3   Step 3: Configuration of Software Product Lines

The last step of the method is the configuration of a software product line by using the feature models for online trustworthiness assessment (Step 3). The configuration can be performed by either using the catalogue structure (Box B) for selecting software features (Step 3.a) or by considering the tree structure of the feature models (Step 3.b). For the catalogue, the preparatory work (Step 0) and the list of trustworthiness facets for the concept feature of a model (Box E) serve as input to consider trustworthiness facets during configuration. Concerning the tree structure, the notation of feature models provides the software engineer a decision basis what software features are mandatory or optional. The output of the configuration is a tailored software product line (Box H).

5.4   Feature Model Catalogue

As mentioned before, a feature model catalogue contains reusable, tailored solution approaches to specific trust problems of an application. As software features may be additionally modelled in terms of conveying a brand image via the application, a catalogue provides input for realising business strategies of the respective service provider. To have consistent information about the software feature available, software engineers shall follow the catalogue structure in Fig. 3 during

Basic Information	
Name	Catfish Protection
Problem	Some social media users are catfish by using fake profiles for fraudulent reasons
Keywords	Catfish, protection, prevention
Requirements	Preventing catfish attacks, protecting users from catfish, warn users about catfish, identify catfish
Problematic characteristics	dishonesty
Desired characteristics	honesty

Information for Trust-Related Software Features	
Feature type	☐ Awareness ☐ Trigger ☐ Empowerment
Target group for online trustworthiness assessment	☐ Users ☐ Application ☐ Service Provider
User Accessibility	☐ Yes ☐ Prerequisite
Sub-Feature Category	☐ Technical Asset ☐ Information ☐ User Interaction
Property Category	☐ Information ☐ Interaction Element ☐ Design Element
Nudging Criteria	☐ Open choice architecture ☐ Guiding information ☐ Explaining behaviour patterns ☐ Solution approaches to unfavourable behaviour ☐ Considering motivational state ☐ Considering user ability ☐ Presenting a behavioural trigger
Trustworthiness facets for individuals	...
Trustworthiness facets for technology	...
Trustworthiness facets for service provider	...

Fig. 3. Catalogue structure for feature models for trustworthiness assessments for the example of catfishing.

modelling (Step 1.1). The structure is divided into basic information and information for trust-related software feature. Based on this information, software features can later be identified or searched within the catalogue. The catalogue structure may be extended by further characteristics than proposed here. The basic information in Fig. 3 is already applied to the example of catfishing from Sect. 6.

The *basic information* of a catalogue aims at the concept feature of a model. Basic information includes the *name* of the concept feature as well as a description of the *problem* that the concept feature addresses. *Keywords* provide an overview about the issue. Furthermore, the software *requirements* that were determined by preparatory work (Step 0) shall be added to document what the concept feature realises. In addition, basic information includes *problematic* and *desired characteristics*, which relate to the identification of trustworthiness facets described in Sect. 2.2.

The second part of the catalog structure contains *information for trust-related software features*, which are presented in the form of characteristics to be checked. Several characteristics of an information category can be applicable at the same time. The information category *feature type* refers to the three software features types awareness, trigger or empowerment from Sect. 3. Moreover, software engineers can select the *target group for the online trustworthiness assessment* for which a feature is intended. The target group can be users, the application or the service provider. Another information category is *user accessibility*. Features can be distinguished between being either user-accessible or being prerequisites for another feature to be user-accessible, such as underlying algorithms of an user interface element. Further information categories are *sub-*

feature and *property category*. Sub-features can be categorized as a technical asset (e.g., algorithm), information (e.g., user data), or user interaction (e.g. confirmation request). Properties can be related to information (e.g., telephone number), interaction element (e.g., button), or design element (e.g., graphical symbol). The information category *nudging criteria* refers to the definitions of nudges and persuasive technologies from Sect. 2.3. Features may comply to the nudging criteria of an open choice architecture, guiding information, explanations of user behaviour patterns or solution approaches to unfavourable behaviour. In terms of persuasive technologies, features may consider users' motivational state, consider users' ability for the targeted behaviour or present a trigger to act in accordance to the target behaviour. The last three information categories of the catalogue structure are the trustworthiness facets for individuals, technology and the service provider. For these, the list of trustworthiness facets of a concept feature (Box E) serve as input. Software engineers may choose facets in which they are interested.

6   Example: "Identity Verification" for Catfish Protection

For demonstrating feature models for online trustworthiness assessments, we chose the scenario of catfishing in online dating. Catfishing is a phenomenon, where online dating users, known as catfish, create user profiles with fake identities for fraudulent reasons [38]. It is a suitable example, because catfish are reason for trust issues among users. Online trustworthiness assessments help users to identify catfish and resolve their concerns. Based on this knowledge, we filled out the basic information of the catalogue structure from Sect. 5.4, Fig. 3. Catfishing is the problem that shall be tackled by catfish protection. Suitable keywords are catfish, protection and prevention. Software requirements for catfish protection can be to prevent catfish attacks, to protect users from catfish, to warn users about them or to identify catfish.

In the following, we demonstrate how the feature models can be used for catfish protection by the feature "identity verification". Identity verification helps to resolve the uncertainty whether another user has created a fake profile [39]. It is known to be an interactive tool for self-presentation, which increases users' reputation and allows them to rate the trustworthiness of other users. Furthermore, it is combined with persistent labelling in a user profile on which basis users can derive whether the identity is verified. Therefore, we classify identity verification as an empowerment feature to perform a trustworthiness assessment. Due to space limitations, the model can be extended by further features. We only explain parts of it.

6.1   Example: Feature Model Creation

Identity verification is introduced as an empowerment feature after the concept feature on the second layer (see labelling <<empower>>, Fig. 4). In the third layer of the model, we refine identity verification in three mandatory features -

a verification algorithm, user profile and the notification about the verification status. Verification algorithms most often try to link a user profile to additional identifying information. Therefore, we connect the verification algorithm with the user profile by a require-link. The verification algorithm has three properties: "photo of ID card", "phone number", and "Facebook account". They represent the additional information that may be used for the verification of the user profile. By the OR-link, the model depicts that the algorithm needs to consider at least one of the options.

If a system has the software requirement to inform its users about the verification status of other users, a notification about the status is a suitable feature to address this requirement. In order to realize notifications, knowledge about the verification status is required. Therefore, we use the require-link to connect the feature notification with the feature verification algorithm. As a next step, we identify three different verification statuses, that are "verified", "not completed" and "fake" (see right sub-tree, layer four of model). For determining features how to express the statuses, we follow the principle of familiarity. It says that the frequency with which users have already encountered design elements like symbols lead to an increased usability and understanding [40]. Therefore, we choose features that are frequently used by other applications and are thus already well-known to users in their appearance and meaning. For the verified status, a graphical symbol in form of a green check mark next to the name of a user profile can be used. Online dating applications such as Tinder[1] already use this symbol for verified profiles. In case of uncompleted identity verification processes, we want to emphasize this by an orange question mark next to the name of a profile. This symbol is inspired by the green check mark described before. If a fake identity has been identified by the verification algorithm, the catfish should no longer be available for matching. Furthermore, users should no longer be able to interact with catfish when they already had a match. To visualise the inactivity of a catfish profile, the profile and the corresponding chat are presented greyed out for the other users.

6.2   Example: Catalogue Information

As part of feature modeling and refinement, the software engineer has to assign trust-related software feature characteristics from the catalogue structure to each feature. For this example, we demonstrate this for the green check mark feature. Belonging to the identity verification feature, the green check mark is an empowerment feature. It is illustrated on the graphical user interface so that users can assess the trustworthiness of other users. Therefore, it is user-accessible. Being a property, the green check mark can be categorized as a design element and information, because it conveys the message that another user has passed the identity verification. Concerning the nudging criteria, the green check mark provides information that may guide user behaviour. For trustworthiness facets that are associated with the green check mark, we refer to Sect. 6.3.

---

[1] www.tinder.com.

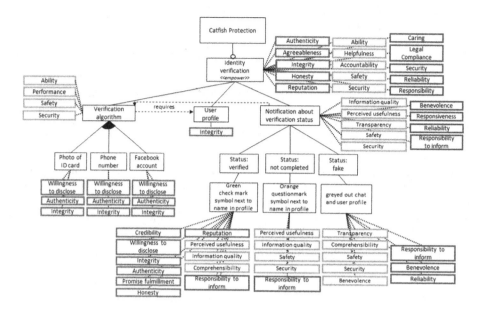

Fig. 4. Feature model for the empowerment feature "identity verification" for catfish protection after the allocation phase. (Color figure online)

6.3   Example: Trustworthiness Facet Attribution Process

After the model has been established, we proceed with the trustworthiness facet attribution. For the allocation phase, we start with the empowerment feature "identity verification". Following the guideline for selecting appropriate trustworthiness facets [19], we first acquire an understanding of the actual problem to which identity verification serves as a solution approach. As mentioned before, identity verification shall resolve users' concerns about fake profiles by proving that an identity is true. Thinking of problematic characteristics of a catfish, catfish are dishonest. We add this information to the catalogue structure for catfish protection (see Fig. 3). Catfish are likely to not perform an identity verification to hide the fraud. Therefore, they would not comply to the application's norms in absolving a verification. Based on this problematic characteristic, we check the overview of trustworthiness facets [19] on semantically opposite trustworthiness facets by definition (Box C, Fig. 2). As a result, we assume that users, who perform an identity verification are associated with authenticity, agreeableness, integrity with the norms of the application, honesty and good reputation (green frames, second layer, Fig. 4).

As a next step, we consider how including identity verification in the system might impact users' perception of the online dating application. Former research has pointed out that websites should be interested in taking the responsibility for their users' safety and security [41]. If the feature was not implemented, users might feel insecure and not well supported. Having this in mind, we check the overview of trustworthiness facets for technology [19] (Box C). Our findings are depicted as the attributes of identity verification in the orange boxes in Fig. 4. By having identity verification implemented, the online dating application presents its ability to address the problem. Furthermore, the application thereby helps its users in countering their catfish concern. In addition, it shows that it is accountable and takes care of the safety and security of its users.

Last but not least, we conclude the trustworthiness facets of the service provider if identity verification was implemented in the online dating application. They are depicted as the attributes of identity verification framed in purple in Fig. 4. The facets are in accordance to the ones for the online dating application as a technology (see Fig. 2 attributes of identity verification, orange frames). We came to the conclusion that service providers express their care for users' safety and security when using identity verification. Furthermore, catfishing has been discussed in court concerning online impersonations [41]. Therefore, service providers would demonstrate their responsibility and legal compliance.

For the rest of the feature model, we proceed in a similar way. Due to space constraints, we do not further explain the following steps. Yet, we want to mention that for the statuses on layer four of the feature model (see right sub-tree in Fig. 4, we have not added trustworthiness facets as attributes. Here, we regard them as specifications of their parent feature, which are expressed in detail by their child features. Therefore, we limit the facet allocation on the child features for this specific case. Figure 4 shows the feature model after allocation phase (Step 1.1, Fig. 2).

After the allocation phase, the propagation phase can be performed. Trustworthiness facets that are not yet allocated to parent features are now propagated. This is for example the case for "reputation" from the green check mark feature, which is added as an attribute to the notification feature.

As an outlook for the configuration process of this feature model, the tree structure of the model points out to the optional properties of the verification algorithm. The software engineer needs to determine whether the ID card, phone number, Facebook account or a combination of them shall be used for checking a match with the user profile.

7   Related Work

As previously introduced, the model for the design of nudges (DINU model) [26] provides a catalogue of existing nudges that can be used as input for the method presented in this work. Additionally, the DINU model relates to our work insofar that it guides practitioners in the analysis, design, and evaluation of nudges and their context. In doing so, it focuses on the nudging criteria that we included in the catalogue structure (see Fig. 3). Compared to our work, the DINU-model misses the model-based approach of feature models. It not only allows software engineers to support users in their online trustworthiness assessment but also to validate trust-related software features in a structured way for software product line engineering.

Another related work is from Martinez et al. [42], who invented a feature model tool to select appropriate features based on their attributes. For that, they introduce algorithms on the basis of petri nets. Similar digital tools for configuring software product lines based on feature models are the FeAture Model Analyser (FAMA) [43] or Requiline - a requirements engineering tool for software product lines [44]. These tools are missing the interdisciplinary trust background, but are valuable for complementing our method. By combining such tools with our catalog structure, configurations of trust-related software product lines can be automated.

8 Discussion

This work introduces a method for software engineers that is based on extended feature models. Its intend is to create reusable catalogues for software features that focus on online trustworthiness assessments. Online trustworthiness assessments are especially relevant for social media users of computer-mediated introductions (CMIs). Based on the assessment, CMI users decide whether to tolerate risks associated with the interaction of other parties such as unknown users, the CMI platform and the CMI service provider. However, users are most often not aware of the assessment's importance or find it too difficult to perform. Therefore, this work uses adapted feature models to derive awareness, trigger and empowerment features for trustworthiness assessment. Feature models are adapted by adding trustworthiness facets as attributes to software features for considering them in the features' specification and design.

Applying the adapted feature models for online trustworthiness assessment has shown that they are suitable to derive and specify awareness, trigger and empowerment features. For each of the features, a huge range of different interaction elements can be considered for realizing associated software requirements. Another key element of the adapted feature models is the large collection of trustworthiness facets related to each software feature. The model further differentiates between the trustworthiness facets of the CMI parties "user", "platform" and "service provider". Thereby, software engineers can ensure to implement cues that foster online trustworthiness assessments regarding all three parties. Catalogues of such feature models lead to comprehensive solution approaches for specific problems and reflect a variety of design options.

Overall, extending feature models by trustworthiness facets provides a solid basis for validating the trustworthiness assessment and trust building. However, the trustworthiness facets may impact more constructs than trust building, which could be taken into consideration for the validation process as well. An example could be the halo effect. The halo effect is a cognitive bias that describes an error in reasoning based on one known trait leading to an overall impression of further traits [45]. In terms of the facet allocation phase for example, a software engineer could assign the facet benevolence to a feature and, based on that alone, simultaneously associate the feature with the facet usefulness. Future work needs to consider the halo effect of trustworthiness facets in the validation process from two perspectives. How does the halo effect may have impacted the software engineer to identify irrelevant facets during the facet allocation phase? How might the halo effect impact CMI users to assess further trustworthiness facets by being exposed to a software feature? Maybe some of the trustworthiness facets impacted by the halo effect have not even been identified by the software engineer in the facet attribution process.

Unidentified trustworthiness facets pose another challenge for validation. Currently, the validation process checks on facets that have been identified by the software engineer in the facet attribution process. Future work needs to consider how feature models can be validated in terms of unidentified facets that are nonetheless relevant for software features.

Unidentified trustworthiness facets and the halo effect point to a limitation of the method introduced here. Feature model creation is subject to the subjectivity of the software engineer applying the method. In order to reduce mistakes, we propose to perform the method in an agile team. Agile methods increase the flexibility and efficiency of software development [46]. Thereby, software features and trustworthiness facets can be easily discussed within the team and changes can be done throughout the whole method. In addition, future work needs to validate how the method is accepted by practitioners. By empirical studies, practitioners might give feedback on how the method can be further improved.

Another aspect that future research needs to tackle regarding the trustworthiness facets is the difficulty to distinguish between facets of the CMI platform and of the CMI service provider. During the facet allocation phase, we recognized the similarity of resulting facets for both types. A reason for that might be that users are oftentimes affected by brand image when it comes to their perception of the software application [47]. Future work could examine the relationship between users' perception of these two facet types. This in turn could provide insights for the facet allocation phase and support engineers in performing it.

In terms of configuration, a main challenge of Software Product Line Engineering is handling the variability of a model [48]. Although validated trustworthiness facets support software engineers in improving users' online trustworthiness assessment, it increases the complexity of configuration. Software feature tools like FAMA [43] or Requiline [44] (see Sect. 7) could aid software engineers in this process of systematically selecting those software features that address desired trustworthiness facets. However, future work might focus on the questions whether including as much trustworthiness facets as possible within software enhances online trustworthiness assessments or whether configuring a certain set of facets provides a better support.

The selection of certain sets of features can further be related to the question of diversity and commonality. Finding a balance between the diversity and commonality of software product lines is tackled in variability management [33]. It is about weighing the reduction of complexity within the product for easy usage and the differentiation of a provider's products from competitors based on underlying business strategies [33]. Future work needs to examine whether a balance of variability and commonality is crucial for trust-related software features as well. Usability testing could be a useful approach for finding answers.

Overall, the great scope of trustworthiness facets as attributes of software features allows engineers to model various options of how to support users in their trustworthiness assessment. Yet, drawbacks can be observed in the overwhelming size of models based on the large amount of features and facets. Handling large-scale variability models is a well-known challenge in Software Product Line Engineering [48]. To counter the problem of cluttered feature models, we again propose to use digital tools as FAMA [43] or Requiline [44] for model creation and configuration. These tools support operators to keep an overview.

9   Conclusion

This work focuses on how software engineers can best support social media users in assessing the trustworthiness of other users, the application, and the service provider by means of software features. For that reason, three different types of software features were identified: awareness, trigger and empowerment features. In order to document such software features for specific problems of social media use, feature models were extended by trustworthiness facets to address users' trust building. Feature models for online trustworthiness assessments can serve as reusable catalogues in order to consider and validate different design options and interaction elements of trust-related software feature. Furthermore, they can be used for the configuration of software product lines in social media. For future work, additional validation techniques need to be developed to evaluate the extent to which software features address trustworthiness facets and impact users' trustworthiness assessments.

References

1. Obada-Obieh, B., Somayaji, A.: Can I believe you? Establishing trust in computer mediated introductions. In: Proceedings of the 2017 New Security Paradigms Workshop, pp. 94–106 (2017)
2. Jozsa, K., Kraus, A., Korpak, A.K., Birnholtz, J., Moskowitz, D.A., Macapagal, K.: "Safe behind my screen": adolescent sexual minority males' perceptions of safety and trustworthiness on geosocial and social networking apps. Arch. Sex. Behav. **50**(7), 2965–2980 (2021). https://doi.org/10.1007/s10508-021-01962-5
3. Yi, J., Yuan, G., Yoo, C.: The effect of the perceived risk on the adoption of the sharing economy in the tourism industry: the case of Airbnb. Inf. Process. Manage. **57**(1), 102–108 (2020)
4. Couch, D., Liamputtong, P.: Online dating and mating: perceptions of risk and health among online users. Health Risk Soc. **9**(3), 275–294 (2007)
5. Son, J.Y., Kim, S.S.: Internet users' information privacy-protective responses: a taxonomy and a nomological model. MIS Q. **32**, 503–529 (2008)
6. Hang, L., Kim, D.H.: SLA-based sharing economy service with smart contract for resource integrity in the internet of things. Appl. Sci. **9**(17), 3602 (2019)
7. Becerra, M., Lunnan, R., Huemer, L.: Trustworthiness, risk, and the transfer of tacit and explicit knowledge between alliance partners. J. Manage. Stud. **45**(4), 691–713 (2008)

8. Lewicki, R.J., Wiethoff, C.: Trust, Trust Development, and Trust Repair. The Handbook of Conflict Resolution: Theory and Practice **1**(1), 86–107 (2000)
9. Bialski, P., Batorski, D.: From online familiarity to offline trust: how a virtual community creates familiarity and trust between strangers. Social Computing and Virtual Communities, pp. 179–204 (2010)
10. Bonnefon, J.F., Hopfensitz, A., De Neys, W.: The modular nature of trustworthiness detection. J. Exp. Psychol. Gen. **142**(1), 143 (2013)
11. Ding, S., Yang, S.L., Fu, C.: A novel evidential reasoning based method for software trustworthiness evaluation under the uncertain and unreliable environment. Expert Syst. Appl. **39**(3), 2700–2709 (2012)
12. Borchert, A., Díaz Ferreyra, N.E., Heisel, M.: Building trustworthiness in computer-mediated introduction: a facet-oriented framework. In: International Conference on Social Media and Society, pp. 39–46 (2020)
13. Cassell, J., Bickmore, T.: External manifestations of trustworthiness in the interface. Commun. ACM **43**(12), 50–56 (2000)
14. Mishra, A.K.: Organizational responses to crisis. Trust in organizations. Front. Theor. Res. **3**(5), 261–287 (1996)
15. Mcknight, D.H., Carter, M., Thatcher, J.B., Clay, P.F.: Trust in a specific technology: an investigation of its components and measures. ACM Trans. Manage. Inf. Syst. **2**(2), 1–25 (2011)
16. Mayer, R.C., Davis, J.H., Schoorman, F.D.: An integrative model of organizational trust. Acad. Manag. Rev. **20**(3), 709–734 (1995)
17. Büttner, O.B., Göritz, A.S.: Perceived trustworthiness of online shops. J. Consum. Behav. **7**(1), 35–50 (2008)
18. McKnight, D.H., Chervany, N.L.: What trust means in e-commerce customer relationships: an interdisciplinary conceptual typology. Int. J. Electron. Commer. **6**(2), 35–59 (2001)
19. Borchert, A., Heisel, M.: The role of trustworthiness facets for developing social media applications: a structured literature review. Information **13**(1), 34 (2022)
20. Hsi, I., Potts, C.: Studying the evolution and enhancement of software features. In: icsm, p. 143 (2000)
21. Anton, A.I.: Goal identification and refinement in the specification of software-based information systems. Georgia Institute of Technology (1997)
22. Glinz, M.: On non-functional requirements. In: 15th IEEE International Requirements Engineering Conference, pp. 21–26. IEEE (2007)
23. User Interface Design Patterns. www.cs.helsinki.fi/u/salaakso/patterns/. Accessed 11 Apr 2022
24. Welie.com - Patterns in Interaction Design. www.welie.com/patterns/index.php. Accessed 11 Apr 2022
25. Zetterholm, M., Elm, P., Salavati, S.: Designing for pandemics: a design concept based on technology mediated nudging for health behavior change. In: 54th Hawaii International Conference on System Sciences, pp. 3474–3483 (2021)
26. Meske, C., Potthoff, T.: The DINU-model-a process model for the design of nudges (2017)
27. Acquisti, A., et al.: Nudges for privacy and security: understanding and assisting users' choices online. ACM Comput. Surv. **50**(3), 1–41 (2017)
28. Fogg, B.J.: A behavior model for persuasive design. In: Proceedings of the 4th International Conference on Persuasive Technology, pp. 1–7 (2009)
29. Thaler, R.H., Sunstein, C.R.: Nudge: Wie man kluge Entscheidungen anstößt. Ullstein eBooks (2009)

30. Sunstein, C.R.: Nudging: a very short guide. J. Consum. Policy **37**(4), 583–588 (2014)
31. Kang, K.C., Cohen, S.G., Hess, J.A., Novak, W.E., Peterson, A.S.: Feature-oriented domain analysis (FODA) feasibility study. Carnegie-Mellon Univ Pittsburgh Pa Software Engineering Inst. (1990)
32. Czarnecki, K., Eisenecker, U.W.: Generative programming (2000)
33. Pohl, K., Böckle, G., Van Der Linden, F.: Software product line engineering: foundations, principles, and techniques, vol. 1. Springer, Heidelberg (2005)
34. Riebisch, M.: Towards a more precise definition of feature models. Model. Variability Object-Oriented Prod. Lines 64–76 (2003)
35. Benavides, D., Trinidad, P., Ruiz-Cortés, A.: Automated reasoning on feature models. In: Pastor, O., Falcão e Cunha, J. (eds.) CAiSE 2005. LNCS, vol. 3520, pp. 491–503. Springer, Heidelberg (2005). https://doi.org/10.1007/11431855_34
36. Xiong, J.: New Software Engineering Paradigm Based on Complexity Science: An Introduction to NSE. Springer, NY (2011). https://doi.org/10.1007/978-1-4419-7326-9
37. Arnowitz, J., Arent, M., Berger, N.: Effective Prototyping for Software Makers. Elsevier (2010)
38. Simmons, M., Lee, J.S.: Catfishing: a look into online dating and impersonation. In: Meiselwitz, G. (ed.) HCII 2020. LNCS, vol. 12194, pp. 349–358. Springer, Cham (2020). https://doi.org/10.1007/978-3-030-49570-1_24
39. Kaskazi, A.: Social network identity: Facebook, Twitter and identity negotiation theory. In: iConference 2014 Proceedings (2014)
40. Mcdougall, S.J., Curry, M.B., De Bruijn, O.: Measuring symbol and icon characteristics: norms for concreteness, complexity, meaningfulness, familiarity, and semantic distance for 239 symbols. Behav. Res. Meth. Instrum. Comput. **31**(3), 487–519 (1999). https://doi.org/10.3758/BF03200730
41. Koch, C.M.: To catch a catfish: a statutory solution for victims of online impersonation. U. Colo. L. Rev. **88**, 233 (2017)
42. Martinez, C., Díaz, N., Gonnet, S., Leone, H.: A Petri net variability model for software product lines. Electron. J. SADIO (EJS) **13**, 35–53 (2014)
43. Benavides, D., Segura, S., Trinidad, P., Cortés, A.R.: FAMA: tooling a framework for the automated analysis of feature models. VaMoS (2007)
44. von der Maßen, T., Lichter, H.: RequiLine: a requirements engineering tool for software product lines. In: van der Linden, F.J. (ed.) PFE 2003. LNCS, vol. 3014, pp. 168–180. Springer, Heidelberg (2004). https://doi.org/10.1007/978-3-540-24667-1_13
45. Thorndike, E.L.: A constant error in psychological ratings. J. Appl. Psychol. **4**(1), 25 (1920)
46. Campanelli, A.S., Parreiras, F.S.: Agile methods tailoring-a systematic literature review. J. Syst. Softw. **110**, 85–100 (2015)
47. Yang, T., Bolchini, D.: Branded interactions: predicting perceived product traits and user image from interface consistency and visual guidance. Interact. Comput. **26**(5), 465–487 (2014)
48. Metzger, A., Pohl, K.: Software product line engineering and variability management: achievements and challenges. In: Future of Software Engineering Proceedings, pp. 70–84 (2014)

I Feel You

Christel De Maeyer[(✉)] [iD] and Minha Lee[iD]

Department of Industrial Design, Future Everyday, Eindhoven University of Technology,
Eindhoven, Netherlands
{c.a.a.d.maeyer,m.lee}@tue.nl

Abstract. Digital twins refer to a digital replica of potential actual physical assets, people, or systems, which are relevant for the future of digital health. These virtual replicas can be used to perform simulations that help assess possible risks, test performance, and optimize processes before applying them in the real world. Applied to the healthcare sector, a digital twin can refer to a replica of a patient or certain aspects of a human, like body parts, body organs or body systems. As a digital twin would age with the owner the question arises as to how we should visualize our digital twin (i.e., how to represent ourselves in a digital way with data). We do not yet know how people want their data (quantitative or qualitative) to be represented as digital twins. We addressed this question using generative design research methods, and more particularly co-design sessions that explored users' perspectives and design preferences on digital twins. Our findings suggest a preference for qualitative representation unless there are emergency alerts, in which quantitative representations were preferred. People were reluctant towards health forecasting through a digital twin and saw it more as a reflection tool to improve quality of life.

Keywords: Digital twins · Visualization · Qualitative displays/interfaces · Affective design · Affective atmospheres

1 Introduction

Today, the potential of digital twins is explored in healthcare. A digital twin (DT) refers to a digital replica of potential and actual physical assets, processes, people, places, systems, and devices that can be used for various purposes [1]. From a healthcare perspective, digital twins are gaining attention for hospital management, simulate surgeries or enabling personalized medicine and personalized patient care [34, 35]. Huang [53], redefined the notion of a DT in healthcare context as followed: "a digital twin for personalized health care service is a data-driven, interactive computerized model that aims to offer health-related information that properly simulates or predicts the health conditions of a particular person" [53, p. 12]. A digital twin (DT) holds information of the past and current state of a person because it is synchronized in real time and serves as a 'living' data object. Lupton [2] defines living digital data objects as data that has a 'life' (i.e., digital data that changes over a lifetime), representing and helping generate knowledge (in this case) about humans. People might consider changing behavior or lifestyle

© IFIP International Federation for Information Processing 2022
Published by Springer Nature Switzerland AG 2022
R. Bernhaupt et al. (Eds.): HCSE 2022, LNCS 13482, pp. 23–43, 2022.
https://doi.org/10.1007/978-3-031-14785-2_2

depending on their personal data that they gathered. As a last component, data can be used and "lives" in different environments such as online advertising or security [2, 3]. Thus, DTs can be predictive, descriptive, and prescriptive. Powered through modern computational approaches enabling forecasts, simulations, and recommendations.

The more information a DT has, the more insights it could generate on a specific human body, specific body organs (e.g., liver, heart) or body systems or function (digestion system). The DT can provide insights on what we care about, what our strengths and weakness are, as it becomes a form of our identity, based on our environment and generated health data, be it heart rate measured by wearable sensors or self-rated mood. Today, personal data presentation from sensors are mostly (if not entirely) presented quantitatively. However, we as humans express ourselves in non-quantitative ways, such as with metaphors or visual language (e.g., 'I slept like a baby' or 'I feel stuffed'). Expressing oneself in metaphors helps us conceptualize abstract feelings that cannot be directly seen, heard, touched, smelled, or tasted [4, 5].

Expressing or presenting quantitative data in a qualitative form might be a "human-centered" [37] approach that captures people's "lived experience" of their health [36]. One could view the human body as a 'qualitative interface', as our bodies adapt to certain situations and provide a non-precise, but clearly understandable, qualitative display of our inner states (e.g., people might blush, and faces can get red). Lockton [58] defines "qualitative displays as being a way in which information is presented primarily through *qualities of phenomena*; a qualitative interface enables people to interact with a system through responding to or creating these qualities" [58, p. 2].

As we move on further into an era of self-managed health [6–8], affective design (i.e., designing with and for emotions) is becoming more important. Furthermore, affective design might lead towards positive affective digital atmospheres, creating more digitally engaged people in the preventive healthcare realm. Through this, individuals might build relationships or dependencies with their self-monitoring devices and mobile apps [32, 33], especially in a healthcare environment that the DTs fit into.

DTs in healthcare have been widely researched from the perspective of healthcare experts. Research shows that experts see a promise in preventive healthcare through DTs [9–11, 41], but a user – design perspective that prizes what people desire, and need has yet to be researched. In this paper, the focus is on the research question: "*How do users experience (young adults, middle aged and baby boomers) a Digital Twin, as a facilitator in presenting a state of now or as a forecasting tool of their wellbeing over 10 to 20 years from now (depending on their age) based on their personal data?*" We approach this through affective design (i.e., designing for emotional experiences) as health and wellbeing is an important parameter that influences quality of life of humans. Therefore, DTs needs to be a desirable and trusted environment, considering the affordance of these technologies and their social, ethical, and political aspects to stimulate engagement with people [7].

We thus conducted co-design sessions through deploying probes such as video explainers and visuals combined with in-depth interviews over a 4-month period. To approach the complexity of DTs, we chose to deploy two different stages in our research method. First, we took an art-thinking process in collaboration with an artist to think about how a DT in healthcare could be visualized as an art object or artefact. This was then proposed as concepts to the participants during the co-design [67] sessions to create a mutual understanding of DTs in healthcare in home setting. Second, design thinking was applied during the process of the co-design sessions with the participants, more elaboration on the rationale for choosing these methods are elaborated on in the research method section.

This paper is structured as follows. Section 2 provides relevant work on affective atmospheres and design in relation to visual data representations for DTs. Section 3 presents our methods on the design workshops and thematic analysis; Sect. 4 brings the results of the workshops and in-depth interviews, with proof-of-concepts of DTs for healthcare at home. Section 5 is our discussion and future direction of this work, and the conclusion.

2   Related Work

Humans tend to get emotionally attached to their digital (health) devices. They trust them, rely on them, especially if they give some kind a confirmation, relief in pain or assurance, especially with medical devices [12, 13]. The opposite is also happening, when technologies fail, or not give a trusting feeling, negative emotions are often the response from users and reasons to stop using them [12, 13]. As digital devices are embedded in our everyday lives today, they are also become actors in the (preventive) healthcare space [33]. As mentioned before, DTs in healthcare is a possible concept because of all the wearable devices, mobile apps and IoT (Internet of Things) devices or implants, either medical validated or not, that are available and widely used now to monitor oneself and one's environments. This creates new relations with human and non-human things, which become a part of an affective atmosphere involving digital technologies.

2.1   Affective Atmospheres

DTs in healthcare can influence one's emotional states by representing one's health data. Designing for emotional experiences, then, should consider today's data environments (i.e., an affective atmosphere of data), being "assemblages of data, code, devices, places, space and time, generating feelings" [27]. As a DT is related to one person for tracking their wellbeing [35], one could think about creating one's own affective atmosphere of data that would allow for more engagement in using a DT in healthcare. Affective atmosphere is understood as an "assemblage of affect, humans and nonhumans that is constantly changing as new actors enter and leave spaces and places" [27, p. 1], [14]. Anderson [15, p. 79], draws from the work of Dufrenne [62] that states "atmospheres are perpetually forming and deforming, appearing, and disappearing, as bodies enter in relation with one another. They are never finished or at rest". As digital devices are becoming our digital *companions*, their aesthetics are becoming increasingly important as well. The visual aspects (i.e., the aesthetic quality of the user interface), are all part of the affective atmosphere, due to the importance of our relations with these devices and the feelings they evoke [16, 27]. Hence, the notion of visualizing our gathered personal data to represent us should get more attention; today, data in DTs are presented in a quantitative matter [37]. As Schwartz [6] mentions, a clear data visualization as a presentation layer is a prerequisite for DTs in healthcare to be widely accepted. This can be in many forms, through colors, icons, or other ways to visualize data and trends within a DT.

2.2 Affective Design and the Feeling of Being Cared for

If technologies could have the ability to identify how we feel and respond with an appropriate emotion, how could we visualize that in a caring and understanding manner? Research shows that when patients are approached by medical professionals in a patient-centered way with respect and care, patients' satisfaction and motivation can improve significantly [38, 39]. The study of Bickmore [17] shows that caring can be explored by considering a set of communicative behaviors such as showing social support, empathy, giving comfort and trust. Verbal communications, like a friendly "hello" and "goodbye", and non-verbal communication, such as facial expressions showing concern or direct gaze can indicate care [18].

Affective communication can be implemented in conversational agents that are not embodied like a chatbot or social robots. Depending on the data these agents get, such agents can respond emotionally. For example, Felix[1], a social robot, helps people to express their feelings, expressing emotional states through colors and expression of its eyes. Other examples are social robots we see in caring homes for the elderly, like Paro[2] a seal robot; Paro is used as a mediator to reduce stress or depression and to create enjoyment and improve quality of life for the elderly [20]. Further examples include intelligent systems that detect emotions and stimulates behavior change to assist ageing well [57].

These social robots relate to DTs because they use affective design to create or provide empathic feelings. Unlike these social robots, a DT is *self-representation*; it aggregates different layers of information of a person to inform their wellbeing. But similarly, to social robots, a DT can benefit from affective design for it to be used in trusted environments (i.e., at home). As the previous examples like Felix or Paro show, we can apply different communication methods, such as colors to represent emotions. In the DT, rather than colors representing the agent, colors can represent the person's emotions that are expressed through the DT.

3   Research Method

3.1   Participants

A purposive sample was applied to recruit the participants with an average age of 48.9 (range 32–63). They were of mixed gender (14 female and 9 male) from the Flemish region in Belgium. The sample was recruited mainly within the professional network of the researcher as they are a pool of participants who collaborated with the first author in

---

[1] https://www.happybots.nl/.

[2] http://www.parorobots.com/.

previous research; this group was selected for reasons of trust as the topic approaches sensitive and private information. In addition, participants had knowledge of self-tracking tools in general, a few were more technical savvy/oriented than others. Participants were contacted directly through a personal mail or MS Teams calls to explain the purpose of the research. This research was approved by the Ethical Review Board of Technical University of Eindhoven, Netherlands.

3.2 Sessions and Probes

In this design study, we chose to use two design methods. First, the design thinking method [24, 40] was used in sessions we organized with the participants. Design thinking allows for a human-centered design approach to look at people's needs, and the possibility of technologies in products and services, including business requirements [24]. Second, the art thinking [56] method was applied to develop the probes for the one-to-one sessions, that could illustrate how a DT in healthcare could be materialized in a home setting. Art thinking allows more a free-thinking approach, as explained later in the methods section. We used these two different approaches because both methods deliver a framework for facilitating design. Design thinking is used towards product or service development with the end-user in mind, and art thinking is more an individual looking at a problem and asks, 'is this possible?' "Art thinking is less customer oriented and more breakthrough oriented" [56, p. 8]. A DT is a complex concept because it operates in a healthcare environment focused on the individual and holds sensitive personal information. Thus, the art thinking method helps to suspend consideration of this complexity and allows to explore the DT concept more as an artform or art object, exploring it in a free-form context, not immediately thinking about the barriers or obstacles that comes with a DT.

We chose a mix of online and live, one-to-one design sessions because of the COVID-19 restrictions together with the consideration that some participants are higher risk patients (hypertension, type 2 diabetes, cholesterol) even though most of them were vaccinated. Nine sessions were carried out live and fourteen were done online (July–October 2021). The one-to-one design sessions were either with single participants (N = 17) or with couples living together in one home (N = 6).

3.3 Art Thinking

What was unique to our approach was involving the artist Eric Joris of Crew[3] to create probes to be used with participants, to get participants all on the same page in constructing a mutual understanding. Working with artists gives more freedom in thinking, as ideas flow more creatively for people, even allowing for "disruptive thinking" towards problems to find a unique approach or design space [54–56]. The first author and the artist collaborated for creative probes that were seen as essential to spark discussions on what DTs can be, beyond how they are envisioned now (i.e., as medical tools). The artist and the first author discussed how humans express their wellbeing and how these metaphors resemble occurrences that appear in nature. For example, we elaborated on

---

[3] https://crew.brussels/en.

how natural beings change form, such as a pufferfish that change form depending on its environment (Fig. 1), or a chameleon that changes color depending on the environment (Fig. 2). As another example, lava lamps with lava blobs that move with heat can visualize aspects of our behavior and well-being, like a chameleon (changing color) and pufferfish (changing form) as metaphors. In the case of the lava lamp, the blobs can represent (e.g., mood (Fig. 3)). All examples show metaphors about how we could visualize qualitative changes with DTs.

Fig. 1. Puffer fish that changes form when in danger or threatened. Photo by Stelio Puccinelli.

Fig. 2. Chameleons' changes color depending on their environment. Photo by Pierre Bamin.

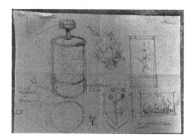

Fig. 3. Sketches by Eric Joris illustrating lava lamp in different forms.

3.4 Design Thinking

The design thinking method[4] [40] was used to empathize, define, and ideate the notion of a DT in healthcare at home. This method is useful because of its iterative process and its

---

[4] https://designthinking.ideo.com/.

human-centered approach towards examining problems or challenges. The empathizing phase allows for discussion of challenges, questioning assumptions, and implications with the participants to define the challenge with more precision. The ideate phase enables brainstorming on a wide range of ideas with the participants looking at the challenge, to converge towards a few prototypes that can be tested and validated by the target users, for this study we applied the empathize and ideate phase for now, as we wanted to explore how participants see the materialization of a DT before going into prototype phase, which is the next step in the process. A 'Miro'[5] online board was setup to explain the concept of DTs for at-home healthcare, used in the online and offline sessions, for introducing the concept to participants and to document the process they took. Each session had a duration of ±45 min.

Ultimately, a DT representing a person's life is a layered technology giving views on the different components in a person's life. Therefore, participants were presented with different probes or designs illustrating different elements such as weight, sleep, physical activity, mood, and location and (limited) medical biomarkers such as blood pressure, glucose, cholesterol, and/or heart rate as individuals' data layers. Within healthcare, these lifestyle data points combined with biomarkers are the components a medical professional may ask during consultations [41]. During the sessions, participants discussed data layers as quantitative, and as qualitative metaphors, an approach based on prior work [42].

3.5   User Involvement

To understand the users' perspectives and their preferences, we involved people, not experts, in the design thinking process for two reasons: 1) the pragmatic rationale to understand their views on the materialization of a DT and 2) the political and ethical rationale that comes with a DT in healthcare [63, 64].

The Pragmatic Rationale

The pragmatic rationale allows co-design to materialize as possible DT options in healthcare in home setting in an early stage. We were interested in how users would envision and experience a DT as a personal coach or health companion, as well as other ideas they may have. We also looked at various affordances and appropriation of the emerging technology from participants' views.

The Political and Ethical Rationale

As a DT in healthcare holds a lot of sensitive information, we wanted to address the underlying concern on what users see as barriers in the appropriation of DTs. DTs might change the current healthcare system, creating new policies, and AI ethical guidelines are already in place on European level [29]. The discourse on these elements can be a part of the conversation in the process, as they have implications on DT designs as well.

3.6   Thematic Analysis

The discussions were recorded either with MS Teams (with video) or mobile phone (only audio) depending on the availability of the technologies with the participants and

---

[5] https://miro.com/.

whether it was an online or live workshop. The recordings were transcribed verbatim and corrected for mistakes. We created mind maps [43] for initial coding. Then we coded themes and subthemes using NVIVO software[6]. We chose for an inductive, data-driven approach without a pre-existing coded framework [44] which allows us to describe (lived) experiences, explanations, and the reality of participants within the thematic analysis approach [26]. As most of the participants already had experiences with self-tracking devices, we chose to identify patterns within our gathered data in relation to participants' lived experience, views, and perspectives, to understand what they think or feel. The findings are on their views about the affective design of DTs for healthcare at home, how their data should be represented qualitatively, and their concerns. This resulted in different themes and subthemes, illustrated in Fig. 4.

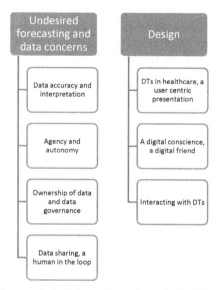

Fig. 4. Themes and subthemes derived from thematic analysis, inductive data-driven without pre-existing framework.

4   Results

4.1   Undesired Forecasting

Typically, a DT is assumed to be useful for forecasting and simulating health status based on historical and current data. However, most of our participants were not interested in forecasting for two main reasons: 1) doubts regarding the data accuracy and the feasibility of modelling human complexity accurately and 2) the confrontation and vulnerability that comes with forecasting. We elaborate on these in the subthemes.

---

[6] https://www.qsrinternational.com/nvivo-qualitative-data-analysis-software/home.

Data Accuracy and Interpretation

As an outlier, one participant, in contrast to the other participants, reasoned that forecasting or better planning upfront could be helpful: *"if you know what your morbidity factors are, eh, to talk about that, then you must take that into account. I'll take that into account, if you have certain conditions, you are more likely to die faster, actually you have to take that into account, so yes, I'm interested in this" (P1)*. However, the remaining participants did not share this perspective, expressing doubts as to the accuracy of the data that the DT is built upon and the complexity of health as a concept which pertains too many variables. Furthermore, predictions can make people feel vulnerable based on what they do know about their family history. For example, P13 said *"I'm coming from a family of cancer and the outcome would be like, look at your 58-year-old you; you will follow your father. That impact, that image, I don't think that is OK", is the data 100% reliable? That is the question and then you might receive a message that is incorrect with all the consequences and mental impact it entails"*. Further P15 argues, *"if the data is unfiltered, I don't see that ending so well, because people will freak out"*. These concerns were also shared with others.

P8 mentioned: *"I don't believe in forecasting because a lot depends on your genes and whether or not you're lucky in certain things, not everything can be explained scientifically. I'm more of the principle of, I don't want to know. Life is what it is, and I take it as it comes" (P8)*. Participants felt that there are too many uncertainties in life. They do not fully trust the data that would be presented as predictions. Accuracy is a major concern and is not necessarily seen to be possible when health depends on "genes" and "luck".

In relation, DTs' forecasting feature can be confrontational. Participants expressed their feelings on vulnerability and how to cope with forecasts. As P9 illustrated *"for me, personally that is scary, I feel more vulnerable than before, friends that are dying, it all becomes so visible"*. P3 stated: *"if you get yourself checked regularly, no, I don't need a digital twin in any form, that would be no good for me, no that would be no good for me, it will stress me out, it will make me sick (laughs)"*. Vulnerability thus comes from confronting the (near or far) future deaths of one's friends (P9), as well as confronting one's own health (P3). There were other arguments. P2 said *"I like the chaos of life" (P2)* referring to unexpected events in life and spontaneous behavior. P2 then refers to the ability to have an unfettered life, not living in a 'nanny' technology world. P16 reasoned that *"I want to have the feeling there is time and space"* (i.e., time and space for life's spontaneity). Overall, participants were not into forecasting; it would limit their life and take away their freedom, perhaps the freedom to not know the future and to live in the present. People want to live in the "now" and use their digital twin more as a reflection tool to optimize their quality of life.

Agency and Autonomy

Most participants pointed out that a DT should be positive, constructive, and not patronizing. If framed positively, they could work on a positive health outcome with their digital twin, which would motivate them to do better in creating a healthier lifestyle, if that is necessary. For example, if a DT could positively create more awareness in one's behavior it could help: *"if it is something where you can better yourself, that could work for me" (P17)*. P1 said *"I now happen to have high cholesterol and high blood pressure, and then I worry. I must take medication for that now, but it would be something that can point to me, just live a bit healthier or pay attention. When you sit in front of your TV in the evening instead of drinking three glasses of wine, take only one".* As a previously mentioned outlier, P1 sees a DT aiding her autonomy, not replacing it.

Some participants had the feeling that a DT would control their life to much: *"I would get stressed from the lifestyle data. I must do this and that is too much. My lifestyle makes me relax. I then lived too much. I don't want that. Then you are not in the here and now (P22). It should not be too controlled. I must have choice in what I can eat, freedom is important".* While self-tracking has the promise of self-empowerment, it could also become an imposed or pushed act by insurers, employers, or just social pressure. Therefore, this can create disempowerment and become more of a surveillance tool for external stakeholders than enabling power for the user/citizen. Another participant argued that it would take away the ability of self-reflection; relying too much on technology could lead to erosion of human agency, natural intelligence versus artificial intelligence: *"strong skills people have will fade away, that makes (us) kind of 'docile' people. Self-reflection, no, I will ask my DT" (P10).* In sum, the positive aspects are the ability to create awareness on current behaviors that might enable behavior change if necessary. The potential negative point is that DTs might erode human agency, and thus less human autonomy. There are two supporting subthemes below.

Ownership of Data and Data Governance

The ownership of data and data governance is a main worry for participants. While data governance on medical data is regulated and in place, healthcare providers and insurers can gather a lot of data via DTs which then can be stored by private companies. The pros and cons were brought up by participants. One couple, P5 and 15 said; *"by using a DT, you will create a new world order. In the end, yes, that data will be used. But I have no problem to make it available for doctors, because it is there then it will be useful'.*

Lifestyle data gathered by mobile apps or wearable devices are mainly developed and designed by private companies and managed by these companies. Transparency is needed to gain trust of the users. P14 stated: *"More and more I'm protecting my data as it is abused. For me an online health system is not an option. If it would be offline, it would be my application and I can update or synchronize it occasional".* Yet, another participant argued that *"where is the data stored, this is important to know, is it protected? This should be transparent otherwise I would be reluctant to use it, although I'm interested in using it"* (P23). Other participants have the same concerns in privacy and ethics on where the data is stored, who can see the data and use the data and for what purpose the data are being gathered. P9 argues *"people do look at the government, you have your 'e-box', 'my health view' in which we already contain a lot of data. The mutuality is the same. If you do your shopping always in the same store (e.g., Colruyt), you save points, because you then get €5 discount. Your diet, they can perfectly extract those products and create a customer profile, we give up a lot of privacy and it is all connected".* Apart from the self-surveillance, there is a danger that these technologies can be used for surveilling a whole population. Developing new policies based on this information can depend on which country you live in these are possible scenarios. On the positive side, this information can also help better a society; it might help to close the gap of inequality, for example, by getting more insights and detail on how to install policies when considering the social determinates of health[7]. These were regular reflections on the usage of a DT in healthcare.

Human-in-the-Loop Data Sharing

Participants want to be in control of their own data. For instance, couples who live together were not so eager to share data with their partners, as they really see it as a private, personal environment. P23 stated *"I think this is a personal decision, I don't think my partner would use this"*. Another participant P16 said *"I really see it as a private thing, it is my private story, I don't see my partner in it or my children, it would be then four different screens, not mingled with each other, I don't even know whether my partner would be interested in this"*. The issue is the feeling of being watched by one's partner when sharing their information: *"seeing that (data) visualized together, yes, I would feel a bit being watched"* (P9). Couples really see the DT as a private environment, something they own and see as private use, their personal space. They are willing to talk about it, but not giving access to their partner. *"I might be willing to share my data and stuff, but I don't want to share my DT as such"* (P7).

In general, participants want to share their data with medical professionals, give consent to access the data, discussing the results, evaluating and interpretating the data, P1 states: *"it is really the GP (General Practitioner) who has followed you closely for years. He knows how that works for you"*, P13 elaborates; *"I think that combination, indeed, because you get a coach who can also put this in perspective and map it out. I would feel more comfortable with that"*. P20 argues *"yes, I would think that is one of the advantages. What you collect is a lot of ordinary data that can be important anyway. The GP sometimes ask that information, but I haven't thought about it (P20). Sometimes you don't know any more what you did in the past week, this could help you with it"* (P20). Depending on the nature, participants are not eager to share the data with their partner, not giving consent to *share* with their partner, they see it as a private environment, but willing to talk about it with their partner. Furthermore, there were some thoughts about sharing a DT with private insurance companies, more specific on hospitalization insurances. It might lead to different scenarios; one participant sees potential: *"In Great Britain, they have insurances where vegetarians are stimulated. If you declare on paper, you are a vegetarian, you get a reduction on your insurance"* (P13). While another participant argues that *"I think it should be protected, if my hospitalization insurance is giving up on me, because according to them I don't fall within the standards, I don't want that, so I don't want them to know, actually"* (P1). In conclusion, people are willing to share data if it can help them (e.g., with medical professionals). But they are cautious about sharing their DT with other external stakeholders such as insurances, even with their partners, in the case of couples. Participants want to talk about their DT but not sharing it in terms of giving consent, which should be solely with the medical professionals. Thus, human-in-the-loop refers to how medical professionals could aid in the process of evaluating and interpreting the data and help in decision making.

---

[7] https://www.who.int/health-topics/social-determinants-of-health.

4.2 Design

DTs in Healthcare: A User Centric Presentation

We aimed to understand participants' preferences in presenting the data and interacting with their DT in general. Participants stated that they want their DT in the background, not invasive and on demand. The DT's awareness of one's health should be subtle: *"if there is no purpose or goal, I would see it in the background. It could be there, but I would pay less attention"* (P19). A DT could be activated in the morning, giving results of one's sleep in a soft glow or use subtle lights: *"something you just pass in your house for instance, like light or a glow, that reflects how you slept would be cool* (P23*).* A qualitative interface or display could allow for personal imaginaries, representing oneself in a concept of a digital twin at a certain moment or over a timeframe. P2 preferred "raw" data presentation, the quantitative way, as stated: *"I'm more the man of figures, I like to know things exactly"*.

While some participants like to see a snapshot of their wellbeing, others are more interested in a timeline where they can see the history of their data. *"Like a timeline of that information over a few years (which) would be extremely helpful [as] the story of my data. I get coughs like twice a year. I would like to track it because I always forget"* (P7). But at the same time, not every countable data should count: *"I hate counting calories, I just hated it. Makes me so sad, but if I could easily without thinking about it, just having an overview of how many calories I had and then something telling me, you might want to cut back on the strawberries, because they give you stomach problems. I really would love that kind a thing"* (P7). What is suggested here is information on, e.g., frequency of getting coughs or calories, with a possible prescriptive suggestion on how one should or could act.

As for a specific example, participants elaborated further on sketches previously prepared by the researcher and the artist (Fig. 3). Discussing the lava lamp (Fig. 5), for instance, P20 explained *"I like the idea of the lamp, but can it hold all the data? Or I can talk to it, and it gives me the results"*. This is a different conception of a lava lamp (i.e., lava lamps normally do not talk or suggest data). P20 recalled that *"I had a lava lamp back in the day, it is soothing and mesmerizing"*. Thus, participants were looking for familiar objects with positive connotations to extend the notion of a DT. According to P1, *"you could give it colors like yellow, orange and red for example"* to represent different data types.

Fig. 5. Colored lava lamp based on a dataset, each blub represents a lifestyle component such as physical activity, sleep and so forth (P 1, 14, 20, and 22 discussed the lava lamp though the drawing was originally created by the researcher).

A Digital Conscience or a Digital Friend

A participant calls a DT as a 'digital friend': *"it is a bit like a friend, they are there when you need them. Sometimes you need them more, depending on the situation"* (P22). This illustrates on the one hand, the temporary use of a DT, when it is 'needed' such as an event that is happening in one's life, and on the other hand a form of dependency towards the technology to consult the DT if necessary to get confirmation and gratification on the components they measured about themselves. Some participants were more philosophical, thinking that a DT could be their 'digital conscience'. As P16 explained: *"I'm triggered by the notion of a 'digital conscience', for me that is the case, although I see it as a sort of reward. Having a DT can be like creating my own artwork, if it goes well, it entails some kind of, yes, beauty. Also, when it (health) is less good, the color palette could adjust accordingly, colors could become darker"* (P16 – Fig. 6). P16 continues: *"if I dream out loud, I'm thinking of a 'digital painting' as it were. But I would also love the ability to turn it around and switch to the pure data."*

Fig. 6. Screen showing qualitative and quantitate data representing weight over a 6-year period. The green color represents things are going well. Pictures can come from the participant (P 16)

While other participants like P1 and P2 were also talking about a 'digital conscience', they saw it slightly differently. P1 stated *"I could see at as my second conscience, but it can't be patronizing, it needs to stay fun and positive to use"*.

Participants want the experience of the DT to differ from their negative experiences within the existing healthcare system. P11 shared an experience with a nurse. After weighing the participant, the nurse bluntly reacted, "you weigh 4 kg more than before" (P11). The participant experienced the feedback as being accusing. This is a negative example of how a DT should not convey information. Another participant (P13) was illustrating that a DT could be gentle in a way, for example: *"instead of saying look, you've gained 10 kg, if you continue, like this, within ten years you will get a heart disease and it's done, there could be stimulating feedback: if you start losing weight you will feel so much better"*. Participants referred towards positive feedback loops and cues stimulating the users, that could be implemented in a DT.

P2 wondered if he wants to see the DT as their own 'conscience': *"What comes to mind is a 'digital conscience', the question is whether I want that. We are all 60 years old or more, we try to live a good life and be aware of things, but do we want to have that mirror every day?"* (P2). This suggests that P2 would not prefer to be always conscious of what is happening as a "mirror" for self-awareness. Two participants reflected on the digital conscience in terms of competing with oneself: *"a DT can be positive, but to compete with myself, I wouldn't feel like that too much"* (P13) while P7 states: *"I think that if I would be kept on seeing red, you know. OK, maybe like I wanted to get green that it would be like a competition with myself. And then I'd be like, OK I did it."* So, some participants see DT as some sort of reward system to improve their quality of life while others see it more as something that could over structure their life and limit their freedom, while others see it as help as long it is not patronizing and that it stays positive and fun to use. The notion of a digital friend or digital conscience suggests that people are envisioning DTs as more than a "data double"; DTs representing who they are or showing who they are to themselves can be explored.

Interacting with DTs

A DT can give (visual) signals or cues as feedback loops and participants described these cues metaphorically: *"I have too little oxygen and you see a few butterflies flying on the wall and they go to the window and there they hang on the window', a very quiet way to say there is too little oxygen, open the window"* (P14).

Other participants described interfaces reacting upon speech, gesture, touch: (P9) comments *"I see myself talking to it, like one of the things with the sleep tracker, I spent too much time to figure it out"*. (P20) states *"I like the lamp idea, but wondering if it can visualize all the data, it would be interesting that I could ask questions to it as well concerning my sleep or physical activity and that it then shows other visualizations as well"*. Yet another participant sees a magic mirror: "Something you touch a magic mirror, the data can be hidden and available when you need it, but the object can just show other presentation forms" (P23).

These quotes refer to Natural User Interfaces (NUI), interfaces that feel natural for the user as they are familiar with speech, gesture, and touch, they come across as very natural, with a promise of ease of use [51, 66]. However, these NUI's need to be carefully designed having their own design challenges [65] asking for some specific settings. Some were against the speech interface, because of the invasiveness on their privacy, which worries (P21): *"yes, talking to an object, is like the object is constantly listen, right, otherwise they cannot react, while with a wearable or a mobile phone I can just touch, and it reacts. I don't want them to listen to what I'm saying all the time"*. In conclusion, the interaction with a DT requires positive experiences and ease of use in the appropriation and affordances of these technologies considering the privacy of the user (i.e., voice, touch or gesture enabled technologies).

5   Discussion

We investigated people's perspectives on DTs for healthcare. Our aim was to understand how users would see the materialization of a DT at home and how they would like to see their data become represented as a digital version of themselves. Data was collected through workshops based on our design-thinking and art-thinking methods. Our thematic analysis resulted in two themes. The first theme was on forecasting with a subtheme on the DT's forecasting ability. The findings also showed concerns on the data accuracy and data governance of a DT. Then the second theme was on the design of a DT with subthemes on digital conscious and interacting with a DT.

We took Grieves definition into account to start, which is a general approach towards DTs in manufacturing mainly, while Huang (2022) refined that definition towards a DT for personalized health care services: "a digital twin for personalized health care service is a data-driven, interactive computerized model that aims to offer health-related information that properly simulates or predicts the health conditions of a particular person" [53, p. 12]. This definition, as our study showed, might not be comprehensive.

5.1 Undesired Forecasting

With Huang's definition in mind, we see a divide on the forecasting ability of a DT. While medical experts show interest in forecasting based on the data models for personalized medicine and predictive treatment [9, 10, 41], the participants in our study showed much less interest in this. It does not encompass the participants' lived experience. Many participants actually felt that forecasting made them feel vulnerable and wanted to prefer to live in the present moment without worrying about their friends or their health or even in some cases, deaths (P9, P3). This demonstrates that the predictive health may not be what people want via their DTs.

DTs can show health-related predictions, but almost none of the participants were interested in forecasting. The main reasons were that the participants doubted the data accuracy and that the complexity of variables that relate to health are difficult to combine. Further, forecasting was not a priority because participants did not want to know what will happen as they want to have room to live in the moment, without projected health-related worries. Furthermore, thinking about 'the future self', such as exploring different hypothetical futures [46] can possibly create hope or fear. These are core motivators for behavior change [45]. But participants in this study tended to see rather the fear component than the hope, especially if they were older. In conclusion, DTs in healthcare for experts has a different application, meaning, and use, compared to our participants. For experts, a DT is a facilitating tool to have a better overview and understanding of a patient [41], while for our participants, it is a facilitating tool for their wellbeing and reflection on the information they get from their DT.

5.2 Quantitative Versus Qualitative Presentation

Among the participants, a dichotomy existed between quantitative and qualitative data presentation of a DT. Some participants were more interested in a quantitative data representation, while others more in qualitative data representation. But there was a consensus in having the ability to have both views. One of the reasons for choosing a qualitative approach is to prioritize different mappings or visualizations of data. This allows for emotional reactions to be qualitatively represented (e.g., as lava lamp blobs or butterflies to represent feelings or mood), compared to the raw data and quantitative presentations, which might result in panic reactions, as users may not always interpretate the data correctly (P13, 15). Only with red alert (i.e., emergencies), participants would like to dig deeper in their data to see what is going on, together with the ability to discuss these results with a medical professional (P13, P15).

A DT could allow for more imaginative understanding of one's wellbeing [23]. Moreover, presenting data according to perceived feelings or emotions of an individual can create active engagement or creativity to look at oneself in a different way, stimulating motivation to adjust oneself for the better, if necessary. As mentioned before, individuals have the tendency to express themselves more in a qualitative manner than a quantitative manner, so presenting data in a qualitative manner might create more data ownership, but also more emotional dependencies.

Participants made clear that they would share and discuss their data with medical professionals to help them interpretate the data that they gathered (P1, P5, P13, P15, P20). They wanted to give more detailed information about themselves to medical professionals to augment what the DT offered. They wanted to be actively involved in designing of their DT, creating a positive affective atmosphere of data; this relates to the assemblage of data (place, space, time, code and data) and how these assemblages generate feelings [27]. Having a say on what their DT would do or look like was interesting for participants; they could create their own data stories or their own artwork (i.e., qualitative representation of personal data) [25].

Some questioned if this technology would take away one's intelligence, like intuitive knowledge about one's health, which relates to concerns about the erosion of human agency and autonomy by over-relying on digital tools [28, 30], as AI systems tend to increasingly act independently and take over control [59]. However, it might give individuals more freedom in making decisions or even give the feeling of self-control, if in people self-design and self-optimize how their DT looks, behaves, and collects and uses their data [60], considering there is still a human-in-the-loop to discuss and support decision making. For example, people can decide when to go to a doctor, what to share with professionals, and how to look for certain treatments. The relationship with the medical professional and patient can change with DTs; patients can be more informed and have a more in-depth conversation with the professional [52]. If people are involved in the design of DTs, it may increase engagement in digital healthcare at home. Involvement in design is understood as using or creating their own imaginaries, creating their own artwork with their data, building up their own story so to speak, being in control in managing their DT. Participants experienced their DT as a reflection tool to help them to improve their quality of life rather than seeing it as a forecasting tool.

5.3 Design Implications of DTs

The design implications of DTs mentioned by participants often referred to natural user interfaces (NUI) [51]. These interfaces feel "natural" or easy to use, but we see that how DTs can become "natural" or they should be grouped under NUIs should be further researched on [65]. In addition, some participants illustrated on the temporary use of a DT (i.e., only being visible when it is 'needed', because of an event that is happening in one's life) [48]. This can form a dependency (i.e., to consult the DT if necessary to get motivation, confirmation, and gratification on the components they measured about themselves) [49]. Furthermore, participants referred to creative representations, such as DTs as objects that glow when they pass them, referring to ambient information systems. While there are various definitions of these systems, Stasko et al. [61] state that "an ambient display resides in the periphery of a person's attention. The display calmly changes state in some way to reflect changes in the underlying information it is representing" [60, p. 19]. Moreover, calming technologies can give an aesthetic dimension to one's personal environment, creating a positive affective atmosphere in home settings. As participants illustrated DTs can be creative presentations of their personal wellbeing, not always active (subtle interaction). These ambient display systems should be explored further in future research to get a more concrete understanding of how to represent holistic views of who we are in DTs.

5.4 Transparency in DTs

In relation, whilst there was enthusiasm on possible designs and materialization of DTs, participants had worries concerning the data. Data concerns were categorized in three different subthemes: 1) ownership and governance of data, 2) data sharing, and 3) data accuracy. DTs in healthcare can bring biomedical data closer to the patient, allowing patients to control and own their biological data. However, complete human oversight and transparency in a DT application is an important requirement [11]. Participants commented on how data are stored, which data are stored, and for what purpose and who has access or how consent is handled within a DT in healthcare. In the context of a DT, several data risk scenarios can rise. Other studies showed that experts were talking about connecting a DT to private insurance companies, enabling reward systems for those individuals who do well; some people could get a cheaper insurance while others who do less well or are ignorant will have to pay more [41, 52]. But our participants commented on how connecting health data to insurance companies would be a risk. While self-surveillance might be helping in prevention, people might be pushed or imposed by external stakeholders to make choices that thwart their autonomy. DTs can enable surveillance in general by external stakeholders.

Surveillance allows for social sorting of a population, allowing new policies based on this information. Depending on which country one lives in, these scenarios can come to the fore [8, 50]. Furthermore, data are a risk for security breaches. If data can be lost or stolen, it is unclear where or with whom the responsibility or accountability lies. There might be considerations such as the location of servers and what legislative domain that falls under. DTs in healthcare deal with sensitive, personal information that demands robust and trustworthy data management. While GDPR (General Data Protection Regulation) law applies and there are AI ethical frameworks as well as expert commissions [29], all such initiatives do not encompass how DTs should be handled legally and ethically. A complete transparency on data use and storage, as well as policies on how to create trustworthy and robust DTs, are a major requirement for the participants. Additionally, participants would share their data with medical professionals, a trusted network, or an appointed, trusted person. But couples in this study were not eager to give access or share the data as such to their partners though they would talk or discuss their health information with each other. They see DTs as private, single-use and personal space or their "digital conscience".

5.5 Limitations

The limitations of this research are mainly in the sample and specific region. It is a sample of 23 participants from the Flemish region in Belgium. Even though Europe has a Directorate-General (DG) Santé, Health and food safety[8] to support EU public health, each EU country has its own versions and adjustments in healthcare. "Health care

---

[8] https://ec.europa.eu/info/departments/health-and-food-safety_en.

systems stem from specific political, historical, cultural, and socio-economic traditions. As a result, the organizational arrangements for health care differ considerably between Member States - as does the allocation of capital and human resources"[9].

Most participants worked already with self-tracking tools in the past and were already familiar with those concepts, so imagining a DT concept was not completely strange. As an extra note, none of the participants had severe health problems. We suggest potential users to be interviewed and consulted from a wide range of backgrounds and places, with different health care needs. In addition, prototyping of a DT for users (non-experts) can be a next step, together with an ethical framework of this concept, which can vary from how current norms and legislation (e.g., GDPR), are conceptualized.

6   Conclusion

We aimed to get an understanding on user' perspectives (as non-experts) and their design preferences of DTs for managing their health at home. As DTs in healthcare are replicas of a physical assets, in this case humans, we covered affective atmospheres of data and affective design with the notion that DTs would be designed and modeled based on these approaches to create more engagement and empowerment for the user. Our findings showed a divide in the conceptualization of a DT. While current, expert norms see a DT in healthcare as a forecasting and simulation tool for predictive health, our participants mostly did not want it as a forecasting tool. They were open to a DT as a reflecting tool to improve their quality of life. In that perspective, participants were in favor of representing aspects of themselves in a qualitative manner rather than in a quantitative manner. But they wanted an option to explore the details of a quantitative presentation, in case there would be red (or emergency) alerts. Apart of the data risks participants brought up, they also saw the added value of using a DT, if their autonomy could be preserved. Some even saw a DT as a "digital conscience" that can positively help them reflect, rather than prescribing what they should do in a patronizing manner. Our view is that the "holy grail" of health forecasting via digital twins can harm, rather than help, if we overlook the emotional vulnerabilities that come with health predictions. Rather than forecasts of what our future can bring, which can bring fear or worries, digital twins can help if we welcome personal reflections for living well in the present.

References

1. Grieves, M.: Digital twin: manufacturing excellence through virtual factory replication. USA (2014)
2. Lupton, D.: Data Selves, More-than-Human Perspectives. Wiley (2019)
3. Smith, G.: Surveillance, data and embodiment: on the work of being watched. Body Soc. **22**, 108–139 (2016)
4. Lakoff, G.: Metaphors We Live By. University of Chicago Press, Chicago (1980)
5. Gibbs, R.: The Poetics of Mind: Figurative Thought, Language, and Understanding. Cambridge University Press, Cambridge (1994)

---

[9] https://ec.europa.eu/commission/presscorner/detail/en/IP_21_1682.

6. Schwartz, S.: Digital twins and the emerging science of self: implications for digital health experience design and "small" data. Front. Comput. Sci. **2**, 31 (2020)
7. Lupton, D.: The digitally engaged patient: self-monitoring and self-care in the digital health era. Soc. Theory Health **11**, 256–270 (2013). https://doi.org/10.1057/sth.2013.10
8. Sharon, T.: Self-tracking for health and the quantified self: re-articulating autonomy, solidarity, and authenticity in an age of personalized healthcare. Philos. Technol. **30**(1), 93–121 (2017)
9. El Saddik, A.: Digital twins: the convergence of multimedia technologies. IEEE Multimed. Comput. Soc. **25**(2), 87–92 (2018)
10. Fuller, A.: Digital twin: enabling technology, challenges and open research. IEEE Access **8**, 108952–108971 (2020)
11. Bruynseels, K.: Digital twins in health care: ethical implications of an emerging engineering paradigm. Front. Genet. **31** (2018)
12. Pols, J.: Caring devices: about warm hands, cold technology and making things fit. In: Care at a Distance: on the Closeness of Technology. Amsterdam University Press (2012)
13. Choe, E.: Characterizing visualization insights from quantified selfers' personal data presentations. IEEE Comput. Graph. Appl. **35**(4), 28–37 (2015)
14. Vannini, P.: Non-representational methodologies: reenvisioning research. Routledge (2015)
15. Anderson, B.: Affective atmospheres. Emot. Space Soc. **2**(2), 77–81 (2009)
16. Ash, J.: Rethinking affective atmospheres: technology, perturbation and space times of the non-human. Geoforum **49**, 20–28 (2013)
17. Bickmore, T.: Towards caring machines. conference on human factors in computing systems. CHI 2004. MIT Media Laboratory, Vienna (2004). https://www.media.mit.edu/people/picard/projects/
18. Argyle, M.: Bodily Communication, 2nd edn. Routledge (1988)
19. Happybots, Felix, een maatje om aan te vertellen hoe je je voelt (2021). https://www.happybots.nl/
20. Hung, L.L.: The benefits of and barriers to using a social robot PARO in care settings: a scoping review. BMC Geriatr **19**(1), 1–10 (2019)
21. Wan, E.: "I'm like a wise little person": notes on the metal performance of woebot the mental health chatbot. Theatre J. **73**(3), E-21–E-30 (2021)
22. Picard, R.: Computers that recognise and respond to user emotion: theoretical and practical implications. Interact. Comput. **14**(2), 141–169 (2002)
23. Murnane, E.: Designing ambient narrative-based interfaces to reflect and motivate physical activity. In: Proceedings of the SIGCHI Conference on Human Factors in Computing systems. CHI Conference (2020)
24. IDEO Design Thinking. https://designthinking.ideo.com/
25. Lockton, D.: Sleep ecologies: tools for snoozy autoethnography. In: Proceedings of the 2020 ACM Designing Interactive Systems Conference. Association for Computing Machinery. ACM (2020)
26. Braun, V.: Using thematic analysis in psychology. Qual. Res. Psychol. **3**(2), 77–101 (2006)
27. Lupton, D.: How does health feel? Towards research on the affective atmospheres of digital health. Digital Health **3**, 1–11 (2017)
28. Anderson, J.: Concerns about human agency, evolution and survival (2018). https://www.pewresearch.org/internet/2018/12/10/concerns-about-human-agency-evolution-and-survival/
29. AI HLEG: Ethics Guidelines for Trustworthy AI. Brussels (2019). https://ec.europa.eu/digital-single-market/en/news/ethics-guidelines-trustworthy-ai
30. Bartneck, C.: An Introduction to Ethics in Robotics and AI. SpringerBriefs in Ethics (2020)
31. EU commission: Europe Fit for the Digital Age: Artificial Intelligence (2021). https://ec.europa.eu/commission/presscorner/detail/en/IP_21_1682
32. Hancı, E.: The impact of mindset on self-tracking experience. Front. Digital Health (2021)

33. Hancı, E., Ruijten, P.A.M., Lacroix, J., Kersten-van Dijk, E.T., IJsselsteijn, W.A.: Are trackers social actors? The role of self-tracking on self-evaluation. In: Oinas-Kukkonen, H., Win, K.T., Karapanos, E., Karppinen, P., Kyza, E. (eds.) Persuasive Technology: Development of Persuasive and Behavior Change Support Systems. vol. 11433, pp. 31–42. Springer, Cham (2019). https://doi.org/10.1007/978-3-030-17287-9_3

34. Xie, Q.: Human-exoskeleton coupling dynamics of a multi-mode therapeutic exoskeleton for upper limb rehabilitation training. IEEE Access **9**, 61998–62007 (2021)

35. Boulos, K.: Digital twins: from personalised medicine to precision public health. J. Pers. Med. **11**(8), 745 (2021)

36. Kaziunas, E., Ackerman, M.S.: Designing for lived health: a practice-based approach for person-centered health information technologies. In: Wulf, V., Schmidt, K., Randall, D. (eds.) Designing Socially Embedded Technologies in the Real-World. pp. 357–381. Springer, London (2015). https://doi.org/10.1007/978-1-4471-6720-4_15

37. Chow, K.K.N.: Designing representations of behavioral data with blended causality: an approach to interventions for lifestyle habits. In: Oinas-Kukkonen, H., Win, K.T., Karapanos, E., Karppinen, P., Kyza, E. (eds.) Persuasive Technology: Development of Persuasive and Behavior Change Support Systems. vol. 11433, pp. 52–64. Springer, Cham (2019). https://doi.org/10.1007/978-3-030-17287-9_5

38. Bellet, P.: The importance of empathy as an interviewing skill in medicine. JAMA **266**(13), 1831–1832 (1991)

39. Levinson, W.: A study of patient clues and physician responses in primary care and surgical settings. JAMA **284**(8), 1021–1027 (2000)

40. Razzouk, R.: What is design thinking and why is it important? Rev. Educ. Res. **82**(3), 330–348 (2012)

41. De Maeyer, C.: Future outlook on the materialisation, expectations and implementation of Digital Twins in healthcare. In: 34th British HCI Conference (HCI2021), pp. 180–191. London: BCS Learning & Development Ltd. Proceedings of the BCS 34th British HCI Conference 2021, UK (2021). https://doi.org/10.14236/ewic/HCI2021.18

42. Menheere, D.: Ivy: a qualitative interface to reduce sedentary behavior in the office context. DIS 2020 Companion - Companion Publication of the 2020 ACM Designing Interactive Systems Confer. ACM (2020)

43. Hanington, B.: Universal Methods of Design. Rockport Publishers, Beverly, MA (2012)

44. Patton, M.: Qualitative Evaluation and Research Methods. SAGE Publications (1990)

45. Fogg, B.: A behavior model for persuasive design. In: Proceedings of the 4th International Conference on Persuasive Technology, pp. 1–7. Association for Computing Machinery, NY (2009)

46. Rapp, A.: Know thyself: a theory of the self for personal informatics. Hum.–Comput. Interact. **32**(5–6), 335–380 (2017)

47. Lupton, D.: Self-tracking modes: reflexive self-monitoring and data practices. Available at SSRN 2483549 (2014)

48. De Maeyer, C.: Exploring quantified self attitudes. HealthINF. Scitepress, Biostec (2018)

49. Shin, D.: Health experience model of personal informatics: the case of a quantified self. Comput. Hum. Behav. **69**, 62–74 (2017)

50. Matthewman, S.: Theorising personal medical devices. In: Lynch, R., Farrington, C. (eds.) Quantified Lives and Vital Data. pp. 17–43. Palgrave Macmillan UK, London (2018). https://doi.org/10.1057/978-1-349-95235-9_2

51. Wigdor, D.: The Natural User Interface. In: Wigdor, D. (eds) Brave NUI World, Morgan Kaufmann (2011)

52. Popa, E.O., van Hilten, M., Oosterkamp, E., Bogaardt, M.-J.: The use of digital twins in healthcare: socio-ethical benefits and socio-ethical risks. Life Sci. Soc. Policy **17**(1), 1–25 (2021). https://doi.org/10.1186/s40504-021-00113-x

53. Huang, P.: Ethical issues of digital twins for personalized health care service: preliminary mapping study. J. Med. Internet Res. **24**(1), e33081 (2022)
54. Withaker, A.: Art Thinking. Haprper Collins Publishers (2016)
55. Bureau, S.: Art thinking: une méthode pour créer de l'improbable avec certitude. ENTREPRENDRE ET INNOVER **3–4**, 88–103 (2019)
56. Robbins, P.: From design thinking to art thinking with an open innovation perspective—a case study of how art thinking rescued a cultural institution in Dublin. J. Open Innov.: Technol. Mark. Complex. **4**(4), 51 (2018)
57. VicarVision: AID2BeWell (2022). https://www.aid2bewell.eu/
58. Lockton, D.: Exploring qualitative displays and interfaces. In: CHI Conference Extended Abstracts on Human Factors in Computing Systems. ACM (2017)
59. Sankaran, S.M.: "It's like a puppet master": user perceptions of personal autonomy when interacting with intelligent technologies. In: Proceedings of the 29th ACM Conference on User Modeling, Adaptation and Personalization. Assoc. ACM Digital Library (2021)
60. Gimpel, H.: Quantifying the quantified self:a study on the motviations of patients to track their own health. In: Thirty Fourth International Conference on Information Systems. ICIS, Milan (2013)
61. Stasko, J., Miller, T., Pousman, Z., Plaue, C., Ullah, O.: Personalized peripheral information awareness through information art. In: Davies, N., Mynatt, E.D., Siio, I. (eds.) UbiComp 2004: Ubiquitous Computing. vol. 3205, pp. 18–35. Springer, Heidelberg (2004). https://doi.org/10.1007/978-3-540-30119-6_2
62. Dufrenne, M.: Experience, the Phenomenology of Aesthetic. Northwestern University Press, Evanston (1989)
63. Kujala, S.: User involvement: a review of the benefits and challenges. Behav. Inf. Technol. **22**(1), 1–16 (2003)
64. Bekker, M., Long, J.: User involvement in the design of human—computer interactions: some similarities and differences between design approaches. In: McDonald, S., Waern, Y., Cockton, G. (eds) People and Computers XIV — Usability or Else!. Springer, London (2000). https://doi.org/10.1007/978-1-4471-0515-2_10
65. Norman, D.A.: Natural user interfaces are not natural. Interactions **17**(3), 6–10 (2010)
66. Liu, W.: Natural user interface-next mainstream product user interface. In: 2010 IEEE 11th International Conference on Computer-Aided Industrial Design & Conceptual Design, vol. 1, pp. 203–205. IEEE (2010)
67. Sanders, E., Stappers, P.J.: Co-creation and the new landscapes of design. CoDesign **4**(1), 5–18 (2008). https://doi.org/10.1080/15710880701875068

Challenges with Traditional Human-Centered Design for Developing Neurorehabilitation Software

Peter Forbrig(✉) ⓘ, Alexandru Bundea ⓘ, and Mathias Kühn ⓘ

Chair of Software Engineering, University of Rostock,
Albert-Einstein-Street 22, 18055 Rostock, Germany
{peter.forbrig,alexandru-nicolae.bundea,
mathias.kuhn}@uni-rostock.de

Abstract. Within our project E-BRAiN (Evidence-Based Robotic Assistance in Neurorehabilitation) we have been developing software for training tasks for patients after stroke. It is the idea of the project that a humanoid robot is instructing and observing the performance of patients. The paper discusses the challenges of developing such interactive system with an interdisciplinary development team. Goals and rules are different for clinicians, psychologists, sociologists and computer scientists. There are different traditions in those sciences. Therefore, evaluations with patients have to be planned much more carefully than with traditional users of interactive systems. The role of task models, storyboards and prototypes in the domain of neurohabilitation are discussed in connection with an experience report of the E-BRAiN project.

Keywords: Task models · Stakeholders · Domain experts · Usability experts

1 Introduction

In 2019 we started our interdisciplinary project E-BRAiN ((Evidence-Based Robotic Assistance in Neurorehabilitation) [2] with colleagues from Medicine, Psychology, Sociology and Computer Science. The goal of this three years lasting project is to explore whether humanoid robots like Pepper can be supportive for rehabilitative training activities of patients after stroke. For this purpose, we implemented apps for four different kinds of rehabilitation treatments. Those groups of training tasks are: 1. Arm Ability training, 2. Arm Basis Training, 3. Mirror Training and 4. Neurovisual Rehabilitation (for a neglect disorder). Within our software engineering group, we have been following the idea of participatory design (PD) and human-centered design (HCD) for several years. The HCD process was specified as standard in 1999 [8]. It consists of five activities that can be characterized as follows:

1. Plan the human centered process
2. Specify the context of use

© IFIP International Federation for Information Processing 2022
Published by Springer Nature Switzerland AG 2022
R. Bernhaupt et al. (Eds.): HCSE 2022, LNCS 13482, pp. 44–56, 2022.
https://doi.org/10.1007/978-3-031-14785-2_3

3. Specify user and organizational requirements
4. Produce design solutions
5. Evaluate against user requirements and continue with 2, 3 or 4 if the requirements are not met.

It was decided for the software development of our project E-BRAiN to follow a Human-Centered Design (HCD) approach. However, we were not aware of the specific aspects for software development in medicine. This is related to ethical aspects, access to patients and design decisions. Our experience report is structured in such a way that we first introduce the four kinds of training tasks we implemented. Second, we describe how we proceeded in our project. Afterwards, we discuss related work and provide a summary with outlook.

2 Therapies Supported by the E-BRAiN-Project

Within the E-BRAiN-Project we developed software for four different classes of rehabilitation training. The first class is called Arm-Ability Training (AAT). It has been especially designed to promote manual dexterity recovery for stroke patients who have mild to moderate arm paresis (Fig. 1).

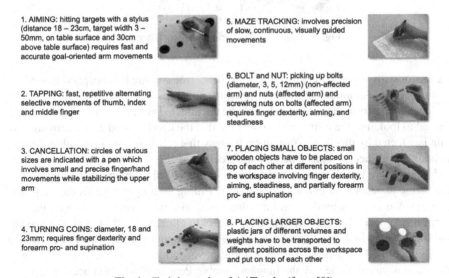

Fig. 1. Training tasks of AAT tasks (from [9]).

Patients with severe arm paresis have to perform first the Arm-Basis-Training (ABT). They need at the beginning the support of a helping hand for exercises. The supporting person will reduce the support from day to day (Fig. 2).

If the health status of a patient is even more severe and s/he cannot move the handicapped arm, a Mirror Therapy might help. In this case, a patient sits at 90 degrees next

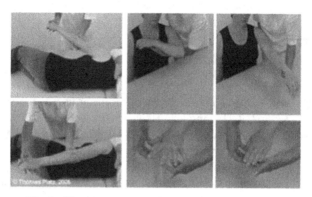

Fig. 2. Situation during an ABT exercises (from [10]).

Fig. 3. Patient acting during a Mirror Therapy.

to a mirror with his healthy arm in front of the mirror and the handicapped behind the mirror (see Fig. 3. Patient acting during a Mirror Therapy.).

A patient performs a training task with the not affected arm. After a while, the patient is asked to look into the mirror and to imagine that the handicapped arm is moving. The brain is affected by this impression in such a way that rehabilitation is possible. Parts of the brain are trained to replace the damaged cells.

Finally, there is a therapy called Neglect. It is a visual problem after a stroke. Left hemiplegic patients have evident difficulties orienting their eyes towards their left field of vision. We implemented several training tasks on a touch screen. They range from identifying objects that are different from others to clicking at all objects of a specific kind like cows, windows or flowers. Figure 4 provides an example where one cow was already identified. If a patient stops without having identified the correct number of objects, hints are provided by the humanoid robot Pepper. First a hint according to the location of an object in one of nine segments ([top, middle, button][left, center, right]). Second a hint is given content wise according already identified objects. Figure 5 gives an impression of the training situation.

Fig. 4. Exploring all cows in a picture during Neglect Therapy.

Fig. 5. Situation where Pepper gives instructions at the beginning of a training task.

3   Our HCD Approach

We started to analyze the context of use by visiting therapies at a clinic for neurorehabilitation. We had a special look at the different training tasks and the support by the therapists. Based on the experiences with task models and our specification environment CoTaSE (Cooperative Task Simulation Environment) we specified models of the behavior of therapists and patients. From this analysis, we envisioned the actions a humanoid robot Pepper has to fulfil. The example of a task model for the robot is presented in Fig. 6. It is specified in the notation of DSL-CoTaL (Domain Specific Language – Cooperative Task Language) [3]. A team model is used to specify the cooperation between different roles. Let us have a look at a specific example of task models for the Mirror Therapy. The team model of Fig. 6 is very simplified and expresses that there is first a greeting part, afterwards the training and finally the end. Pepper and patient can greet in any order (||| - interleaving). The same is true for the end of the exercises. However, in the train part pepper has to show a video before a patient can perform exercises.

During a mirror therapy, the robot has first to greet, afterwards to introduce the training task, to support the training later and finally to end the exercise. The temporal operator >> means enabling. Additionally, the operator ||| (interleaving) allows parallel executions of tasks. While the robot tells the introduction two pictures are shown on its tablet. When the training starts a video is shown and the robot says: "Train three times".

```
⊖team coop {
    root training = greeting >> train{*} [> end_exercise
        task greeting = pepper.greet ||| patient.greet
        task train = pepper.show_video >> patient.goto_next_task
        task end_exercise = pepper.end_exercise ||| patient.finishes_exercises
}
⊖role pepper {
    root roo1 = greet >> instruct >> train{*} [> end_exercise
        task instruct = tell_introd ||| show_pict1 ||| show_pct2
        task instruct pre patient.allInstances.greet
⊖       task train = show_video ||| tell_repeat_3_times >>
                        wait_10_seconds >> train_imagine
        task end_exercise pre patient.allInstances.finishes_exercises
            task train_imagine = tell_repeat_10_times ||| imagine
⊖           task imagine = wait_15_seconds >> tell_look_at_mirror >>
                            tell_imagine_it_is_your_handicapped_arm
}
⊖role patient {
⊖   root root2 = greet >> listens >> performs_exercises{*} [>
                    finishes_exercises >> bye
        task listens pre pepper.oneInstance.instruct
⊖       task performs_exercises = perform_correct [] perform_wrong >>
                            goto_next_task
}
```

Fig. 6. Simplified task models for the mirror therapy (from [4])

After waiting 10 further seconds the task train_imagine follows. It starts with sentence: "Repeat the movements ten times". In parallel the robot waits 15 s and says afterwards: "Look at the mirror" and "Imagine it is your handicapped arm". The robot can end the exercise if all patients finished their exercises.

From our DSL-CoTaL, code for different tools can be generated. In this way, it is possible to visualize the model of pepper from Fig. 6 as a model in CTTE. Figure 7 provides the corresponding result.

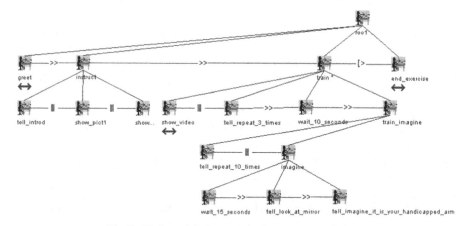

Fig. 7. Task model of pepper in the notation of CTTE.

We were also able to generate code for CoTaSE and animate the models. Figure 8 gives an impression of the situation at the very beginning of the animation. Pepper and patient Illi can execute the task greet. All other tasks are disabled because of temporal relations.

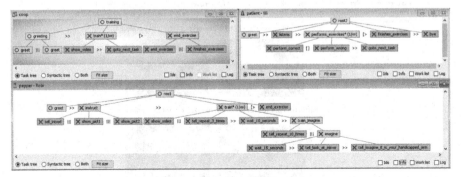

Fig. 8. Animated task models in CoTaSE at the very beginning.

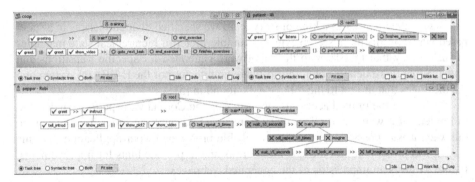

Fig. 9. Animated task models in CoTaSE after some task executions.

In the captured situation of Fig. 9, one can see in the upper left corner of the animated team model describing the general situation. In the upper right corner one can see the task model of patient Illi that greeted and listened already. As next task an exercise can be performed correctly or wrong. Additionally, the exercises can be finished. Pepper Robi greeted, showed two pictures and a video. The humanoid robot can say: "train three times" next.

Discussing the animated models helped us to find a common understanding how the cooperation of robots and patients could work.

After the first experiment with models, detailed manuals were specified by the expert for neurorehabilitation in our project group. They combined medical expressions with instructions for the software design. This includes phrases that the humanoid robot should say and pictures and videos that have to be presented. Figure 10 presents parts of an example for a training task.

Kind of movement	Designation for the patient
Combined shoulder/elbow movements	Push your hand forward and back
(Flexion/Extension and Extension/Flexion)	

Instruction

Please place your forearm on the table and slide your hand forward up the arm fully extended and then pull your hand back on the table. You do three times please Now please do this movement ten more times while watching in the mirror. (After five movements:) Try to imagine that the hand that you see in the mirror is your paralyzed hand, which moves normally.

Instruction photos for a right arm workout (left arm paralyzed):

Instruction photos for a left arm workout (right arm paralyzed):

Fig. 10. Part of a manual specification

Having the manuals as a kind of storyboard we specified dialogue scripts in a state-based way. For this purpose, we extended an interpreter of hierarchical state machines in such a way that messages to the robot were generated for specific transitions and states. Some more details about the software architecture of the E-BRAiN system and the messages that are set to the robot can be found in [5].

Because of the limited access to robots during the Corona virus period, we decided to implement a web-based client that can receive and send messages like a robot. In this way, it was possible to provide a clickable prototype of our applications. In this way, it was possible to test the specified scripts and to provide hints for improvements. Figure 11 gives an impression of the generated webpages.

State - Welcome
Display@Pepper:

Spoken text: "Good morning <patient salutation and name>"

Next states: Introduction   transition after two seconds

Fig. 11. Generated webpage of a dialogue specification

Clicking at <u>Introduction</u> of the webpage of Fig. 11 results in the transition into the corresponding state. This kind of prototype allowed to identify and resolve a lot of problems in the dialogs of therapy sessions. The very good thing was that updates were performed on the Python scripts that are the basis of the prototype but at the same kind the basis of the control of the real robot. We iterated several cycles of the HCD framework.

However, when it came to the state where we wanted to perform training tasks with real patients there were different opinions in our project team. Our colleagues from medicine wanted to approach patients only if the software was nearly perfect and they did not want to evaluate one training task only. They wanted to evaluate a series of training tasks and wanted to measure the success of the training by medical indicators. It was not possible to follow the incremental development process with evaluations by patients we were used to. Additionally, we had to cope with ethical problems that we did not know from projects in other domains. Certain committees and panels protect patients.

Patients are not Simply Users!

For our development process, we identified clinicians, usability experts and patients as the main sources of information. Figure 12 tries to visualize the hierarchy of those stakeholders. The training tasks are designed based on research in neurorehabilitation. Usability plays a minor role. Arguments from the usability point of view are overruled by arguments from neurorehabilitation. Let us have a look at two examples for this purpose.

1. For the crossing out of Os a patient is not allowed to put the arm on the table, which would be much more comfortable. The arm has to be moved freely in the air. The reason for that is to put more stress on the brain with the goal of a better rehabilitation. Usability is not the main purpose of the app.
2. For the neglect therapy we had to work with about three hundred pictures. In one series of exercises patients have to identify windows of buildings. Several buildings have two windows and one building has 50 windows. From the point of view of usability 50 windows seem to be too much and two windows not challenging enough. However, the experts from medicine are more important than usability experts.

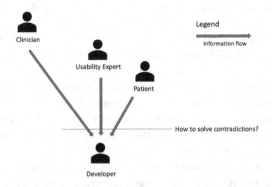

Fig. 12. Main stakeholders for the development process of the E-BRAiN software

In our project, we followed more or less a domain-expert driven approach. One can consider this as a specific participation-driven technique. However, the methods are very different and we did not expect the consequences from the very beginning. Usability experts can provide arguments pro and cons of certain features. Nevertheless, the final decision is made by a clinician. The clinician specified in detail together with developers and usability experts the training tasks and the related dialogs.

We also learned that patient involvement has to be planned carefully for a long time before an experiment can start. Certain committees have to check ethical rules and to agree to the experiments. One has to specify in detail what one wants to reach with the experiments. A fact, we were not aware of.

We also recognized that certain techniques that we used most in usability engineering like thinking aloud were totally impossible with patients. Post-stroke patients have problems with pronunciations and they are distracted from their training task if they are forced to explain their activities. Observation was the best what we were able to reach and this was even difficult to perform.

4 Related Work and Discussion

Hamzah und Wahid [3] provide a literature review of participatory design in the development of healthcare systems. They analyzed 71 papers published between 2010 and 2015. Those papers came from computer science (52 papers), medicine (23), engineering (17), health professions (13) and mathematics (8). The further analysis was focused on the 52 papers from computer science. They determined eight principles for participatory design that were grouped into four themes: (a) the actors' habits and perspectives; (b) the actors' relationship; (c) the designer's mastery of techniques, language and technology; and (d) the implementation process and context. Even though the paper is interesting to read we did not find specific aspects related to the health domain.

In contrast to the literature review Rothmann et al. [12] state: "The aim of this workshop is to reflect on the challenges and dilemmas which are emerging when participatory design is used in Healthcare, because the epistemological, cultural, methodological assumptions of participatory design collide with the traditionally well-established science tradition, language, culture and biomedical approach in health science". This is fully in line with our experiences. It seems to be very problematic to confront patients with prototypes because this does not fit to well-established science tradition.

Balka et al. [1] report about challenges with politics and the problem of combining very complex systems. The project was very well prepared by our colleague from medicine. Therefore, we did not have such problems. All necessary forms related to ethical application were presented to the corresponding panels and committees.

Wechsler [13] mentions: "There were significant challenges with recruiting health consumers for the design research activities. Lengthy ethics applications were required as this was an academic study, and the ethics application was submitted prior to the engagement of the design team. Ethnographic-inspired design research approaches such as one-on-one interviews and home visits (contextual enquiry) were unfortunately not permitted impacting the quality of the insights generated". It seems to be much more complicated to contact patients than ordinary users of interactive systems. An experience we had as well.

While we focus on software products Harte et al. [6] discussed adaptations of HCD for health devices. Nevertheless, they analyzed six requirements from ISO 9241–210 [7] that is dedicated to computer-based interactive systems. Additionally, they identified three further requirements. We would like to highlight requirement no 6:

"The design team includes multidisciplinary skills and perspectives. We will incorporate multiple perspectives from disciplines within the design team, from stakeholders, and from experts. Here we define stakeholders as any person involved in the project who is affected by the activities or outcomes related to the product in question. An expert is defined as any person with an expert knowledge of the product, the end user, or of usability and human factors."

This requirement is true for all applications. However, the role of domain experts is different in business administration than in neurorehabilitation. Figure 12 gives a visual impression of the importance of stakeholders that influenced the development of the E-BRAiN system. In contrast to the traditional participatory design we followed an expert-driven strategy.

Harte et al. [6] did not report about problems with testing with end users. However, they also did not explain in detail whether they worked with patients or with general older people.

One big problem are regulations about medical devices like [11]. It allows to confront patients with devices like the E-BRAiN system only if they are characterized (evaluated) as medical devices. You can combine medical devices to new medical devices. However, you cannot use devices that are not intended for medical use like Pepper. This is possible only with very much administrative efforts. Innovation is in some way restricted by such regulations.

5   Summary and Outlook

We reported about a Human-Centered Design Approach of our project E-BRAiN. We started analyzing the training tasks, modelling them with task models and providing prototypes of dialogs with the humanoid robot Pepper. At this stage, we recognized that it is much more difficult to get access to patients than to users of general interactive systems. Therefore, we followed a domain-expert driven development process. Unfortunately, patients came very late into the loop. For projects in neurorehabilitation and maybe general in medicine the participation of patients has to be planned precisely very early and differently to general HCD projects. Additionally, experiments designed by computer scientists should be separated from those from clinicians because otherwise they can be performed too late in the development process. Patients are not ordinary users. They are much more protected in the environment of a Clinique than computer scientists can imagine. This can result in problems for evaluations.

To provide a web-based prototypical implementation based on specifications that later run the final application was a little bit required by the COVID circumstances of our project. However, this helped a lot to experiment with the already specified parts of the E-BRAiN system. This could be a strategy that further applications with humanoid robots should follow.

We identified a hierarchy of clinicians, usability experts and patients as sources of knowledge. We accepted in this way that domain experts overrule the opinions of other stakeholders. A situation that was not known to us in other domains.

The application of our DSL-CoTaL helped us to provide different perspectives on our specifications (textural, visual and animated). In the meantime, we specified a specific language called DSL-Pepper. It contains specific task models for robots that contain commands like **say**, **show**, **present**, **raiseArms** or **blinkEyes**.

Figure 13 gives an impression how the language looks like. Long text passages can be defined separately without disturbing the structure of the specification in the different tools.

We are extending the interpreter of CoTaSE in such a way that commands are sent via messages to Pepper. It works already for some commands like say. The robot can be controlled in this way by its task model. In the future, it might be possible to integrate sensors that can be used as triggers for specific tasks. In this way, it can be distinguished whether a task was performed correctly. We have to evaluate how useful such specific language can be.

```
target=CoTaL, CTT
team coop {
  root training = greeting >> train {*} [> end_exercise
    task greeting = pepper.greet ||| patient.greet
    task train = pepper.instruct >> patient.goto_next_task
    task end_exercise = pepper.end_exercise ||| patient.finishes_exercises
}
role pepper {
  root roo1 = greet >> instruct >> train{*} [> end_exercise
    task instruct = say introd ||| show pict1 ||| show pict2
    task instruct pre patient.allInstances.greet
      task train = play v ||| say "Repeat the movements three times" >>
                   wait 10 >> train_imagine
      task end_exercise pre patient.allInstances.finishes_exercises
        task train_imagine = say "Repeat the movements ten times" ||| imagine
          task imagine = wait 15 >> say "look_at_mirror" >>
                         say imagine
}
role patient {
  root root2 = greet >> listens >> performs_exercises{*} [>
               finishes_exercises >> bye
    task listens pre pepper.oneInstance.instruct
    task performs_exercises = perform_correct [] perform_wrong >>
                              goto_next_task
}
const t1 = 15
text  introd = "Please move your arm up and down"
text  imagine = "imagine it is your handicapped arm"
video v = "st_13_1.mp4"
image pict1 = "abt_pic_10_1.jpg"
image pict2 = "abt_pic_10_r.jpg"
```

Fig. 13. Example of the Pepper-DSL with commands of the robot.

Acknowledgements. This joint research project "E-BRAiN - Evidence-based Robot Assistance in Neurorehabilitation" is supported by the European Social Fund (ESF), reference: ESF/14-BM-A55–0001/19-A01, and the Ministry of Education, Science and Culture of Mecklenburg-Vorpommern, Germany. The sponsors had no role in the decision to publish or any content of the publication.

References

1. Augstein, M., Neumayr, T., Schacherl-Hofer, I.: The usability of a tabletop application for neuro-rehabilitation from therapists' point of view. In: Proceedings of the Ninth ACM International Conference on Interactive Tabletops and Surfaces (ITS 2014). Association for Computing Machinery, New York, pp. 239–248 (2014). https://doi.org/10.1145/2669485.2669516
2. E-BRAiN Homepage. https://www.ebrain-science.de/en/home/. Accessed 29 Mar 2022
3. Forbrig, P., Dittmar, A., Kühn, M.: A textual domain specific language for task models: generating code for CoTaL, CTTE, and HAMSTERS. In: EICS 2018 Conferences, Paris, France, pp. 5:1–5:6 (2018)
4. Forbrig, P., Bundea, A.-N.: Modelling the collaboration of a patient and an assisting humanoid robot during training tasks. In: Kurosu, M. (ed.) HCII 2020. LNCS, vol. 12182, pp. 592–602. Springer, Cham (2020). https://doi.org/10.1007/978-3-030-49062-1_40
5. Forbrig, P., Bundea, A., Bader, S.: Engineering the interaction of a humanoid robot pepper with post-stroke patients during training tasks. EICS **2021**, 38–43 (2021)
6. Harte, R., Glynn, L., Rodríguez-Molinero, A., Baker, P.M., Scharf, T., Quinlan, L.R., et al.: A human-centered design methodology to enhance the usability, human factors, and user experience of connected health systems: a three-phase methodology. JMIR Hum. Factors **4**(1), e8 (2017)
7. ISO 9241–210 Ergonomics of human-system interaction -- Part 210: Human-centred design for interactive systems. https://www.iso.org/standard/52075.html
8. ISO 13407: Human centred design processes for interactive systems (1999)
9. Platz, T., Lotze, M.: Arm ability training (AAT) promotes dexterity recovery after a stroke-a review of its design, clinical effectiveness, and the neurobiology of the actions. Front. Neurol. **9**, 1082 (2018). https://doi.org/10.3389/fneur.2018.01082
10. Platz, T.: Impairment-oriented training - official homepage, May 2019. Accessed 24 Feb 2021 (2019). http://www.iotraining.eu/kurse.html
11. Regulation (EU) 2017/745 of the European Parliament and of the Council of 5 April 2017 on medical devices, amending Directive 2001/83/EC, Regulation (EC) No 178/2002 and Regulation (EC) No 1223/2009 and repealing Council Directives 90/385/EEC and 93/42/EEC (Text with EEA relevance)Text with EEA relevance (2017). https://eur-lex.europa.eu/eli/reg/2017/745/2020-04-24

12. Rothmann, M.J., Danbjørg, D.B., Jensen, C.M., Clemensen, J.: Participatory design in health care: participation, power and knowledge. In: Proceedings of the 14th Participatory Design Conference: Short Papers, Interactive Exhibitions, Workshops – vol. 2 (PDC 2016). Association for Computing Machinery, New York, pp. 127–128 (2016). https://doi.org/10.1145/294 8076.2948106
13. Wechsler, J.: HCD mobile health project: post collaboration reflection of researcher and designer. In: Proceedings of the Asia Pacific HCI and UX Design Symposium (APCHIUX 2015). Association for Computing Machinery, New York, pp. 16–21 (2015). https://doi.org/10.1145/2846439.2846442

Dissecting the Security and Usability Alignment in the Industry

Bilal Naqvi[⊠] [iD]

Software Engineering, LENS, LUT University, 53850 Lappeenranta, Finland
Syed.naqvi@lut.fi

Abstract. Security and usability are two important characteristics often in conflict with each other. This paper presents challenges related to alignment between security and usability in the industry. The challenges were identified after analyzing the data from 12 semi-structured interviews. There were nine different challenges in industrial practices which were identified after the interviews, moreover, two recommendations for future solutions were also identified. The paper also presents a framework for addressing the identified challenges within the industry context. The framework presented in the paper has been tailored for the agile development context and aims at identifying minimal trade-offs between security and usability.

Keywords: Usability · Security · Usable security · Framework · Trade-offs

1 Introduction

The human facet of security more commonly referred to as usable security aims at bridging the aspects of usability (effectiveness, efficiency, and satisfaction while using the system [3]) and principles of security (confidentiality, integrity, and availability, among others [19]) in the development of software systems. Despite the realization that security systems should be usable, humans are often blamed as the weakest link in the security chain. Research on human psychology identifies that all the mistakes people commit are predictable. Either these mistakes occur due to latent failures (organizational conditions and practices) or due to active failures (individual human factors) [1]. The factors leading to latent failures include productivity-driven environments, lack of training, interruption in tasks, poor equipment, etc. However, the active failures which occur due to human errors are also influenced by the organizational conditions in addition to individual human factors such as risk-taking attitudes, inexperience, limitations of memory, etc. One example in this regard is the successful cyber-attack on Victorian regional hospitals in Australia, where the need for effective usable security was realized as the human facet of security was compromised leading to a ransomware attack [18]. The attack affected all hospital systems including patient records, booking, and management systems, doctors were not able to access patients' health records either. A combination of latent and active failures led to a successful attack.

R. Bernhaupt et al. (Eds.): HCSE 2022, LNCS 13482, pp. 57–69, 2022.
https://doi.org/10.1007/978-3-031-14785-2_4

One important aspect which contributes to most security failures is the lack of user-centered design of security mechanisms [2]. The development approach has been focused on fixing the humans to be able to use the system, rather than designing the systems duly considering appropriate mental models and user perceptions about security [1]. However, there is a realization that it is vital to consider the aspects of usability in the security design as a key factor of security hygiene. Otherwise, the developed systems and services despite being secure against external threats could be susceptible to user mistakes leading to a security failure.

The latent failures are induced due to malpractices in the organizational conditions and practices, however, there is also an impact of these organizational practices in determining the active failures. To elaborate on this aspect this paper reports findings from semi-structured interviews conducted with front-end developers, user experience experts, security engineers, and product owners working in a leading European IT organization. The paper reports the gaps in organizational practices (latent failures) which lead to the development of complex secure systems thereby making the systems susceptible to active failures. During the interviews with experts, it was intended to identify the importance of security as a product quality characteristic and that of usability both as product quality and as a quality characteristic in use (*usability in use*) [3]. It was also intended to identify how security and usability issues specifically conflicts between the two are aligned during the system development life cycle, the intent was to identify best practices and mechanisms for handling the conflicts from the industry.

Furthermore, based on the findings of the interviews the paper presents a framework for improving the current state of the art. The framework is an adapted version of the framework presented in [4], however, a significant difference is that the current framework is applicable for agile development contexts. The initial version of the framework considering the challenges identified after the interviews was subject to validation by involving the interviewees in a workshop where the interview findings and the framework were presented. However, after incorporating the comments, the framework was updated which is also presented in this paper.

The remainder of the paper is organized as follows. Section 2 presents the background. Section 3 presents the interview protocol and results. Section 4 presents the framework, and Sect. 5 concludes the paper.

2   Background

Before presenting the challenges related to alignment between security and usability in the industry, one additional challenge related to alignment between security and usability was identified after analyzing the existing literature on the topic. Different communities and interest groups including usable security community, traditional computer security community, human-computer interaction (HCI) community, and software engineering community have been studying the relationships between security and usability. The study of security and usability dependencies by different communities and interest groups from their respective viewpoints has led to inconsistent perceptions [5].

2.1 Trade-offs

Most of the work on security and usability dependencies advocates the existence of trade-offs [6–10]. A case study on iOS and Android was conducted to find an answer for "what is more important: usability or security" [6]. The results identify that the importance of security and usability is purely situation-based and that the trade-offs are sometimes in favor of security and vice versa. Furthermore, based on the comparison of the two platforms, the study identified that android takes the lead in usability as compared to iOS. However, security is a preferred feature in iOS devices.

Concerning the dimensions of the conflict discussed earlier, sometimes the trade-offs are in favor of security and vice versa. From the usability of security dimension, password masking is implemented in most of the authentication mechanisms to protect against shoulder surfing, but at the cost of the usability element of 'feedback.' Other conflicts leading to trade-off situations may arise when critical security decision-making is reliant on the users. Security developers do not consider the fact that the users are less knowledgeable than the implementers, and that the users should be presented with high-level yet comprehensive information. The trade-off between security and usability is because security is considered a burden both by the developers and by the system users [7].

From the security of usability dimension, the location awareness capability of smart-phones remains enabled until disabled manually. This is done to ensure UX in applications like maps, weather updates, options near me, etc. This comes at the cost of privacy and has security implications as well since the users' location data can be subjected to unauthorized disclosure using one of the prevalent mechanisms.

Irrespective of the type of system under consideration, there is evidence of the existence of trade-offs between security and usability [8, 9], for instance, security and usability trade-offs in end-to-end email encryption. The results of the study [8] identified that the participants in their choice of the preferred system deliberately made trade-offs between security and usability. Another case study [10] for handling security and usability in database systems identifies that the systems designed with tight security have limited usability. In other words, robust security comes at the cost of usability. Therefore, it is a trade-off versus usability.

Furthermore, researchers extend the argument of trade-offs to propose that quantification of trade-offs can contribute to achieving an effective balance between security and usability [9]. Therefore, a study was conducted to test and quantify possible usability and security trade-offs using three different schemes for e-voting systems [11]. The results reveal that the voters were in favor of more secure systems and were willing to sacrifice a maximum of 26 points (scale of 0 to 100) on usability for a system that provides higher security. The authors state, "nevertheless, the security gains come at the cost of usability losses".

2.2 No Trade-offs

In parallel to the research identifying the existence of trade-offs, some researchers classify usability and security trade-offs as mere myths, and that security and usability are not inherently in conflict.

A special issue 'the security-usability trade-off myth' features a discussion of researchers and practitioners in usable security [12]. The participants were of the view that decreasing usability can lead to less security. The participants discussed the example of two-factor authentication involving a one-time password (OTP) and its consequences if the length of OTP is increased from 6 to 8 characters, which represents the case of a false trade-off. There are cases where increased usability can lead to increased security, for example making the security functionality more understandable can lead to improved user decision-making and increased security. Overall, the participants were of the view that "security experts simply invoke the myth of trade-off between usability and security and use this as a cover to avoid the exercise of saying precisely what security benefit in precisely what scenarios this usability burden is going to deliver".

As a step further from the argument of no trade-offs, there is a need to incorporate the aspects of user value-centered design [13]. A framework to identify user values associated with security systems and services is required. There is a need for shifting the approach of fixing the users to be 'able to use' security. Therefore, incorporating value-sensitive design, which can help, requires the following actions, (1) identify and document user behavior drivers, trends, and patterns, which might conflict with security mechanisms. (2) conduct value-sensitive conceptual and empirical analyses for the security application. The authors state "identifying the root causes of disengagement can only be done by studying users' rationales for not using a security mechanism, not by studying how they, or others, fail to use it when they already want to."

With the discussion, above it was highlighted that there is a difference in perceptions concerning the existence of trade-offs between security and usability. The divided opinions of the community pose a challenge imperative to be addressed.

3 Interview Protocol and Findings

3.1 Data Collection

The data was collected using 12 semi-structured interviews and discussions with members of the 2 leading product lines of a major European software development organization. The participants included product owners, architects, developers, security engineers, and UX developers. The interview had 3 major themes: (1) how are security and usability aligned during the development lifecycle of the products, (2) who handles the conflicts between security and usability during the development, and (3) how it is ascertained that the product is secure AND usable? The interviewees also shared instances of the conflicts they encountered in their product lines and challenges faced in the alignment between security and usability. Each interview lasted approximately one hour. The interviews were audio-recorded for analysis purposes and due ethical concerns were considered in this regard. The interview data was later transcribed and co-related with the notes taken by the researcher during the interviews.

3.2 Analysis Methodology

The interview data was analyzed using the Gioia method [14]. The Gioia method is a qualitative data analysis method with an inductive approach. One of the reasons for its choosing was its inductive nature as it allows making broad generalizations based on informants' understanding of the organizational events. In line with the specifics of the Gioia method, a 3-stage analysis method was followed. In the first stage, the interview transcripts were read thoroughly followed by listening to the audio recordings of the interviews. The intent was to assign first-order codes to the interview data. Codes were assigned to repeated statements, surprise responses, aspects stressed by the interviewees, or something similar as reported in the previous studies, and related to some theory/model. Table 1 shows the codes created during this stage along with the example quotes by the interviewees.

After this exercise, the first-order trends were finalized. In the second stage, the related codes were merged to develop broader categories and abstract concepts. Finally, in the third stage, the second-order concepts were aggregated to form broader themes relevant to alignment between security and usability in the industry. The second-order concepts and the aggregated themes are presented in Fig. 1.

3.3 Findings

With reference to the content presented in Sect. 3.2, after analysis of the interview data, two aggregated concepts were identified as (1) current gaps in the management of the conflicts, and (2) consideration for future solutions. Current gaps in the management of the conflicts relate to gaps in the industrial practices and procedures regarding alignment between security and usability. These gaps include:

– less emphasis on usability as compared to security, despite the fact that both usability and security are equally desired characteristics in software systems.
– there are conflicts between security and usability the trade-offs always favoring security.
– there are no designated roles for management of the conflicts, the roles vary across different teams.
– there are no formal communication mechanisms between the security and usability teams for concerns to be integrated from both sides,
– usability aspects are not well integrated into the design and development phase of the systems and services.
– there are no existing practices and methods that guide the developers in the management of conflicts.
– there is no specified phase in the product development lifecycle for management of the conflicts, although the interviewees agree the earlier the better management of conflict approach, in practice it's often late in the product development lifecycle.

Furthermore, it was identified that the use of design patterns can help the developers in the management of conflicts more effectively. The idea is to support the developers in handling security and usability conflicts by using the design patterns. Patterns provide benefits like means of common vocabulary, shared documentation, and improved communication. Also, the pattern can be incorporated during the early stages of system development in contrast to considering usability and security later in the development

Table 1. Key concepts and associated codes during stage 1

Concepts	Example of codes	Example quotes
Security and usability are inter-related	Conflicts, value, reputation, trade-offs	"Security is really important, so is usability, bad UX can lead to bad security." "Security is very important from a management perspective; however, usability can help bring competitive advantage. Yes, there are conflicts between the two."
Security is more important than usability	Weight, competitive advantage, cost, value	Security is most important for the whole product both in terms of value and reputation of the company, usability is very important, but security has more weight." "Security is critical to ensure that the data remains safe, "Do the secure things, if not easy then the next easiest thing". Usability is required to serve need/business goals. There are conflicts."
Lack of formal communication mechanisms between teams	Discussion, informal communication, issue-specific results	"There are different roles for handling usability and security in a project and there are no communication mechanisms specifically for usability and security developers. It's the same as all others." "There are different teams for both and discussion is done when there are issues."
Security has the final say	Usability aspects, integration of concerns	"There is a discussion for communication, it is informal, and security has the final say." "There are different roles for each aspect, UX people sketches are discussed, security people raise a hand to change. Does not happen the other way round."

(continued)

Table 1. (*continued*)

Concepts	Example of codes	Example quotes
Frequency of occurrence of the problem	Every day, often, repetitive, commonly	"Frequently encountered conflicts, they are repetitive, when trying to solve security issues it adds usability issues in the product." "Commonly encounter security and usability conflicts, especially when starting to design new systems."
Lack of practices of methods for handling conflicts	Practices and methods, informal communication	"No practices and methods used for handling usable security exist, discussion-based approach is used." "No practices and methods used for handling usable security exist, informal communication."
Different roles involved in the process	Developers, product owners, UX specialists, security engineers, architect	"Developer and product owner handle the conflicts in case they arise." "UX specialist, security engineer, product lead architect discuss, and final verdict often favors security over usability." "Product owner, architect discuss. Trade-offs are situational security is very critical."
No specified phase in the development life cycle during which conflicts should be handled	Requirements, design, implementations, testing	"Should be during the requirements and design but does not happen often, its worst when it happens during the QA and testing." "Ideally should be during the design phase, but currently during the implementation and testing phase"

(*continued*)

Table 1. (*continued*)

Concepts	Example of codes	Example quotes
There is a business impact of compromise on usability due to security	Number of users using the system, business impact	"Usability of security could impact the number of users using the system." "It does have a business impact."
No efforts and costs were spent on engineering the conflicts	Not determined, very little, not measured	"No cost and effort spent on engineering the conflicts, if it is there it's very small but there should be." "Very tiny/not applicable sometimes, there is already a security framework no deviations allowed."
Not assessing the usability of security features	No means, metrics, independent assessments	"There is no means to assess the usability of security." "Independent assessments are done, nothing for usable security."

lifecycle. It is perceived that handling the usable security problem earlier in the development lifecycle will help in saving significant costs and delays associated with re-work. Moreover, patterns' ability to be improved over time and incorporate multiple viewpoints make them suitable for interdisciplinary fields like usable security [5].

Patterns can be effective in assisting the developers in making reasonably accurate choices while dealing with conflicts. Each pattern expresses a relation between three things, context, problem, and solution. Patterns provide real solutions, not abstract principles by explicitly mentioning the context and problem and summarizing the rationale for their effectiveness. Since the patterns provide a generic "core" solution, their use can vary from one implementation to another. A usable security pattern encapsulates information such as name, classification, prologue, problem statement, the context of use, solution, and discussion pertaining to the right use of the pattern. More details on how a usable security pattern looks like are presented in [5]. A challenge in this regard is collecting such patterns and making a catalog to be disseminated to the developers.

In addition, it was also identified that there is a need for metrics for the assessment of the usability of security. Usability-only measurement strategies do not hold equally good for the usability of security systems [9]. There is a need for the development of metrics for measuring the adequacy of usable security. To do so, there can be two options: (1) develop a set of usable security metrics, and (2) evolution of the existing usability evaluation metrics to hold good for measurement of security. In this regard, the evolution of the existing usability metrics seems to be a more feasible option. For instance, one such metric could measure the degree of conflict between sub-characteristics of security and usability, respectively. Moreover, in usable security research, there has been an

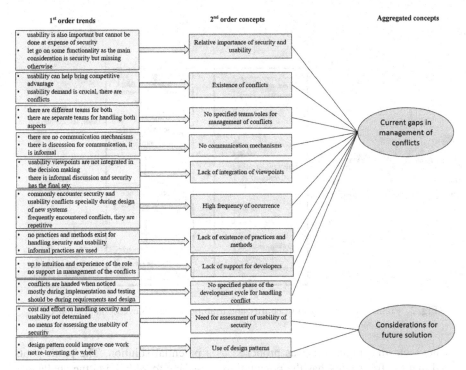

Fig. 1. Challenges in alignment between security and usability in the industry

emphasis on determining the deviation from the user's primary task, which would also require a set of metrics to determine such a deviation. A measurement methodology [15] identifies metrics such as NUC (number of user complaints). However, the efficacy and completeness of the set of such metrics is something that needs to be explored further.

4   Framework for Addressing the Challenges

Based on the challenges identified after the interviews, the framework presented in Fig. 2 was created based on the elements of design science research (DSR). Design science research is a method focused on the development of artifacts to solve existing problems. DSR has a dual mandate: (1) it attempts to generate new knowledge, insights, and theoretical explanations, and (2) it allows the utilization of existing knowledge to solve problems and improve existing solutions [17]. Design science attempts to create artifacts that serve human purposes [16].

The framework has been developed considering its application in agile development contexts specifically Scrum. Though, the framework is inspired by the work [4]; the difference lies in the fact that some of the stages have been left out to support the agile development model. It is relevant to mention that the framework after its creation was subjected to validation from the interviewees during a post-interview workshop. The workshop was held online where the challenges identified after the interviews were

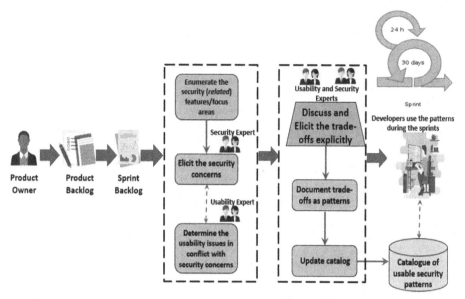

Fig. 2. Framework for aligning security and usability in agile development contexts

presented and the framework was proposed as a potential solution. The participants agreed that the framework has the potential to contribute to addressing the challenges faced by the industry.

The framework addresses the challenges of no designated roles for management of the conflicts by assigning different responsibilities to different roles, for instance, the product owner (scrum master) maintains the product backlog based on which the sprints are planned. Other roles and activities as presented in Fig. 2 are discussed as follows.

– *Enumerate the security features and focus areas:* The security experts working on the project assess the sprint backlog to identify the security requirements. This is done to ensure a specific focus on requirements directly affecting security and its usability.
– *Elicit the security concerns:* For the enumerated security requirements, a specification of what is required from the security point of view is explicitly identified by the security experts. This involves the identification of affected sub-characteristics of security (including confidentiality, integrity, and availability, among others). While eliciting the concerns, it is important to consider both internal and external threats.
– *Determine the usability issues in conflict with security concerns:* Once the security concerns are known, the requirements associated with each of the security concerns are subjected to usability analysis to identify instances of potential conflicts. A matrix of sub-characteristics of security (rows) and sub-characteristics of usability (columns) are created (see Fig. 3). Each element of the matrix describes a potential conflict.
– *Discuss and elicit the trade-offs explicitly:* Once the security and usability concerns are known, the trade-offs are elicited explicitly with the objective of having minimum possible compromise to any of the characteristics and their relevant sub-characteristics. For eliciting the trade-offs, the security and usability experts can use (1) goals from

the security and usability perspectives identified earlier, and (2) standards and best practices concerning security and usability. This may sound like an optimistic approach but by integrating concerns from both perspectives minimal trade-offs have been achieved, practically the example for these includes a single sign-on where a client after the first sign-in can access different systems without having to sign in each of them.

- *Document trade-offs as patterns:* The trade-offs thus identified are documented as design patterns. The patterns can then help other developers solve security and usability alignment issues occurring in similar contexts. More details on patterns' documentation as well as the example of usable security patterns are presented in [4, 5].
- *Update catalog:* Whenever a new design pattern is documented, it is added to the catalog. This has two advantages, (1) developers working on different projects can use these patterns in case they face the same problem with a similar context, and (2) the patterns enter their validation and evolution phase where it is subjected to validation and comments by other developers who use it, and in case it does not serve the needs, the solution proposed by the pattern can be updated or a new pattern can be documented.

Furthermore, the approach targets to address the gaps identified after interviews. The gaps addressed include no specified teams/roles for management of conflicts, no communication mechanisms, lack of integration of viewpoints, lack of existence of practices and methods, and lack of support for developers, among others. Moreover, it also captures the considerations for future solutions by documenting the identified trade-offs as patterns. However, for the assessment of the usability of security solutions, the framework partially considers this aspect due to fact that patterns evolve with time and as better solutions are identified the patterns can be updated, however, the need for metrics (for instance) for measurement of the degree of trade-offs is something which needs to be considered as part of the future work.

Security	Usability		
	Effectiveness	Efficiency	Satisfaction
Confidentiality			
Integrity			Place an "X" in the cell where there is a potential conflict
Availability			
Authentication			

Fig. 3. Matrix for describing a potential conflict at a sub-characteristic level

5 Conclusion

This paper presents an analysis of the state of the art considering the alignment between security and usability in the industry. The paper presents findings after conducting a series of semi-structured interviews with different roles at a leading European development organization. The interviews identified several gaps in the state of the art including no specified teams/roles for management of conflicts, no communication mechanisms, lack of integration of viewpoints, lack of existence of practices and methods, and lack of support for developers, among others. The paper also presents a framework to be incorporated during the product development lifecycle for improving the current state of the art. It is worthwhile to mention that the version of the framework presented in the paper was validated during a post-interview workshop conducted with the interviewees.

References

1. Sasse, A., Rashid, A.: The Cyber Security Body of Knowledge — Human factors knowledge area v 1.0. The University of Bristol (2019). https://www.cybok.org/media/downloads/Human_Factors_issue_1.0.pdf. Accessed 23 Dec 2021
2. Garfinkel, S., Lipford, H.R.: Usable Security: History, Themes, and Challenges. Morgan & Claypool Publishers, USA (2014)
3. International Standardization Organization (ISO) (2011). Systems and software engineering – systems and software quality requirements and evaluation (SQuaRE) – system and software quality models, ISO 25010
4. Naqvi, B., Clarke, N., Porras, J.: Incorporating the human facet of security in developing systems and services. Inf. Comput. Secur. 29(1), 49–72 (2020)
5. Naqvi, B., Seffah, A.: Interdependencies, conflicts, and tradeoffs between security and usability: why and how should we engineer them? In: 2019 1st International Conference HCI-CPT held as part of the 21st HCI International Conference, HCII 2019, pp. 314–324 (2019)
6. Garg, H., Choudhury, T., Kumar, P., Sabitha, S.: Comparison between significance of usability and security in HCI. In: 2017 3rd International Conference on Computational Intelligence Communication Technology (CICT), pp. 1–4 (2017)
7. Barlev, S., Basil, Z., Kohanim, S., Peleg, R., Regev, S., Shulman-Peleg, A.: Secure yet usable: protecting servers and Linux containers. IBM J. Res. Dev. 60(4), 12:1–12 (2016)
8. Bai, W., Kim, D., Namara, M., Qian, Y., Kelley, P.G., Mazurek, M.L.: Balancing security and usability in encrypted email. IEEE Internet Comput. 21(3), 30–38 (2017)
9. Wang, Y., Rawal, B., Duan, Q., Zhang, P.: Usability and security go together: a case study on database. In: 2017 Second International Conference on Recent Trends and Challenges in Computational Models (ICRTCCM), pp. 49–54 (2017)
10. Nwokedi, U.O., Onyimbo, B.A., Rad, B.B.: Usability and security in user interface design: a systematic literature review. Int. J. Inf. Technol. Comput. Sci. 8(5), 72–80 (2016)
11. Kulyk, O., Neumann, S., Budurushi, J., Volkamer, M.: Nothing comes for free: how much usability can you sacrifice for security? IEEE Secur. Priv. 15(3), 24–29 (2017)
12. Sasse, M.A., Smith, M., Herley, C., Lipford, H., Vaniea, K.: Debunking Security–Usability Tradeoff Myths, p. 7 (2016)
13. Dodier-Lazaro, S., Sasse, M.A., Abu-Salma, R., Becker, I.: From paternalistic to user-centered security: putting users first with value-sensitive design. In: CHI 2017 Workshop on Values in Computing, p. 7 (2017)
14. Gioia, D.A., Corley, K.G., Hamilton, A.L.: Seeking Qualitative rigor in inductive research: notes on the gioia methodology. Organ. Res. Methods 16, 15–31 (2013). https://doi.org/10.1177/1094428112452151
15. Naqvi, B., Seffah, A., Braz, C.: Adding measures to task models for usability inspection of the cloud access control services. In: Bogdan, C., Kuusinen, K., Lárusdóttir, M., Palanque,

P., Winckler, M. (eds.) Human-Centered Software Engineering. HCSE 2018. Lecture Notes in Computer Science, vol. 11262, pp. 133–145. Springer, Cham (2019). https://doi.org/10.1007/978-3-030-05909-5_8

16. Peffers, K., Tuunanen, T., Rothenberger, M.A., Chaterjee, S.: A design science research methodology for information systems research. J. Manag. Inf. Syst. **24**(3), 45–78 (2007)

17. Baskerville, R.L., Kaul, M., Storey, V.C.: Genres of inquiry in design-science research: justification and evaluation of knowledge production. MIS Q. **39**(3), 541–564 (2015)

18. Guan, L.: Cyberattack hits regional Victoria hospitals, Patient records and booking system shut down. https://ia.acs.org.au/article/2019/cyberattack-hits-regional-victoria-hospitals-.html. Accessed 28 Jun 2022

19. Avizienis, A., Laprie, J.C., Randell, B., Landwehr, C.: Basic concepts and taxonomy of dependable and secure computing. IEEE Trans. Dependable Secure Comput. **1**(1), 11–33 (2004)

Models-Based Analysis of Both User and Attacker Tasks: Application to EEVEHAC

Sara Nikula[1] , Célia Martinie[2(✉)] , Philippe Palanque[2] , Julius Hekkala[1] ,
Outi-Marja Latvala[1] , and Kimmo Halunen[3]

[1] VTT Technical Research Centre of Finland, Kaitoväylä 1, 90571 Oulu, Finland
{sara.nikula,julius.hekkala,outi-marja.latvala}@vtt.fi
[2] ICS-IRIT, Université Toulouse III - Paul Sabatier, Toulouse, France
{martinie,palanque}@irit.fr
[3] University of Oulu, Oulu, Finland
Kimmo.Halunen@oulu.fi

Abstract. The design and development of security mechanisms, such as authentication, requires analysis techniques that take into account usability along with security. Although techniques that are grounded in the security domain target the identification and mitigation of possible threats, user centered design approaches have been proposed in order to also take into account the user's perspective and needs. Approaches dealing with both usability and security focus on the extent to which the user can perform the authentication tasks, as well as on the possible types of attacks that may occur and the potential threats on user tasks. However, to some extent, attacker can be considered as user of the system (even if undesirable), and the analysis of attacker tasks provides useful information for the design and development of an authentication mechanism. We propose a models-based approach to analyse both user and attacker tasks. The modeling of attacker tasks enables to go deeper when analysing the threats on an authentication mechanism and the trade-offs between usability and security. We present the results of the application of this models-based approach to the EEVEHAC security mechanism, which enables the setup of a secure communication channel for users of shared public computers.

Keywords: Task modeling · Usable security · Human understandable cryptography · Visual channel

1 Introduction

Security mechanisms have an impact on human performance because they add additional activities to users that do not correspond to their main goals [28]. For example, when the main purpose of a user is to check a bank account statement on a website, the user will not directly consult the statement after having

© IFIP International Federation for Information Processing 2022
Published by Springer Nature Switzerland AG 2022
R. Bernhaupt et al. (Eds.): HCSE 2022, LNCS 13482, pp. 70–89, 2022.
https://doi.org/10.1007/978-3-031-14785-2_5

entered the service web page. Before that, the user will have to authenticate and thus to perform additional actions that aim to grant access to the bank account statement. These additional activities require to engage additional resources (e.g. temporal, cognitive, motor...) and decrease the user global performance. However, these mechanisms may be necessary when they correspond to threats to be avoided. In our example, the authentication mechanisms aims to avoid that user's data be stolen, compromised, destroyed or used for malicious purposes. All of the authentication mechanisms do not have the same impact on user tasks, and thus are not equal in terms of level of usability. In the same way, all of the authentication mechanisms are not equal in terms of level of security. When designing authentication mechanisms, both usability and security aspects have to be taken into account [7], in order to explore the possible trade-offs, as well as to perform informed design choices. Existing research work on the engineering of usable and secure authentication mechanisms focuses on the extent to which the user can perform the authentication tasks (using empirical or analytical approaches), as well as on the possible types of attacks that may occur and the potential threats on user tasks [7]. It is acknowledged that a specific feature of an authentication mechanism may have an important impact on user's tasks, and as a consequence, trigger its integration or removal. But a specific feature of an authentication mechanism may also have an important impact on attacker's tasks, either making them almost impossible or trivial to perform. To some extent, attacker can be considered as (undesirable) user of the system, and the authentication mechanism should be designed to make impossible the attacker's task.

This paper presents a models-based approach to analyse both user and attacker's tasks when designing and developing an authentication mechanism. The capital S in the end of the word model stands for the different types of models required to apply the proposed approach. It combines task models, to describe explicitly user and attacker's tasks, and attack tree models to describe explicitly alternative paths of attacks. The article is organized as follows. Section 2 introduces the main theoretical aspects of the proposed approach. Section 3 presents the two types of models required for the application of the proposed approach and how they complement each other. Section 4 presents the results of the application of the proposed approach to the EEVEHAC authentication mechanism. Section 5 presents the related work on methods and techniques to usable and secure authentication mechanisms. Section 6 concludes the paper.

2   Towards Humans Centric Security Engineering

The engineering of usability and security require to take into account the user tasks to ensure usability and to identify potential security threats on these tasks. But users may not be the only humans involved while the authentication system executes. An attacker may also interact with the authentication system and thus authentication mechanisms design and development approaches have to deal with attacker tasks.

2.1 Generic Requirements for Engineering Authentication Mechanisms for Usability and Security

The ISO standards defines usability as *"the extent to which a system, product or service can be used by specified users to achieve specified goals with effectiveness, efficiency and satisfaction in a specified context of use"* [19]. The analysis of effectiveness requires to identify precisely and exhaustively user tasks, in order to check that all of them are supported by the authentication mechanism [23]. Moreover, ensuring effectiveness requires to check that the appropriate function is available at the time when the user needs it. The analysis of efficiency also requires a precise identification and description of user tasks. In the case of predictive assessment of efficiency (e.g. Keystroke Level Model prediction techniques [10,13,18]), the task types and their temporal ordering are required to be identified in order to associate a standard predicted value and to calculate the estimated time. In the case of empirical assessment of efficiency, tasks also have to be identified to prepare the user testing protocol. The analysis of satisfaction requires user feedback because it is a subjective criteria that relies on the individual characteristics of the user, though it is dependent on effectiveness and efficiency. The analysis of satisfaction also requires the identification of user tasks as the user feedback may be referring to a particular task [4].

Security analysis highly relies on the identification and description of potential threats [9]. The analysis of possible threats on user tasks requires precise and exhaustive description of user tasks [7]. In particular, it requires to identify the user task types (a threat can arise from a type of user action, e.g. drawing a gesture password on a tactile screen is subject to smudge attacks whereas typing a password on a keyboard is subject to key-logging attack), their temporal ordering (a threat can arise from the specific ordering of user tasks, e.g. leave the credit card in the automated teller machine once having withdrawn the notes), and the information, knowledge, objects and devices being manipulated while performing the tasks (a threat can arise from an information, knowledge or object that the user has lost, forgotten or misused, e.g. a credit card lost in a public space).

2.2 Generic Requirements for Engineering the Attacker Tasks to Be as Complex as Possible

The analysis of complexity of attacker tasks requires the precise and exhaustive identification of the tasks to attack the authentication mechanism. Precise and exhaustive description of tasks enable to analyse effectiveness and efficiency, and as such to ensure a very low level of effectiveness and efficiency for an attacker. In the same way that the analysis of effectiveness and efficiency requires the identification of the user tasks types, of their temporal ordering, as well as of the information, knowledge, objects and devices manipulated while performing the tasks, the analysis of the attacker tasks also does.

3 Models-Based Analysis of Both User's and Attacker's Tasks

The production of task models of both user and attacker tasks enable to systematically and exhaustively analyse the effectiveness and efficiency of the user and of the attacker with an authentication mechanism, provided that the task modeling notation is expressive enough to fulfill the requirements presented in the previous section.

3.1 Task Model Based Analysis of User Tasks Using HAMSTERS-XL

Task models consist of a graphical, hierarchical and temporally ordered representation of the tasks the users have to perform with an interactive application or system in order to reach their goals. Task models are one of the very few means for describing user tasks explicitly and exhaustively [22]. Task models support several different stages of interactive systems design and development (e.g. user roles identification, system functions identification, user interface design, testing, training program design...). We selected the HAMSTERS-XL notation [22] because it enables to describe the required types of tasks such as user task (cognitive, perceptive, and motor), abstract tasks, interactive tasks (input, output), and system tasks, as well as their temporal ordering and the information, knowledge, objects and devices manipulated while performing the tasks.

3.2 Attack Tree Based Analysis of Possible Attacks

An attack tree [29] describes the possible attacks or combination of attacks on a system. It is composed of a main goal for an attack, which is represented by the top root node, and of a combination of leaves that represent different ways to achieve that goal. In the original notation [29], OR nodes (presented in Fig. 1) refer to alternatives of attacks to achieve the attack whilst AND nodes refer to combination of attacks. The notation has been extended to enable the description of the potential effects of attacks, as well as to enable the description of the combination of attacks, using the SAND logical operator. Other elements of the notation include a rectangle to represent an event (such a threat or attack), an ellipse to represent an effect and a triangle to represent the fact that a node is not refined. All elements of the attack tree notation are shown in Fig. 1. Attack trees enable to systematically identify possible attacks on an authentication mechanism.

3.3 Task Model Based Analysis of Attackers' Tasks

An attack tree describes attack goals, but does not describe the possible tasks and their temporal ordering to reach these attack goals. It thus presents a partial view on attacker's tasks. Although attack trees represent the main attack goal

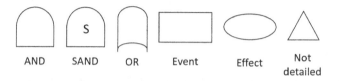

Fig. 1. Elements of notation for the attack trees from [27]

and its associated possible combination of ways to reach the main goal of the attack, the attacker tasks to reach an attack goal may be very different from the tasks to reach another attack goal. For example, the tasks to perform a video attack are very different from the tasks to perform a shoulder surfing attack. In the first case, the attacker has to identify a location where the camera could be installed, as well as means to either trigger the recording at the appropriate time or to extract the video sample when the user was authenticating if the record covers a long time period. Several specific preparation tasks are required and specific devices are required too. In the other case, the attacker has to stand behind the user at the right time, but does not need special devices.

Task models of attackers tasks that provide exhaustive description of the tasks as well as of information, data, objects and devices thus help to identify whether the authentication mechanism is worth to implement, by explicitly highlighting the complexity of the attack.

4   Validation of the Approach: Models-Based Analysis of Usability and Security of EEVEHAC

In this section, we present the results of the application of the proposed approach for the analysis of the EEVEHAC (End-to-End Visualizable Encrypted and Human Authenticated Channel) secure communication channel mechanism [17].

4.1   EEVEHAC: End-to-End Visualizable Encrypted and Human Authenticated Channel

EEVEHAC uses human understandable cryptography and has been designed to enable users to safely recover and use sensitive private data (e.g. bank account statement) when using public untrusted devices (e.g. public desktop in libraries or cybercafés). EEVEHAC establishes a secure communication channel and warns the user about the possibility of corruption of the public device if necessary. EEVEHAC is actually implemented for smartphones but targets smaller wearable devices such as smart glasses.

Overview of EEVEHAC. Modern cryptographic mechanisms are based on complicated mathematics that regular human users cannot understand. However, for a regular user, the common experience of using it is completely opaque: after they type in their password, there is no further interaction and no indication of whether the cryptographic protocols behind the scene have executed in a correct manner and without interference from attackers. Because cryptography is mathematically complicated, it is fully done by machines and there is no immediate way for a user to know if the results are correct or corrupted. In order to mitigate this issue, there has been some previous research in developing human understandable cryptography. An early example of this is visual cryptography [26], where the user can decrypt a secret message simply by looking at it. A recent review [16] presents more examples of the use of human abilities in cryptographic systems. There are certain key building blocks that utilize human capabilities in cryptography, but no complete end-to-end communications systems existed, until EEVEHAC was proposed [17]. EEVEHAC composes of two security protocols: HAKE (Human Authenticated Key Exchange) [5] and EyeDecrypt [15]. The user first sets up a long term key, also referred to as "the long time secret", with a trusted server. Based on this long term secret, the user then setups of a secured communication channel using a smartphone which implements the HAKE protocol. The second security protocol, EyeDecrypt, provides a visual channel to communicate securely using a public terminal. By visual channel, we mean that it provides to the user visual indication about the possible corruption of the communication channel.

Main Steps for Configuring the Long Term Key. The steps for the configuration of the long term key are presented in Table 1. The authentication information contains a story and a mapping between six colors and numbers, which the user needs to memorize. These compose the long term key and are acquired during registration to the service. The story is mostly computer generated, but the user has an option to change one word for each sentence. The intention is to balance the strengths and weaknesses of both machine and human generated stories [30]. Once the long term key (story and color code) is configured, the server and the user's trusted device (smartphone) have matching keys (AES [11] and HMAC [20]) and the second protocol of EEVEHAC can be used.

Main Steps to Log in to a Service Including the Set up of a Secure Communication Channel. The steps for initiating a secure communication channel in order to log in to a service, i.e. performing a HAKE protocol leading to UAN (Unique Authentication Number) code, are presented in Table 2. The smartphone authentication application presents sentences from the original story where one word is replaced, so that the sentence remains grammatically correct but the meaning is changed. The user needs to spot the changed words and take note of their colors. They then recall the corresponding numbers, count their sum and use the modulo 10 of the sum as the first digit of the UAN. This process is iterated 3 times more (one iteration for each digit of the UAN code which is 4 digit long). Once the UAN code is entered and validated by the smartphone application, the secure channel is ready and the user can log in to the target

Table 1. Main steps for configuring the long term key.

Step	Screenshot of the application	Description
1		This screen welcomes the user to the registration process. The user clicks the light red button to start the process.
2		Instructions appear on the screen. The user is supposed to fill in a missing word in each sentence.
3	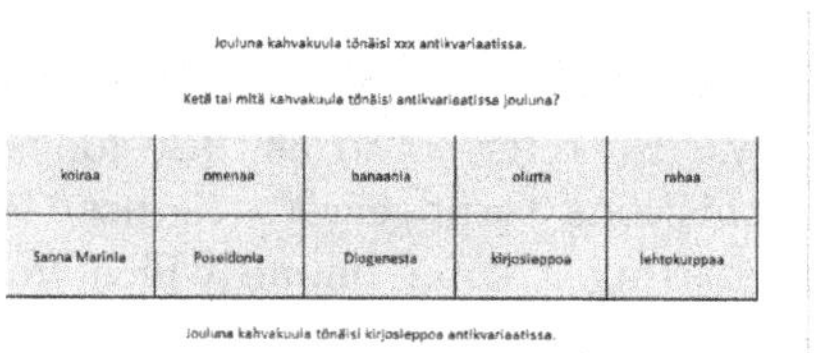	First sentence appears on the screen. The uppermost sentence is to be filled. Alternative words are shown on the light red buttons. The user picks one of these by clicking it. The filled sentence is shown on the bottom line. This is repeated eight times.
4	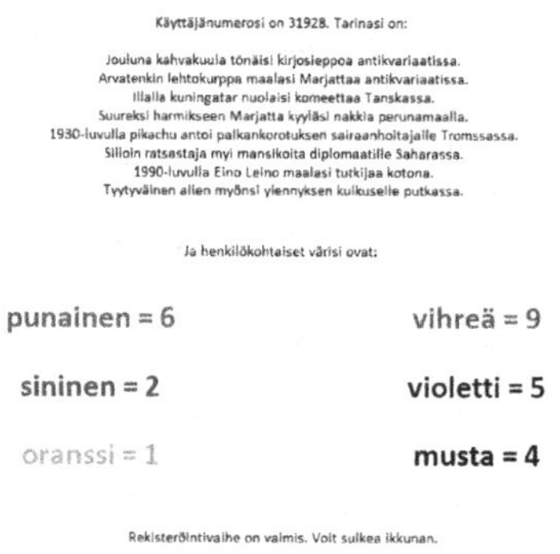	After the user has completed all sentences, user specific user number is shown on the uppermost row. The user specific story, consisting of the eight sentences completed in the previous step, is shown below. The user specific color-number-mapping is shown on the colored lines: the number corresponding to red is 6, the number corresponding to blue is 2, and so on. The last row states that the registration phase is ready and the user can close the window.

Table 2. Main steps to setup the secure communication channel.

Step	Screenshot of the application	Description
1	EEVEHAC EEVEHAC APPLICATION SCAN FOR QR CODES KEY EXCHANGE	The user opens the application and clicks the key exchange button to start the HAKE protocol.
2	CONNECT TO SERVER User name:	The user fills in their user number.
3	Jääkauden aikana abstrakti olio valmisti illallista sairaanhoitajalle kuola valuen. Samaan aikaan auto arvosteli ahventa päiväkodissa. Aivan yllättäen auringonkukka parturoi leipäveistä raivokkaasti. Mutta sotkan muna ihaili postimiestä nakkikioskilla.	The application connects to the server and starts the HAKE protocol. The user must first detect which two sentences belong to the story and which words have been changed. The user then recalls the numbers corresponding to colors of these words. They then sum these colors and count modulo 10 of this sum.
4	UAN code should be 4 digits long at this point UAN: ·· NEXT QUIT AND RETURN	The user inputs the result in the UAN field shown under the sentences. After every set of sentences, the user inputs one number, the length of the UAN code increases by one after every screen. This is done four times. After the last screen, the user is either informed that the protocol was successful or that they must try again.

service (e.g. bank account). Table 3 presents the steps to log in the target service using the secured channel. The server sends encrypted messages to the untrusted device (public desktop), which shows them in their respective grid positions as QR codes. The user points the camera of their smartphone to the screen of the laptop to scan the grid. The EEVEHAC application processes the QR codes, checking their position and trying to decrypt the contents. Correct positioning of the codes is indicated with green outlines on top of the camera feed. Red outlines are used for incorrect positions. Uncorrupted QR can be successfully decrypted and the results shown to the user in the camera feed. Conversely, if the application cannot process the QR codes and show the results, the user can deduct that something has gone wrong in the process and that an attack may be going on. By referencing the camera feed, the user can now input a short PIN code through the untrusted device to access the underlying service provided by the server.

Table 3. Main steps to input service PIN code while using the visual channel by scanning QR codes.

Step	Screenshot of the application	Description
1	EEVEHAC EEVEHAC APPLICATION SCAN FOR QR CODES KEY EXCHANGE	The user clicks the Scan QR codes button.
2		The user sees QR codes on the terminal and points at them with the camera of their mobile device. If green rectangles appear around the QR codes, the user knows that everything is OK. Based on the decrypted content shown in the application the user can select the right QR code.

4.2 Task Models of User Tasks with EEVEHAC

In this section, we present the main task models that were produced to analyse usability of EEVEHAC. For the explanation of the application of the approach, we present the high-level parts of the task models. We also focus on specific branches of the task models, for which we present the details of the tasks, in order to highlight how we use them for the analysis presented in Sect. 4.5.

Figure 2 presents the task model that describes the main user tasks to configure the long term key. These consist of building (with application support) a story, memorizing the story and memorizing the color codes. The task model reads from left to right and from top to bottom. The main goal is represented by the abstract task at the top of the model "Configure long term key (story and color code)". To reach this main goal the user has to perform a sequence of four sub-goals, also represented by abstract tasks. All of the abstract tasks are refined in concrete user tasks. For example, the user first starts the configuration (abstract task "Start configuration" on the left of the model). This abstract task decomposes in a sequence ('>>' operator) of the cognitive task "Decide to start", the interactive input task "Click on start" and the interactive output task "Display welcome message". The abstract task "Select a word for the story" is iterative. The user manipulates several information (green boxes) to configure the long term key (e.g. story, value for orange color...). In the end, the user has to memorize this information, which is described by the production of declarative knowledge (represented with violet boxes names "Story" and "color codes").

Figure 3 presents the task model that describes the main user tasks to log in to the service with EEVEHAC. Under the main goal labelled "Log in to the service" at the top of the task model, a sequence of tasks has to be accomplished (temporal ordering operator "sequence" represented with ">>"). The main high-level sub goals are, that first, the user starts the service provider application on his smartphone, then, the user performs the UAN authentication and the last subgoal is to insert the PIN code. The abstract task "Select QR code" is represented as folded (with the symbol '+' at the bottom right of the task name). This means that this tasks decomposes in several tasks (not presented here).

4.3   Attack Tree

In this section we focus on an extract of the attack tree of EEVEHAC, for which we present the details of the attack, in order to highlight how we used it for the analysis presented in Sect. 4.5. A full description and a threat analysis of the EEVEHAC system is presented in [17].

Figure 4 presents the extract of the attack tree of EEVEHAC for the attacker goal "Impersonate the server or the user". The attacker goal may be to impersonate the server or the user (rectangle labelled "Impersonating the server or the user" on the top of the attack tree). This attack may have 3 effects (3 ellipses on the top of the attack tree): the communication channel is compromised, sensitive user data is stolen and the user device is infected with malware. If the attacker gets access to the encryption key, which is used to encrypt and decrypt the communication channel, the channel is no more secure. To reach the attack goal, the attacker must conduct a man-in-the-middle attack and uncover the long term key (story and color code). This is represented with the two rectangles under the "AND" operator. The man-in-the-middle attack is very unlikely because the attacker must simultaneously impersonate trusted devices (the server and the

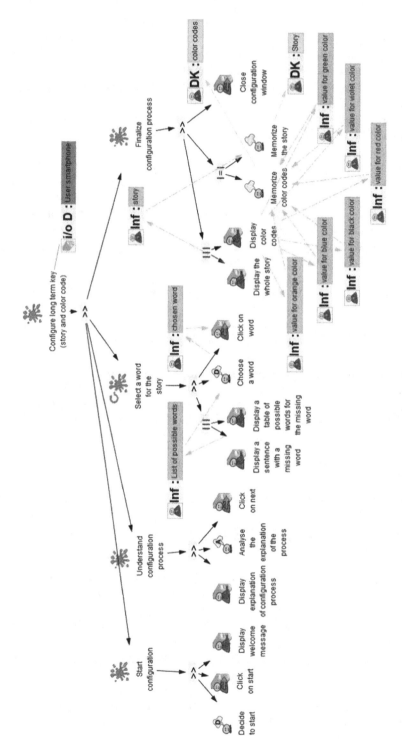

Fig. 2. Task model describing the task to "Configure the long term key (story and color code)" (Color figure online)

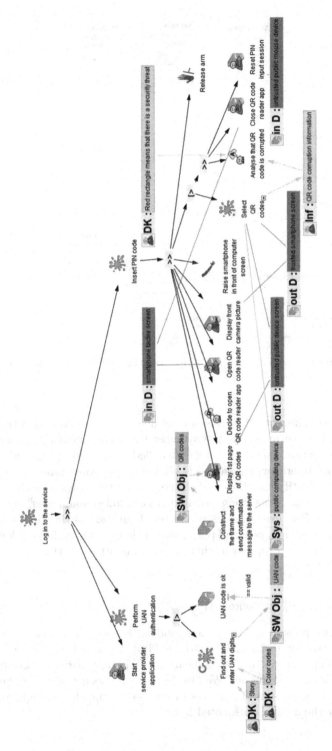

Fig. 3. Task model describing the task to "Log in to the service" (Color figure online)

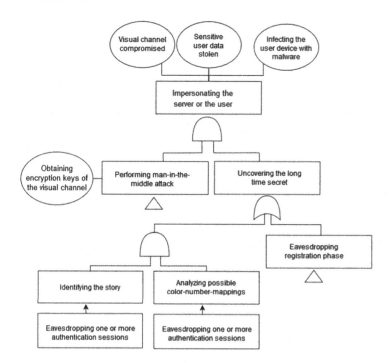

Fig. 4. Attack tree for the attacker goal "Impersonating the server or the user" (Color figure online)

user smartphone). This attack is thus not detailed (represented with a triangle). To uncover the long term secret, the attacker can either steal the information during the registration phase (rectangle labelled "Eavesdropping registration phase") or ("OR" operator) eavesdrop HAKE protocol communication channel setup sessions to identify the story and the color code (rectangles labelled "Identifying the story" and "Analyzing possible color-number-mappings" under the "AND" operator). Because the registration (configuration of the long term key) is supposed to be done in a peaceful place, such as home, it is highly unlikely that the information is eavesdropped in this phase. This attack is thus not detailed (represented with a triangle).

4.4 Task Models of Attacker Tasks

In this section, we present the main task models that were produced to analyse complexity of attacker tasks for the attack "Impersonating the server or the user". For the explanation of the application of the approach, we present the high-level part of the task model. We also focus on a specific branch of the task model, for which we present the details of the tasks, in order to highlight how we use them for the analysis presented in Sect. 4.5.

Figure 5 presents the task model of the attacker to reach the goal "Uncover the long time secret by eavesdropping". This goal in the task model corresponds to the main attack goal presented in the attack tree in the previous section.

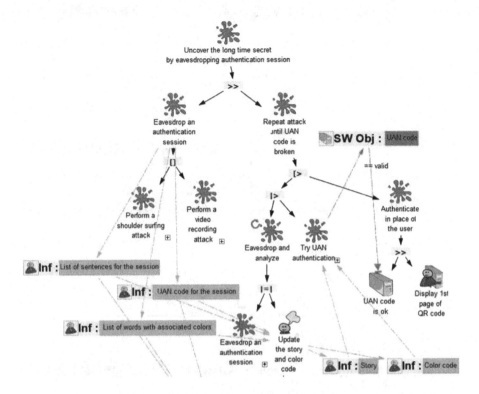

Fig. 5. Upper part (sub-goals) of the task model describing the attacker task "Uncover the long time secret by eavesdropping" (Color figure online)

The task model presented in Fig. 5 is the upper part of the whole task model for the attacker tasks. The attacker has to eavesdrop an authentication session (abstract task labelled "Eavesdrop and authentication session"), using a shoulder surfing attack or a video recording attack (folded abstract tasks labelled "Perform a shoulder surfing attack" and "Perform a video recording attack"). This first attack enables to get the first version of the list of possible sentences, as well as the corresponding UAN code and a first version of the list of possible words with their associated colors. Every iteration of this attack gives the attacker more information and thus, if the first attack is complete, the attacker has to repeat the attack until the long term key is broken (abstract task "Repeat attack until UAN code is broken"). This task decomposes in the abstract iterative task "Eavesdrop and analyze", that may be interrupted (temporal ordering operator '| >') by the task "Try UAN authentication". The abstract task "Authenticate in place of the user" may disable the abstract task "Try UAN authentication"

84   S. Nikula et al.

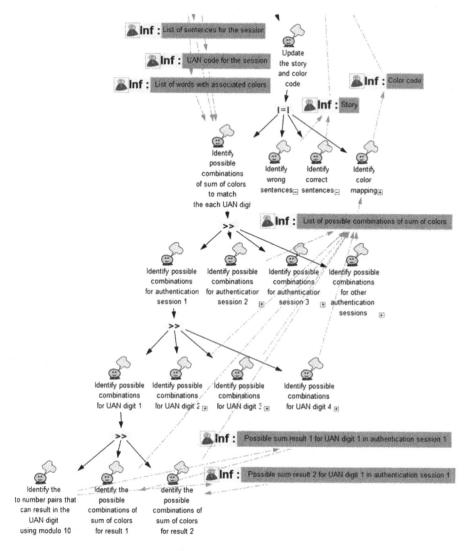

Fig. 6. Extract of the task model of the attacker task "Uncover the long time secret by eavesdropping" for the sub-goal "Update the story and color code" (Color figure online)

if the UAN code is valid. In this case, the attacker reached the main goal of the attack. The abstract iterative task "Eavesdrop and analyze" decomposes in the folded (not presented in detail in the paper) abstract "Eavesdrop and authentication session" and in the cognitive task "Update the story and color code". They can be performed in an order independent way (temporal ordering operator '| = |').

Figure 6 presents an extract of the description of the attacker task "Update the story and color code". The attacker has to perform several cognitive tasks to find out the story and the color code. The attacker has to "Identify the possible combinations of sum of colors to match each UAN digit", to "Identify wrong sentences", to "Identify correct sentences", and to "Identify color mapping". The folded tasks are not presented in detail in the paper. In order to identify the possible combinations of sum of colors to match each UAN digit, the attacker has to identify the combinations for several authentication sessions. And for each authentication session, the attacker has to identify the possible combinations for each UAN digit. And for each UAN digit, the attacker has to identify the possible combinations for the two possible number pairs that can result in the UAN digit using modulo 10. Figure 6 details the attacker tasks for 1 branch for each task. We present here a subset of the tasks because the full model does not fit in a page, and embeds more than sixty tasks, providing an evidence that the attacker will have a lot of work to perform to uncover the story and the color codes.

4.5 Task Models Based Analysis of Tradeoffs Between Usability and Security for EEVEHAC

About the usability of EEVEHAC, we analysed the two task models: "Configure the long term key" (Fig. 2) and "Log in to the service" (Fig. 3). For the first one, user tasks consist of building the story and memorizing it, as well as memorizing the color codes. There are several cognitive tasks, including memory tasks. The cognitive load for choosing words for the story may not be very high, but for the memory task, from the task model, we see that several information has to be memorized (chosen words, value for orange color, value for blue color, value for black color, value for red color, value for violet color and value for green color). All of this information has to be recorded in long-term memory, and turned into declarative knowledge (color codes and story in the task model). This implies that the user has to be willing to spend time on the configuration of the long term key. However, remembering a story can be easier than remembering an arbitrary password. The work of [30] takes advantage of the human ability to better remember stories than characters and numbers and the authors suggest a system where the secret key is a story in form of a text adventure. At last, configuration of the long term key is done only once.

For the second task model, "Log in to the service" (Fig. 3), the user has also to perform several cognitive tasks in order to recall and recognize the story words, identify the wrong words, recognize the colors and recall the color codes and to calculate the UAN temporary code. These tasks include cognitive calculation tasks that may take time depending on the user. This is supposed to be less efficient than a textual password, which only requires to remember the code before inputting it (if the user remembers it correctly). There thus may be an efficiency issue for the mechanism. This analysis is consistent with previous studies on the topic. Visual recognition of information has also been used in graphical passwords such as Passface [8]. Usability studies have demonstrated that they outperform passwords and PIN but the that graphical and interaction design might jeopardise their usability [12].

About the security, we analysed that the task is very complex for the attacker. From the task models (Fig. 5 and 6), we see that eavesdropping several full sessions are required to uncover the story and color code. Furthermore, the attacker can compromise the attack when trying the story and color code if the temporary guessed story and color code are wrong. From the task model, we also analyzed that there are more than fifty cognitive tasks for trying to find out the story and color code. Moreover, it is very unlikely that an attacker can eavesdrop several complete sessions and complete all of the tasks required to uncover the story and password. To make a comparison with textual password, EEVEHAC is more secure. For a textual password, a single eavesdrop is enough to uncover the password (the task model would be one branch only for the textual password).

To summarize, although the user tasks are numerous, with a potentially high cognitive load that may decrease efficiency, the tasks to attack it are complex. EEVEHAC thus enables to setup a secure communication channel between the user and the target services, in the case where the user needs to use an untrusted computer.

5   Related Work

We did not find any existing approach that explicitly targets usability and security, and that explicitly support the description of attacker tasks. In this section, we present the results of the comparison of the proposed approach with existing model-based approaches to analyse both usability and security, and with existing approaches to take into account attacker tasks.

5.1   Model-Based Approaches to Analyse Both Usability and Security

Braz et al. [6] proposed a so called "Metrics Based-Model", which is a conceptual framework gathering a set of criteria for assessing usability and security. They propose to use it to analyse systematically the usability and security of interactive systems. This approach is based on scenarios of the usage of the system, and it thus cannot cover all the possible user tasks and all of their possible temporal orderings, as scenarios are partial selections of sequences of user tasks. Mona et al. [25] proposed a meta-model of the relationships between usability and security, as well as a knowledge elicitation technique to ensure that required knowledge for the user is taken into account when designing the security mechanism. Our approach also takes into account the user knowledge: procedural knowledge with the hierarchy and temporal ordering of tasks and declarative knowledge with information to be memorized (e.g. a story). Al Zahrani et al. [1] target healthcare software and proposed a framework, composed of a set of metrics for usability and security and of a fuzzy logic based modeling techniques to produce probabilistic estimations of usability and security of a software. It aims to support decision making for security managers. It takes as input data from security and usability experts. Prior to its application, this approach thus requires a usability and security analysis. Broders et al. [7] proposed a task model based approach focusing on user tasks and on potential threats on these user tasks. In this approach, attack trees are also produced as a mean to ensure that every potential threat on user tasks has been identified. Martinie et al. [21] target the cybersecurity of maritime supply chain and proposed to integrate task modelling to the MITIGATE risk assessment method in order to identify threats on user tasks, whether they root in malicious attacks or in human errors. None of these model-based approaches deal with the attacker tasks.

5.2 Approaches to Take into Account Attacker Tasks

Encina et al. [14] proposed a catalog of misuse patterns, that can inform designers and developers when proposing new security mechanisms. This catalog gathers a set of threats and enables to build use cases of attacks. It neither mentions attacker tasks explicitly, nor the attacker in the attack workflow. Ben Othmane [3] et al. proposed to use information about attacker capabilities for risk assessment and mitigation. Such sets of information can be useful but have to be maintained up to date and provide incomplete information about the attacker tasks. Atzeni et al. [2] proposed a method to produce attacker personas, and Moeckel et al. [24] completed the method by adding an attacker taxonomy. Attacker personas aim to raise awareness about threats for the designers and developers, but also more generally in an organisation, to make the security issues more concrete to the users, for example. Personas rarely contain information about tasks, thus they are not sufficient to analyze the complexity of an attack.

6 Conclusion

We presented a models-based approach to analyse both user and attacker tasks when designing and developing a security mechanism. The EEVEHAC case study enabled us to show that attack trees are not enough to analyse the security of an authentication mechanism because the attacker tasks for uncovering a key are very complex and this cannot be foreseen from the attack tree. This can only be analysed if attacker tasks are systematically and precisely described. The modeling of attacker tasks enables to identify whether a specific security feature is worth to be implemented. For example, this approach enables to justify that usability could be decreased if there is no other option to reach the required security level. Another example is that if a security mechanism decreases usability but does not make the attacker tasks more complex, it should not be an acceptable design choice. The proposed approach enables to build evidences to argue for design choices.

References

1. Al-Zahrani, F.A.: Evaluating the usable-security of healthcare software through unified technique of fuzzy logic, ANP and TOPSIS. IEEE Access 8, 109905–109916 (2020). https://doi.org/10.1109/ACCESS.2020.3001996

2. Atzeni, A., Cameroni, C., Faily, S., Lyle, J., Flechais, I.: Here's Johnny: a methodology for developing attacker personas. In: 2011 Sixth International Conference on Availability, Reliability and Security, pp. 722–727 (2011). https://doi.org/10.1109/ARES.2011.115
3. ben Othmane, L., Ranchal, R., Fernando, R., Bhargava, B., Bodden, E.: Incorporating attacker capabilities in risk estimation and mitigation. Comput. Secur. **51**, 41–61 (2015). https://doi.org/10.1016/j.cose.2015.03.001
4. Bernhaupt, R., Martinie, C., Palanque, P., Wallner, G.: A generic visualization approach supporting task-based evaluation of usability and user experience. In: Bernhaupt, R., Ardito, C., Sauer, S. (eds.) HCSE 2020. LNCS, vol. 12481, pp. 24–44. Springer, Cham (2020). https://doi.org/10.1007/978-3-030-64266-2_2
5. Boldyreva, A., Chen, S., Dupont, P.A., Pointcheval, D.: Human computing for handling strong corruptions in authenticated key exchange. In: 2017 IEEE 30th Computer Security Foundations Symposium (CSF), pp. 159–175. IEEE (2017)
6. Braz, C., Seffah, A., M'Raihi, D.: Designing a trade-off between usability and security: a metrics based-model. In: Baranauskas, C., Palanque, P., Abascal, J., Barbosa, S.D.J. (eds.) INTERACT 2007. LNCS, vol. 4663, pp. 114–126. Springer, Heidelberg (2007). https://doi.org/10.1007/978-3-540-74800-7_9
7. Broders, N., Martinie, C., Palanque, P., Winckler, M., Halunen, K.: A generic multimodels-based approach for the analysis of usability and security of authentication mechanisms. In: Bernhaupt, R., Ardito, C., Sauer, S. (eds.) HCSE 2020. LNCS, vol. 12481, pp. 61–83. Springer, Cham (2020). https://doi.org/10.1007/978-3-030-64266-2_4
8. Brostoff, S., Sasse, M.A.: Are Passfaces more usable than passwords? A field trial investigation. In: McDonald, S., Waern, Y., Cockton, G. (eds) People and Computers XIV – Usability or Else!. Springer, London (2000). https://doi.org/10.1007/978-1-4471-0515-2_27
9. Carbone, R., Compagna, L., Panichella, A., Ponta, S.E.: Security threat identification and testing. In: 2015 IEEE 8th International Conference on Software Testing, Verification and Validation (ICST), pp. 1–8 (2015). https://doi.org/10.1109/ICST.2015.7102630
10. Card, S.K., Moran, T.P., Newell, A.: The model human processor: an engineering model of human performance. In: Handbook of Perception and Human Performance, pp. 1–35 (1986)
11. Daemen, J., Rijmen, V.: The Design of Rijndael, vol. 2. Springer, Heidelberger (2002). https://doi.org/10.1007/978-3-662-60769-5
12. De Angeli, A., Coventry, L., Johnson, G., Coutts, M.: Usability and user authentication: pictorial passwords vs. PIN, pp. 240–245. Taylor and Francis, UK (2003). https://doi.org/10.1201/b12800
13. El Batran, K., Dunlop, M.D.: Enhancing KLM (keystroke-level model) to fit touch screen mobile devices. In: Proceedings of the 16th International Conference on Human-Computer Interaction with Mobile Devices and Services, pp. 283–286. MobileHCI 2014, Association for Computing Machinery, NY (2014). https://doi.org/10.1145/2628363.2628385
14. Encina, C.O., Fernandez, E.B., Monge, A.R.: Threat analysis and misuse patterns of federated inter-cloud systems. In: Proceedings of the 19th European Conference on Pattern Languages of Programs. EuroPLoP 2014, Association for Computing Machinery, NY (2014). https://doi.org/10.1145/2721956.2721986
15. Forte, A.G., Garay, J.A., Jim, T., Vahlis, Y.: EyeDecrypt—private interactions in plain sight. In: Abdalla, M., De Prisco, R. (eds.) SCN 2014. LNCS, vol. 8642, pp. 255–276. Springer, Cham (2014). https://doi.org/10.1007/978-3-319-10879-7_15

16. Halunen, K., Latvala, O.M.: Review of the use of human senses and capabilities in cryptography. Comput. Sci. Rev. **39**, 100340 (2021)
17. Hekkala, J., Nikula, S., Latvala, O., Halunen, K.: Involving humans in the cryptographic loop: introduction and threat analysis of EEVEHAC. In: Proceedings of the 18th International Conference on Security and Cryptography - SECRYPT, pp. 659–664. INSTICC, SciTePress (2021). https://doi.org/10.5220/0010517806590664
18. Holleis, P., Scherr, M., Broll, G.: A revised mobile KLM for interaction with multiple NFC-tags. In: Campos, P., Graham, N., Jorge, J., Nunes, N., Palanque, P., Winckler, M. (eds.) INTERACT 2011. LNCS, vol. 6949, pp. 204–221. Springer, Heidelberg (2011). https://doi.org/10.1007/978-3-642-23768-3_18
19. ISO: ISO 9241-11:2018 ergonomics of human-system interaction part 11: Usability: Definitions and concepts. International Organization for Standardization
20. Krawczyk, H., Bellare, M., Canetti, R.: HMAC: keyed-hashing for message authentication (1997)
21. Martinie, C., Grigoriadis, C., Kalogeraki, E.M., Kotzanikolaou, P.: Modelling human tasks to enhance threat identification in critical maritime systems, pp. 375–380. PCI 2021, Association for Computing Machinery, NY (2021). https://doi.org/10.1145/3503823.3503892
22. Martinie, C., Palanque, P., Bouzekri, E., Cockburn, A., Canny, A., Barboni, E.: Analysing and demonstrating tool-supported customizable task notations. Proc. ACM Hum.-Comput. Interact. **3**(EICS), 1–26 (2019)
23. Martinie, C., Navarre, D., Palanque, P., Fayollas, C.: A generic tool-supported framework for coupling task models and interactive applications. In: Proceedings of the 7th ACM SIGCHI Symposium on Engineering Interactive Computing Systems, pp. 244–253. EICS 2015, Association for Computing Machinery, NY (2015). https://doi.org/10.1145/2774225.2774845
24. Moeckel, C.: From user-centred design to security: building attacker personas for digital banking. In: Proceedings of the 10th Nordic Conference on Human-Computer Interaction, pp. 892–897. NordiCHI 2018, Association for Computing Machinery, NY (2018). https://doi.org/10.1145/3240167.3240241
25. Mohamed, M.A., Chakraborty, J., Dehlinger, J.: Trading off usability and security in user interface design through mental models. Behav. Inf. Technol. **36**(5), 493–516 (2017). https://doi.org/10.1080/0144929X.2016.1262897
26. Naor, M., Shamir, A.: Visual cryptography. In: De Santis, A. (ed.) EUROCRYPT 1994. LNCS, vol. 950, pp. 1–12. Springer, Heidelberg (1995). https://doi.org/10.1007/BFb0053419
27. Nishihara, H., Kawanishi, Y., Souma, D., Yoshida, H.: On validating attack trees with attack effects. In: Casimiro, A., Ortmeier, F., Bitsch, F., Ferreira, P. (eds.) SAFECOMP 2020. LNCS, vol. 12234, pp. 309–324. Springer, Cham (2020). https://doi.org/10.1007/978-3-030-54549-9_21
28. Sasse, M.: Computer security: anatomy of a usability disaster, and a plan for recovery (2003)
29. Schneier, B.: Attack trees. Dr. Dobb's J. **24**(12), 21–29 (1999)
30. Somayaji, A., Mould, D., Brown, C.: Towards narrative authentication: or, against boring authentication. In: Proceedings of the 2013 New Security Paradigms Workshop, pp. 57–64 (2013)

On the Potentials of Realtime Sentiment Analysis on Text-Based Communication in Software Projects

Lennart Schroth[1], Martin Obaidi[2], Alexander Specht[2],
and Jil Klünder[2]($\boxtimes$)

[1] Leibniz Universität Hannover, Hanover, Germany
`info@lennart-schroth.de`
[2] Software Engineering Group, Leibniz Universität Hannover, Hanover, Germany
`{martin.obaidi,alexander.specht,jil.kluender}@inf.uni-hannover.de`

Abstract. Sentiment analysis is an established possibility to gain an overview of the team mood in software projects. A software analyzes text-based communication with regards to the used wording, i.e., whether a statement is likely to be perceived positive, negative, or neutral by the receiver of said message.

However, despite several years of research on sentiment analysis in software engineering, the tools still have several weaknesses including misclassifications, the impossibility to detect negotiations, irony, or sarcasm. Another huge issue is the retrospective analysis of the communication: The team receives the results of the analysis at best at the end of the day, but not in realtime. This way, it is impossible to react and to improve the communication by adjusting a message before sending it.

To reduce this issue, in this paper, we present a concept for realtime sentiment analysis in software projects and evaluate it in a user study with twelve practitioners. We were in particular interested in how real-time sentiment analysis can be integrated in the developers' daily lives and whether it appears to be helpful. Despite the still missing long-term case study in practice, the results of our study point to the usefulness of such kind of analysis.

Keywords: Sentiment analysis · Social aspects · Software project · Team mood · Realtime feedback

1 Introduction

In modern software development, several project leader strive to obtain an overview of what is going on in the teams [8,17]. This overview is not only limited to the technical aspects such as development progress, but also includes social aspects as they have been proven to influence the productivity of the team [4–6,24]. So-called sentiment analysis tools are one possibility to observe text-based communication that are widely used in software engineering [28]: Applying

© IFIP International Federation for Information Processing 2022
Published by Springer Nature Switzerland AG 2022
R. Bernhaupt et al. (Eds.): HCSE 2022, LNCS 13482, pp. 90–109, 2022.
https://doi.org/10.1007/978-3-031-14785-2_6

such tools to chats or other communication channels returns the polarity of each statement, i.e., whether it is positive, negative, or neutral, or an aggregated value for the whole team (e.g., [3,10,11]). Assuming that the used language reflects the general mood of a team member (happy team members are likely to communicate more friendly and positive, whereas a dissatisfied team member is likely to write more negatively), these values allow project leaders or managers to get an overview of the team mood without investing much time [3]. Due to the involvement of tools, this mood is kind of objectively measured.

However, such sentiment analysis tools have some weaknesses ranging from general problems with the accuracy of the detected polarity [12,21] to the impossibility to handle negotiations, irony, sarcasm, and the like [2,9,13,14,25,26]. Another problem is the time frame: The text-based communication is analyzed afterwards, e.g., at the end of a day, to draw conclusions about what was going on during the day (e.g., [7,23]). Hence, realtime interventions, i.e., adjusting the negative text-based message to be less negative, are almost impossible. However, another problem in software projects is the missing awareness of team members about the possible influences of their (interpersonal) behavior, including inadequate communication [17]. Even more, they are often not aware about how they communicate, i.e., whether it is likely that other team members perceive their text-based communication as positive and friendly or negative and unfriendly [16,17]. Consequently, providing them with information about how their message might be perceived before they send it to the rest of the team allows them to adjust it. Such kind of realtime feedback allowing team members to react has proven to be valuable for software development team [19].

As a first attempt to solve this problem, in this paper, we introduce a concept for realtime sentiment analysis for text-based communication between developers. This concept enables an analysis of all kind of input via the keyboard and returns the sentiment polarity of the input (independent of whether it is a word or a statement) so that the sender of the message receives a sentiment score representing how the receiver might perceive his text. This allows the sender to adjust the used language if necessary (e.g., if the message appears to be unintentionally negative). We evaluate the concept according to its applicability and its possible usefulness in a user study with twelve practitioners. Summarizing, we contribute the following key findings:

- The study participants agree that the core idea of realtime sentiment analysis is useful for industry.
- They would be willing to share their personal results in order to calculate an average team mood despite some security concerns.
- The participants' suggestions to improve the software point to an integration of established techniques that are already used in retrospective sentiment analysis into the concept of realtime sentiment analysis.
- We as experimenters observed an increasing awareness on how the participants communicate over the course of the study.

Context. This paper is based on the master's thesis [29] by Lennart Schroth with the title *"Concept for a preventive sentiment analysis of messages in software development teams"*.

Outline. This rest of this paper is structured as follows: In Sect. 2, we present background and related work. The concept of realtime sentiment analysis is outlined in Sect. 3. Section 4 summarizes our study design with the research questions, the instrument development, the data collection, and the data analysis. In Sect. 5, we present our results which we discuss in Sect. 6. Section 7 concludes the paper.

2   Background and Related Work

The idea of realtime sentiment analysis extends the core idea of sentiment analysis that is an established and frequently used method in software engineering [20,28]. There are several existing tools to analyze text-based communication, some of which are especially designed for the use in the software engineering domain [1,3,10,11,14,15].

The application of sentiment analysis in software engineering is not new [20,28]. Already in 2010, Thelwall et al. [30,31] presented SentiStrength which is a lexicon-based tool that searches for positive or negative words in a sentence (according to a pre-defined lexicon) and calculates the overall polarity based on these words. SentiStrength-SE is an adjusted version of SentiStrength that is specifically designed for the software engineering domain [14]. Comparing SentiStrength and SentiStrength-SE, Islam et al. [14] showed that the latter one provides more accurate results in software engineering contexts.

Klünder et al. [16] developed a sentiment analysis tool for classifying textual communication in a development team. They collected their data based on digital correspondence in German between developers working in the industry [16]. Their tool can detect polarities and is based on different machine learning algorithms like support-vector machine, random forests and an evolutionary algorithm for selecting suitable metrics to achieve the best performance.

Herrmann and Klünder [10,11] developed a sentiment analysis tool called SEnti-Analyzer which can analyze text-based communication data for their polarities as well as audio recordings and meetings in real time. The tool also assigns polarities and works with English and German language. SEnti-Analyzer includes several lexicon-based as well as machine learning based tools and combines them in a majority voting, which consists of the median label of each tool.

Calefato et al. [3] developed a tool called Senti4SD and enabled training and also classification of models specific to the SE domain. They implemented both a specialized word lexicon and also a support-vector machine. They were able to classify an input document in one of the three polarities *positive, negative, and neutral*.

Novielli et al. [26] also compared different sentiment analysis tools in a software engineering context. They tested the tools on data from GitHub, Jira, and

Stack Overflow. According to their results, lexicon-based methods provide better results, with, e.g., SentiStrength-SE having an accuracy of 75 to 80%.

Zhang et al. [33] compared the performance of different pre-trained neural network models (e.g., RoBERTa [22]) with those tools using more classical machine learning approaches or lexicon based tools (e.g., SentiStrength-SE [12]). They evaluate the classification accuracy of all these tools on many the data sets. They observed that the RoBERTa model [22] most often had the highest scores on average among the pre-trained transformer models.

In their replication study, Novielli et al. [27] explained some sentiment analysis tools (e.g. Senti4SD [3]) in great detail and described the underlying data. They also calculated an interrater agreement between sentiment analysis tools with each other and also with manual annotations from a gold standard of 600 documents. Based on their results, they suggest platform-specific tuning or retraining for sentiment analysis tools [27].

However, all these tools or studies did not perform a realtime sentiment analysis. But in order to be able to address the social factors such as negative mood in teams at an early stage, realtime sentiment analysis could be a solution. Our approach is based on such existing tools as they have been proven to provide adequate results with a sufficient accuracy.

3 Concept: Realtime Sentiment Analysis in Software Projects

Our concept for realtime sentiment analysis strives to detect the mood transported in a text-based message. So far, sentiment analysis on text-based communication requires time afterwards and the results are presented retrospectively [28]. The concept includes a window that is displayed in parallel to the already used communication software and calculates and visualizes a sentiment score based on the typed words. With our approach, we want to minimize the time required to analyze the message by presenting the results before sending a message, locally on a terminal without central analysis service. This helps highlighting how a receiver of a message may perceive it (and allows adjusting the wording if necessary). Resulting from this line of thoughts, our approach consists of the following three steps:

1. **Data collection:** We need to collect the written messages either in one specific channel (e.g., Microsoft Teams) or in general.
2. **Data analysis:** The collected data needs to be analyzed using different (already existing) mechanisms.
3. **Data processing:** We need to visualize and evaluate the results of the analysis.

These three steps result in the following requirements for the software system that implements our concept:

- The software tool shall run locally on a terminal device (offline).
- After having started the tool, it analyzes all messaging inputs from the user.
- The tool shall provide the results of the analysis in a short time (<1 s).
- All user data has to be deleted when stopping the tool.

These steps and the requirements should be implemented as individual modules. A high degree of modularity and interchangeability should be ensured in order to enable future improvements with low effort. For further improvements, we wanted to allow the deactivation, editing, or replacement of modules while the system is running. For this reason, an Internet of Thinks (IoT) protocol was used to ensure future-oriented data traffic. Message Queuing Telemetry Transport (MQTT) is a solution for short messages between different services, supervised by the MQTT-Broker as node for data traffic and quality of service[1]. The dependency and connections of the individual modules is shown in Fig. 1. In the following, we describe each of the steps in more detail.

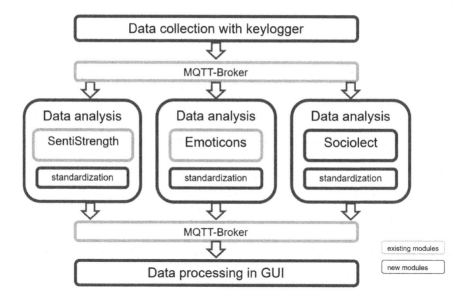

Fig. 1. Concept overview realtime sentiment analysis

3.1   Data Collection

In order to analyze different kind of text-based communication, we need to capture text or drafts of a message in realtime. As communication varies remarkably across teams (while one team prefers the communication via mail, while another

---

[1] https://mqtt.org/.

one prefers group chats [18]) and due to the wide variety of communication tools used in teams, we decide to use a keylogger that collects all types of keyboard inputs in the background. The keylogger helps identifying and collecting every input made using the keyboard and processes the input to be usable for the next step. The collected characters from the keyboard input are transformed to sentences to analyze the message as a whole instead of word-by-word. These were published on a MQTT-Broadcast channel respectively MQTT-Topic.

3.2 Data Analysis

For the data analysis, we use messages as input. For this step, we use a combination of existing tools consisting of an established sentiment analysis tool, the analysis of emoticons, and the analysis of the sociolect. Each of these methods was realized as a module to allow to activate or deactivate single tools. The following tools were considered for the sentiment analysis.

1. **SentiStrength**
   SentiStrength is a tool that detects mood in sentences by inferring positive or negative utterances from the polarity of words. E.g. "Good (+1) work". This tool has already been used in various studies and classifies quite reliably. Due to the evaluation of our approach in German companies with German as main language, we integrated the German version of SentiStrength in our concept. We integrate two versions of SentiStrength: SentiStrengh-DE (for German language) and SentiStrength-EN (for English language).
2. **Emoticons**
   An emoticon is the combination of different characters used in short messages to express the mood. E.g. "(^ ^)" (+1) ; "=(" (−1) ; "o.O" (0).
   We collected those emoticons in a look-up table with a sentiment value. The implemented script analyzes the incoming messages and calculate an average if multiple emoticons are used.
3. **Sociolect**
   During the pre-study, some statements were not recognized by SentiStrength, since they were neutral in terms of the polarities of the words, but are perceived negatively or positively in teams. A keyword-based analysis tool was then developed to classify such statements. In order to adapt this concept to different user groups, individual statements can be added manually to a lookup table.

The individual analyses had to be standardized for further data processing. In this context, the sentiment values were converted to a range from −1 (negative) to +1 (positive). In order to recognize why a message was interpreted in what way, the analyses also presents a reason for a calculated value.

3.3 Data Processing

We developed a user interface (in C#) that can be opened alongside an existing messenger service, such as Microsoft Teams. This slim display collected and displayed the results of the realtime sentiment analyses. In addition to displaying the individual analyses with explanation, an overall average was also calculated and shown central.

3.4 Prototype

We implemented these core ideas regarding the data collection, analysis, and processing in a software prototype. A screenshot of the general functionality is visualized in Fig. 2. In the upper half of the screen, we see the results of the different sentiment analyses over time. Below, we see the most recent sentiment score of the message, and an overview of explanations about how the score was calculated in the bottom. Note that, as we conducted the study in Germany, we also integrated the German version of SentiStrength and just translated the input for this screenshot. Typically, SentiStrength-DE would not be able to provide any information for English inputs. However, both analyses run in parallel. That is, if the used words are present in the German lexica, the German version is used. However, as computer science is a field in which English words are omnipresent, we also look into English lexica (provided by SentiStrength-EN) to increase the richness of the information. Nevertheless, this parallelity of the both languages introduces some difficulties as there are words that have different meanings in the languages. For example, the word "war" (past tense form of "be" in German) has a neutral meaning in German, but a negative meaning in English. Further research is required to solve such issues.

4   Study Design

In the following, we present our study design with the research questions and goals, the experiment structure, and the data collection.

4.1 Research Goal and Research Questions

Our overall research goal is to *evaluate realtime sentiment analysis with regard to its applicability and usefulness in practice*. In particular, we strive to answer the following research questions:

Research Question 1

> *How can realtime sentiment analysis be integrated in the daily lives of software developers?*

This question strives to analyze whether the concept presented before is useful for realtime sentiment analysis.

Research Question 2

> *How useful is realtime sentiment analysis perceived by practitioners?*

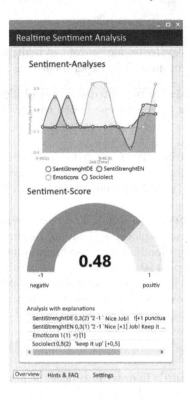

Fig. 2. Screenshot of the software prototype translated to English

This question clarifies if realtime sentiment analysis adds perceived value to software projects. In addition, it also shows how this added value looks like and how it can be achieved.

Research Question 3

> *Would team members be willing to share their aggregated data to allow an analysis on team level?*

This questions deals with the further data processing to not only reflect the mood of single team members, but also of the whole team, which is the main use case of retrospective sentiment analysis, but which needs to be adjusted to a realtime analysis.

4.2 Instrument Development

In order to evaluate the usefulness of realtime sentiment analysis, we implemented the aforementioned concept in a prototypical tool consisting of a *keylogger* to collect all keyboard inputs (in order to analyze them independently from the used messenger), three different analysis tools described in Sect. 3 and the visualization of all collected data over time.

4.3   Experiment Structure

We used the prototype to evaluate our concept of realtime sentiment analysis in an experiment with practitioners. The experiment consisted of five steps:

1. **Introduction (5 min):** We presented our overall idea of the realtime sentiment analysis and how the prototype works that they are about to use. We paid particular attention to a (brief) overview of the data processing and the further storage of the data.
2. **Questionnaire 1 (5 min):** The participants answered a questionnaire asking about demographic information (years of experience, their role in the team, etc.) and about their typical communication behavior (the use of different channels).
3. **Exploring the prototype (5 min):** The participants were asked to get to know the prototype in an exploratory fashion. In particular, they were asked to write something to get familiar with the main functionality of the software.
4. **Testing the prototype (10–20 min):** As the study strived to analyze the concept (i.e., the core idea of realtime sentiment analysis) rather than the prototype itself, we presented fictive scenarios that are possible use cases of the tool. As part of these scenarios, the participants were asked to write an answer to a received message. They were asked to write this answer in a positive, negative, or neutral way and to compare their perception with the response of the tool.
5. **Questionnaire 2 (5 min):** In order to collect the perceptions and opinions of the participants, they were asked to answer a second questionnaire to report on general feedback and their perceived usefulness of the tool. In addition, we integrated the "I wish, I like, I wonder" methodology to collect ideas for future research (*I wish*), core ideas that are good (*I like*), and potential for improvement or the need for explanations (*I wonder*).

4.4   Data Collection

As a first step, we collected data in a pre-study evaluating the overall concept and to allow for necessary improvements of the software prototype before testing it in a broader scope. In December 2021 four experts (project leader, quality assurance, or researchers with several years of experience with working in industry) participated in the pre-study. We used the feedback to make improvements to the prototype for analysis accuracy and user acceptance.

The pre-study followed the same process as described above, but strived to lay a foundation for the main study rather than to evaluate the idea from several viewpoints. That is, we conducted the pre-study to get a basis for the main experiment. We applied the think-aloud approach in order to collect as much feedback as possible. That is, participants were asked to verbalize their thoughts as fine-grained as possible. Resulting from the insights we gained during the pre-study, we improved the user interface and the sentiment analysis itself, as almost all participants faced problems with a few unclear classifications of messages: Team-specific statements were identified as neutral, although these were perceived negative by the experts. As a consequence, we included an analysis of the sociolect[2] with the option to add typical phrases (with a polarity value) to a so-called look-up table to adjust the tool to the team-specific language. For example "keep it up" was analyzed as *neutral*, although it was meant to be *positive*, and "if it has to be" ("wenn es sein muss" in German) has no negative polarity words but is meant negatively.

The main study was then conducted in the end of January 2022 with twelve participants from industry that did not participate in the pre-study. Depending on the preferences of the respective participant, the study was either conducted in person or in an online setting. The experiments had a duration of 45–55 min. The twelve participants work in three medium-sized companies (with 50 to 250 employees) in the domain of information systems and telecommunication. All participants work in software development teams. Seven participants work as software developer, two as project leaders, two as technical designer, and one as an IT consultant. In total, four female and eight male team members participated in our study. On average, the participants had 10 years of experience with working in the IT domain with a minimum of one year and a maximum of 24 years.

During the study, we applied the think-aloud approach and took notes. In addition, the participants answered two questionnaires that were also used for the later data analysis.

These questionnaires consisted of three question on demographics, 13 items that were rated on a Likert scale, two open questions on communication behavior in general, and some space for feedback divided into *I wish* (ideas for improvement), *I like* (good core ideas that are useful), and *I wonder* (needs for explanations or adjustments).

4.5   Data Preprocessing and Data Analysis

To answer our research questions, we mainly used two data sources: (1) The answers to open questions on communication behavior and feedback in the questionnaire (together with our notes resulting from the think-aloud process) and (2) Ratings on Likert scales on statements to different aspects concerning our research questions.

(1) The answers to the open questions were coded using open coding. That is, we categorized all answers (both from the questionnaires and from our notes) as long as we were sure that each statement was assigned the best matching category. These categories then helped us draw conclusions on the usefulness, missing functionalities, and potential for improvement (among others). These open questions also include the feedback presented on the questionnaires.

---

[2] Sociolect is a form of language (non-standard dialect, restricted register) or a set of lexical items used by a socioeconomic class, a profession, an age group or other social group.

(2) For the Likert scales, we calculated the median values for each of the six statements presented in Table 1. Note that, although we present the English translation of the statements, the statements were provided in the native language of the participants.

Table 1. Items rated by the participants

ID	Item	Questionnaire
1	I receive sufficient information to solve my tasks	Q1
2	There are several team meetings for exchanging relevant information for the projects	Q1
3	I try to spread a positive mood in the team	Q1
4	I try to formulate messages in a positive way	Q1
5	The results of the analysis coincide with my perception	Q2
6	The different analysis mechanisms detected different moods adequately	Q2
7	Such kind of software might be helpful in the future	Q2
8	I had few security concerns when using the software	Q2
9	To improve the team mood, I would share the average results of the analysis of my data with the project lead	Q2
10	I would like to know the average team mood	Q2

5 Results

We conducted the study as described in the previous section. In the following, we present the results.

5.1 Characterizing the Participants

Regarding the typical information exchange in the companies, the participants reported on generally receiving sufficient information for their tasks (Statement: *I receive sufficient information to solve my tasks*; median: 4, min: 3, max: 5). That is, typically, they receive the required information to solve their tasks. In addition, there are several meetings to ensure sufficient information exchange (statement: *There are several team meetings for exchanging relevant information for the projects*, median: 5, min 4, max: 5). The participants also try to spread a positive mood in the team (statement: *I try to spread a positive mood in the team*, median: 4, min: 3, max: 5) and to write positively (statement: *I try to formulate messages in a positive way*, median: 4, min: 3, max: 5).

At the time of the study (and likely influenced by the CoVID19-pandemic) participants report on using online-video meetings most often for communication (avg: 34,6%, SD[3]: 11,6%), followed by chat messages (22,1%, SD: 8,53%), e-mails (19,6%, SD: 11,4%), and face-2-face communication (18,3%, SD: 17,1%). Phone calls are barely used (5,4%, SD: 8,28%).

Text-based communication, that is analyzed by our tool, is used on average for 42% of the communication. Some participants use messages up to 60% to exchange information.

5.2   Perceived Accuracy of the Tool

Regarding the tools' accuracy, the participants were mostly satisfied (statement: *The results of the analysis coincide with my perception*, median: 4.5, min: 3, max: 5). However, note that this is only the perceived accuracy as we did not calculate some objective measure such as an interrater reliability between each participant and the tool. When analyzing social aspects in development teams, the perceived accuracy is much more important than the objective accuracy: If the participants' perception deviates too far from the results, they will likely neglect the results. Therefore, we opted for the perceived accuracy rather than for the objective measure. Nevertheless, we ensured objective accuracy by using established sentiment analysis tools.

In addition, the participants reported that the different mechanisms (SentiStrength, emoticons, and sociolect) detected the mood adequately (statement: *The different analysis mechanisms detected different moods adequately*, median: 4, min: 3, max: 5).

5.3   Perceived Helpfulness

The participants reported on a potential helpfulness of the software in future (statement: *Such kind of software might be helpful in the future*, median: 4.5, min: 3, max: 5). In order to improve the usability, they suggested to analyze the chats on project-level or to just consider specific chats of groups or teams, which is the current state of sentiment analysis, but retrospectively [28]. In addition, two participants recommended to provide the results comparable to a spell check underlining the words in red or green, respectively. Half of the participants were also interested in a live presentation of the results aggregated on chat-level right in the respective chat window.

---

[3] SD is the abbreviation for standard deviation.

5.4   Data Aggregation on Team Level

However, the participants had some security concerns when using the software (statement: *I had few security concerns when using the software*, median: 3, min: 2, max: 5). This also goes along with one participant reporting on the feeling of being monitored or observed. This feeling is also omnipresent if the aggregated results are shared with the project leader. Nevertheless, the participants reported on agreeing to share their data (statement: *To improve the team mood, I would share the average results of the analysis of my data with the project lead*, median: 4, min: 3, max: 5), as they are also interested in the average team mood (statement: *I would like to know the average team mood* , median: 5, min: 4, max: 5). However, ten out of twelve participants stated that they are only willing to share their average data if the whole team can see the results on team level, and not only the project leader.

5.5   Observations of the Experimenters

Regardless of the team sentiment level, the study showed that awareness of a positive way of communicating can be increased with the help of such a tool. We observed an improved self-reflection and the careful selection of the wording in text messages. As soon as the participants perceived some kind of familiarity with the tool, they started to write messages as positive or as negative as possible in order to test the tool. Afterwards, they started adjusting their wording in order to be at least neutral, but not negative – also when trying to write some negative message in the fictive scenario.

6   Discussion

In the following, we discuss and interpret our results as well as threats to validity.

6.1   Answering the Research Questions

Based on our results, we can answer the research questions as follows:

Answer to RQ1: Using our rudimental and prototypical concept consisting of a keylogger and a joint sentiment analysis, it is possible to integrate realtime sentiment analysis in the daily lives of software developers. However, in order to ease the use of the concept, an integration of the concept into different platforms (such as Microsoft Teams or Skype) would be helpful. Nevertheless, a real use in practice is still missing. With our study, we just prove that the general concept works.

Answer to RQ2: The core idea is perceived helpful by our twelve study participants. However, the practitioners proposed different extensions to increase the helpfulness of the results, such as the integration into existing chat tools instead of the decentralized idea followed by our approach. These insights and the promising results motivate further research on realtime sentiment analysis.

Answer to RQ3: The participants also stated to be willing to share their aggregated scores to allow the calculation of an average team score (under the condition that they get to see the results). However, our study was conducted in an experimental setting. Thus, we got impressions from practitioners, but only reflecting on a hypothetical use in practice.

6.2   Interpretation

Summarizing, the results of our study motivate the further exploration of real-time sentiment analysis.

The results of our study indicate that realtime sentiment analysis is help-ful and was well-accepted by the study participants. The median value was 4.5 (between agree and absolutely agree) when asked if such a tool could help in the future. The fact that this is not a "traditional", i.e., retrospective, sentiment analysis, but feedback when writing a message, means that realtime sentiment analysis does not contradict the current use of sentiment analysis. The estab-lished tools provide insights about sentiments by observing the textual commu-nication of developers. The concept presented in this paper provides feedback on the sentiment of a self-written message with the option to adjust it appropriately before sending the message to the team. This helps to convey the perception a developer wants to convey accordingly and thus avoid possible misunderstand-ings. This means that, for example, developers can adjust their message from negative or neutral to positive if the message is not meant to have such polarity. On the other hand, it is possible to change a positive message to neutral, if this effect is desired, for example, due to poor results in the current development or inadequacy of positive mood due to other social factors.

Regarding the combination of realtime and "typical" sentiment analysis, there is the threat that messages are changed after the feedback of the tool, e.g., from negative towards positive, although the negative wording reflects the actually existing emotional mood of the sender. Regarding the reduced risk of negative mood in the team due to a too rough communication, this is the desired out-come. But teams need to be aware that a retrospective sentiment analysis would then not adequately reflect the real team mood. This means that the messages sent are somewhat manipulated and introduce a bias. Thus, sentiment analysis tools applied to written communication might not measure the true sentiment in this case. However, a combination between realtime and retrospective sentiment analysis is still useful to have more data to get closer to the real sentiment of a developer team. This was also requested by our study participants. In addition, the analysis of what has already been written can also have a different focus, e.g. instead of sentiment in the actual sense, it can be more of a content-based analysis, e.g. whether negative or positive events are mentioned. This also goes along with Graziotin et al. [5] results, which show that satisfied developers are better at solving problems. So if many negative events were mentioned in the communication, this can be an indication of possibly dissatisfied developers. This means that our feedback tool analyzes how a message might be perceived by the recipient, while another tool analyzes the communication, focusing on how it was communicated. Nevertheless, these ideas require future research.

However, the security concerns mentioned by the participants must not be ignored. Therefore, a company or project leader should be very transparent with the tool (e.g., how it works and determines the sentiment) as well as with the analysis of the messages in order to avoid that the developers feel observed or do not feel comfortable writing messages. It also makes sense to regularly measure the mood and emotional state of developers to see whether such a feedback tool has a negative impact on the developers or not.

6.3 Threats to Validity

In the following, we present threats to validity according to our paper. We categorize the threats according to Wohlin et al. [32] as conclusion, internal, construct, and external validity.

Our study had only 12 participants (construct validity), and not all of them were pure developers (external validity). Consequently, the results must not be overinterpreted. We gained insights from twelve practitioners that imagined using such a tool in their daily lives. They answered the questions based on their experiences. However, already the study with such a small sample size provided interesting insights that motivate further research. As a first proof of concept, in our opinion, such a small study suffices. Nevertheless, future studies are required to strengthen the results.

The study was conducted in a fictive situation (construct and external validity) which limits the generalizability of our results.

The perceived accuracy of the realtime feedback tool offers potential for improvement, partially due to the lack of recognition of sarcasm and irony. These statements were mostly classified as neutral (internal and construct validity). However, as far as we know, this issue has not been resolved in research, but has been frequently identified as a problem [20,28].

When developers know that what they write is analyzed by a tool, this can influence their behavior. They would not write certain things or think about what they write before writing and sending it (external validity). However, this was not a threat of our study, but of the generalizability of the results. In this controlled settings, participants reported on a potential usefulness and it was not an "observation" of their behavior and what they write. They were just neutrally asked to try the tool. However, the fact of observation and monitoring will influence the use of the tool in reality.

Although all written communication is considered in the concept by a keylogger, written communication only accounts for 42% according to the surveys (conclusion validity). This can also include communication beyond the computer, e.g. via smartphone. Meetings, for example, are often also a component of communication. However, our concept covers a large part of the communication. And often misunderstandings and therefore problems and bad moods arise from written communication, where sender and receiver do not see each other and do not hear each other's voice.

In the study, only SentiStrength (for English and German) was used as a sentiment analysis tool (construct and internal validity). However, the tool was supplemented by further data analysis using emoticons and a self-created lexicon by the study participants. Nevertheless, the accuracy of the analysis results strongly depends on the selected analysis techniques. This accuracy, in turn, has an influence on the perceived helpfulness of the tool, because unreliable results would be neglected and will not provide any benefit for a hypothetical use in practice.

Open coding of the survey's responses to open questions was conducted by only one author (construct validity). However, the categories were reviewed by the other authors to increase the accuracy of the results.

Summarizing, these threats point to weaknesses of the reliability and the validity of our study's results. Future research is required to solve these issues, to provide deeper insights, and to strengthen the results. In particular, a real case study in practice is required to provide insights on the real usefulness and not only on the potential usefulness.

6.4   Future Work

The threats presented before and the results of our study point to potential for further research. For our study we used a keylogger to get access to the written message. In future work it is possible to develop a framework which can get access to other services like Microsoft Teams or Telegram. With this framework it should be possible to also handle emoticons which are integrated in the operated system and to also analyze reactions to specific messages. In our study we used only text-based emoticons. Operating systems have much more smileys with different meanings which can be analyzed. It is also possible that we receive better accuracy when we do not use lexicon-based sentiment analysis but a machine learning based algorithm. In the SLR from Obaidi and Klünder [28], we see that machine learning sentiment analysis offers a better performance, so we get better results.

To show the sentiments we present a prototype in Sect. 3 and there are much more possibilities to integrate the sentiment in other messengers. One of them could be a, e.g., highlighting-system like a spell checker. Sentiment words with positive meaning could be green and negative ones red.

Some of our participants wish to perform a long-time study to evaluate if the usage behavior is changing over time. In the future it is useful to conduct such a study. Furthermore, it can also be investigated to what extent the software has an influence on the users over time. For this purpose, interview studies or surveys on various aspects such as behavior, mood, etc. should be carried out before, during, and after the study.

Another point was that some users reported on being disappointed when writing a long message and only getting back an "okay". In future works it is possible to evaluate if an assistant can give suggestions for improvement e.g., "You got a long message. Don't you want to write more words in your response?" and if it is useful while writing messages. Another point to increase the effectiveness of our prototype is that the sentiment analysis can (and should) also be improved, because we analyze only the text which is written but without any context analysis. If someone is writing ironically it is likely that the sentiment detection is wrong. Also, short messages without context could be wrong detected.

In order for the prototype to be used in a real scenario, certain aspects such as practicality must be taken into account. This may include ease of installation (or installation instructions), maintenance, and support for the software. This may include adapting the tool to the particular developer team. Communication between developer friends may be different than between the developer and the project manager.

The suggestions provided by our participants also point to the idea of combining realtime with retrospective sentiment analysis. As discussed before, this combination has potential, but requires a profound analysis of the real usefulness, as both analysis methods analyze the same aspect (the mood in the team) from different viewpoints and with different goals. Nevertheless, the combination might provide more sound insights than each of the methods (realtime and retrospective sentiment analysis) in a stand-alone setting.

7   Conclusion

As there is an increasing interest on analyzing social aspects in development teams, sentiment analysis is widely used in research to get an overview of what is going on in a development team. However, in order to provide the possibility for adjustments and interventions, some kind of realtime sentiment analysis is required.

Our concept for realtime sentiment analysis offers this opportunity by analyzing messages before they are sent. This avoids sending messages that raise some negative feeling with the receiver and increases the awareness of how some message might be perceived by others.

We evaluated our prototypically implemented concept in an experimental setting with twelve participants from industry. Despite the small sample size and the preliminary nature of this study, we observe that participants expect the idea of realtime sentiment analysis to be helpful in industry. In addition, they also stated to be willing to share their data to calculate the mood aggregated on team-level. Nevertheless, they provided ideas on how to extend the concept of realtime sentiment analysis pointed to already established approaches when doing retrospective sentiment analysis.

Future research will focus on the suggestions of the participants and requires a case study in industry in order to prove the usefulness in a real setting.

Acknowledgment. This research was funded by the Leibniz University Hannover as a Leibniz Young Investigator Grant (Project *ComContA*, Project Number *85430128*, 2020–2022).

References

1. Ahmed, T., Bosu, A., Iqbal, A., Rahimi, S.: SentiCR: a customized sentiment analysis tool for code review interactions. In: 2017 32nd IEEE/ACM International Conference on Automated Software Engineering (ASE), pp. 106–111 (2017). https://doi.org/10.1109/ASE.2017.8115623
2. Cabrera-Diego, L.A., Bessis, N., Korkontzelos, I.: Classifying emotions in stack overflow and JIRA using a multi-label approach. Knowl.-Based Syst. **195**, 105633 (2020). https://doi.org/10.1016/j.knosys.2020.105633
3. Calefato, F., Lanubile, F., Maiorano, F., Novielli, N.: Sentiment polarity detection for software development. Empir. Softw. Eng. **23**(3), 1352–1382 (2017). https://doi.org/10.1007/s10664-017-9546-9
4. De Choudhury, M., Counts, S.: Understanding affect in the workplace via social media, pp. 303–316. Association for Computing Machinery, NY (2013)
5. Graziotin, D., Wang, X., Abrahamsson, P.: Happy software developers solve problems better: psychological measurements in empirical software engineering. PeerJ **2**, e289 (2014). https://doi.org/10.7717/peerj.289
6. Graziotin, D., Wang, X., Abrahamsson, P.: Do feelings matter? On the correlation of affects and the self-assessed productivity in software engineering. J. Softw.: Evol. Process **27**(7), 467–487 (2015). https://doi.org/10.1002/smr.1673
7. Guzman, E., Azócar, D., Li, Y.: Sentiment analysis of commit comments in GitHub: an empirical study. In: Kim, S., Pinzger, M., Devanbu, P. (eds.) 11th Working Conference on Mining Software Repositories. 31 May–1 June 2014, Hyderabad, pp. 352–355. ACM (2014). https://doi.org/10.1145/2597073.2597118
8. Guzman, E., Bruegge, B.: Towards emotional awareness in software development teams. In: Meyer, B., Mezini, M., Baresi, L. (eds.) 2013 9th Joint Meeting of the European Software Engineering Conference and the ACM SIGSOFT Symposium on the Foundations of Software Engineering (ESEC/FSE). 18–26 August 2013, Saint Petersburg, Russia, pp. 671–674. ESEC/FSE 2013, ACM (2013). https://doi.org/10.1145/2491411.2494578
9. Guzman, E., Maalej, W.: How do users like this feature? A fine grained sentiment analysis of app reviews. In: 2014 IEEE 22nd International Requirements Engineering Conference (RE), pp. 153–162 (2014). https://doi.org/10.1109/RE.2014.6912257
10. Herrmann, M., Klünder, J.: From textual to verbal communication: towards applying sentiment analysis to a software project meeting. In: 2021 IEEE 29th International Requirements Engineering Conference Workshops (REW), pp. 371–376 (2021). https://doi.org/10.1109/REW53955.2021.00065
11. Herrmann, M., Obaidi, M., Klünder, J.: Senti-analyzer: joint sentiment analysis for text-based and verbal communication in software projects. Tech. rep. (2022). https://arxiv.org/abs/2206.10993
12. Imtiaz, N., Middleton, J., Girouard, P., Murphy-Hill, E.: Sentiment and politeness analysis tools on developer discussions are unreliable, but so are people. In: Proceedings of the 3rd International Workshop on Emotion Awareness in Software Engineering, pp. 55–61. SEmotion 2018, Association for Computing Machinery, NY (2018). https://doi.org/10.1145/3194932.3194938
13. Islam, M.R., Zibran, M.F.: Leveraging automated sentiment analysis in software engineering. In: 2017 IEEE/ACM 14th International Conference on Mining Software Repositories (MSR), pp. 203–214 (2017). https://doi.org/10.1109/MSR.2017.9

14. Islam, M.R., Zibran, M.F.: DEVA: sensing emotions in the valence arousal space in software engineering text. In: Haddad, H.M., Wainwright, R.L., Chbeir, R. (eds.) Applied Computing 2018, pp. 1536–1543. Association for Computing Machinery Inc. (ACM), NY (2018). https://doi.org/10.1145/3167132.3167296

15. Islam, M.R., Zibran, M.F.: SentiStrength-SE: exploiting domain specificity for improved sentiment analysis in software engineering text. J. Syst. Softw. **145**, 125–146 (2018). https://doi.org/10.1016/j.jss.2018.08.030

16. Klünder, J., Horstmann, J., Karras, O.: Identifying the mood of a software development team by analyzing text-based communication in chats with machine learning. In: Bernhaupt, R., Ardito, C., Sauer, S. (eds.) HCSE 2020. LNCS, vol. 12481, pp. 133–151. Springer, Cham (2020). https://doi.org/10.1007/978-3-030-64266-2_8

17. Klünder, J., Schneider, K., Kortum, F., Straube, J., Handke, L., Kauffeld, S.: Communication in teams - an expression of social conflicts. In: Bogdan, C., et al. (eds.) HESSD/HCSE -2016. LNCS, vol. 9856, pp. 111–129. Springer, Cham (2016). https://doi.org/10.1007/978-3-319-44902-9_8

18. Kortum, F., Klünder, J., Schneider, K.: Don't underestimate the human factors! exploring team communication effects. In: Felderer, M., Méndez Fernández, D., Turhan, B., Kalinowski, M., Sarro, F., Winkler, D. (eds.) PROFES 2017. LNCS, vol. 10611, pp. 457–469. Springer, Cham (2017). https://doi.org/10.1007/978-3-319-69926-4_36

19. Kortum, F., Klünder, J., Schneider, K.: Behavior-driven dynamics in agile development: the effect of fast feedback on teams. In: 2019 IEEE/ACM International Conference on Software and System Processes (ICSSP), pp. 34–43. IEEE (2019)

20. Lin, B., Cassee, N., Serebrenik, A., Bavota, G., Novielli, N., Lanza, M.: Opinion mining for software development: a systematic literature review. ACM Trans. Softw. Eng. Methodol. **31**(3), 1–41 (2022). https://doi.org/10.1145/3490388

21. Lin, B., Zampetti, F., Bavota, G., Di Penta, M., Lanza, M., Oliveto, R.: Sentiment analysis for software engineering: how far can we go? In: Proceedings of the 40th International Conference on Software Engineering, pp. 94–104. ICSE 2018, Association for Computing Machinery, NY (2018). https://doi.org/10.1145/3180155.3180195

22. Liu, Y., et al.: RoBERTa: a robustly optimized BERT pretraining approach (2019)

23. Freira, M., Caetano, J., Oliveira, J., Marques-Neto, H.: Analyzing the impact of feedback in GitHub on the software developer's mood (2018). https://doi.org/10.18293/SEKE2018-153

24. Graziotin, D., Wang, X., Abrahamsson, P.: How do you feel, developer? An explanatory theory of the impact of affects on programming performance. PeerJ Comput. Sci. **1**, e18 (2015)

25. Novielli, N., Girardi, D., Lanubile, F.: A benchmark study on sentiment analysis for software engineering research. In: 2018 IEEE/ACM 15th International Conference on Mining Software Repositories (MSR), pp. 364–375 (2018)

26. Novielli, N., Calefato, F., Dongiovanni, D., Girardi, D., Lanubile, F.: Can we use SE-specific sentiment analysis tools in a cross-platform setting? pp. 158–168. Association for Computing Machinery, NY (2020)

27. Novielli, N., Calefato, F., Lanubile, F., Serebrenik, A.: Assessment of off-the-shelf SE-specific sentiment analysis tools: an extended replication study. Empir. Softw. Eng. **26**(4), 1–29 (2021). https://doi.org/10.1007/s10664-021-09960-w

28. Obaidi, M., Klünder, J.: Development and application of sentiment analysis tools in software engineering: a systematic literature review. In: Evaluation and Assessment in Software Engineering, pp. 80–89. EASE 2021, Association for Computing Machinery, NY (2021). https://doi.org/10.1145/3463274.3463328

29. Schroth, L.: Konzept für eine präventive Stimmungsanalyse von Nachrichten in Software-Entwicklungsteams (concept for a preventive sentiment analysis of messages in software development teams) (2022)
30. Thelwall, M., Buckley, K., Paltoglou, G.: Sentiment strength detection for the social web. J. Am. Soc. Inform. Sci. Technol. **63**(1), 163–173 (2012). https://doi.org/10.1002/asi.21662
31. Thelwall, M., Buckley, K., Paltoglou, G., Cai, D., Kappas, A.: Sentiment strength detection in short informal text. J. Am. Soc. Inform. Sci. Technol. **61**(12), 2544–2558 (2010). https://doi.org/10.1002/asi.21416
32. Wohlin, C., Runeson, P., Höst, M., Ohlsson, M.C., Regnell, B., Wesslén, A.: Experimentation in Software Engineering. Springer, Berlin (2012). https://doi.org/10.1007/978-3-642-29044-2
33. Zhang, T., Xu, B., Thung, F., Haryono, S.A., Lo, D., Jiang, L.: Sentiment analysis for software engineering: how far can pre-trained transformer models go? In: 2020 IEEE International Conference on Software Maintenance and Evolution (ICSME), pp. 70–80 (2020). https://doi.org/10.1109/ICSME46990.2020.00017

Little Stakeholder Communication in Distributed Scrum Projects During the Covid-19 Period

Hrund Valgeirsdóttir, Marta Lárusdóttir(✉) ⓘ, and Helgi Þór Ingason ⓘ

Reykjavik University, Menntavegur 1, 102, Reykjavik, Iceland
marta@ru.is

Abstract. Agile methods have recently been popular by software development teams, with Scrum being the prominent process over the last decade. In Scrum, the Scrum Master serves the developers, the Product Owner, and the organization by coaching, leading, mentoring, planning, removing impediments, etc. Additionally, the Scrum Master is accountable for establishing the developer's effectiveness. The global pandemic of Covid-19 changed the world unexpectedly in March 2020. Work has mostly shifted to a remote setting, and meetings have mostly transferred to being remote. People have had to adapt to these new circumstances worldwide. This research aimed to explore the changes that Scrum Masters and their teams have had to face during the first year of the Covid-19 period by increasing distributed working and the changes in the Scrum Master's responsibilities. The results indicate that the most significant change has been decreasing communication with stakeholders and users after working more distributed. Additionally, not meeting socially, as the teams did before, has been a big challenge for the Scrum Teams.

Keywords: Scrum Master · Stakeholder communication · Distributed work

1 Introduction

The work environment of many professions has undergone many changes since early 2020 worldwide. People have been working from home a lot more under different circumstances. Some have their spouses also working from home and children taking their school lessons through virtual tools. Some people had to do their work from their kitchen or their bedrooms with different equipment and privacy standards which can depend on circumstances, and affect people's focus on work routines.

According to the annual State of Agile Survey, 95% of organizations surveyed practice Agile development. Of all the Agile frameworks and methodologies, Scrum is the most popular method or used by 58% of organizations. The same survey informs that 81% of organizations have Agile teams where all the team members do not work at the same location. Distributed teams may become a "new normal" due to the current worldwide health crisis [23].

© IFIP International Federation for Information Processing 2022
Published by Springer Nature Switzerland AG 2022
R. Bernhaupt et al. (Eds.): HCSE 2022, LNCS 13482, pp. 110–126, 2022.
https://doi.org/10.1007/978-3-031-14785-2_7

In Scrum methodology, a Scrum Team consists of three different roles: the Scrum Master (SM) role, the Product Owner (PO) role, and the Scrum Team (ST) role, a development team of 10 or fewer developers. The PO is accountable for maximizing the value of the product resulting from the work of the developers. His/her focus is on building the right product. The ST developers have the skills required to deliver the business value requested by the PO as their focus is mainly on building the product right [16, 19].

The Scrum Master role is described by him/her: *being a coach*, coaching the team members in self-management and cross-functionality, *being a servant leader*, leading the Scrum Team to ensure the highest priority needs are met; and *having process authority*, which involves that the Scrum Master should ensure that the team enacts and adheres to the Scrum values, principles, and practices, along with the team's specific approach [6, 16, 19, 20]. Schwaber and Sutherland additionally mention that the Scrum Master's role is to be leading, supporting training, and coaching for the organization, especially while the organization is adapting to using Scrum [19]. Additionally, the role of the Scrum Masters includes planning, ad advising on the implementations of Scrum within the organization [19]. Noll et al. did a systematic review to identify activities performed by Scrum Masters. These activities were process facilitation, ceremony facilitation, and impediment removal [15]. Another study on the Scrum Master's responsibilities by Bass reveals six most common activities: process anchoring, stand-up facilitating, impediment removing, sprint planning, Scrum of Scrum facilitating, and integration anchoring [3]. An online survey from 2019 revealed that 91% of IT professionals with Scrum experience think that the Scrum Master role is important for the success of the Scrum methodology [9].

The scope of this paper is to study how the change that Scrum Masters and their teams have experienced from being entirely or partially co-located to being a fully distributed team during the Covid-19 period. The focus is on the role of the Scrum Master, studying particularly, if and then how, the responsibilities of the Scrum Masters, changed while their work was more distributed during the Covid-19 period. Distributed work entails that all team members are working from different locations. The rationale behind the selection of focus is that the Scrum Master acts as a bridge between the developers and the Product Owner and therefore is aware of the changes that have impacted the Scrum Team since working from home. We ask the following research question:

What changes did distributed work during the Covid-19 period entail for factors included in the responsibilities of the Scrum Master role?

In this paper, we first give a short overview of the background literature, including summarizing the responsibilities of the Scrum Masters listed in core literature on the subject and the effects already described by the Covid-19 period on distributed work. We describe the data gathering conducted with interviews, the participants, and the data analysis method. We describe the results in six themes: the responsibilities of the Scrum Masters, the work environment and procedures, meeting and Scrum events, communication and social interaction, productivity, and the future. We conclude by discussing our results.

2 Background

This section gives a short overview of the literature on Scrum, the Scrum Master's responsibilities, and related work in the field of Scrum in a distributed work environment.

2.1 Scrum Methodology

Scrum is an agile approach for developing innovative products and services [16]. It was defined in 1986 by Takeuchi and Nanaka while studying methods to create new products [21]. Ken Schwaber and Jeff Sutherland developed Scrum as it is known today in the early 1990s [19]. They presented it first at the OOPSLA conference in 1995.

At the beginning of a project, the Product Owner creates a product backlog in collaboration with the other Scrum Team members and stakeholders. The backlog is a prioritized list of features and other capabilities needed to develop a successful product. It is a constantly evolving artifact [16].

The work within Scrum is in iterations that are called sprints, which are fixed lengths of events of one month or less. A new sprint starts immediately following the conclusion of the previous sprint. Within each sprint, there is Sprint Planning, Daily Scrums, Sprint Review, and Sprint Retrospective. Sprint Planning is for laying out the work in the upcoming sprint and can take about four to eight hours, depending on the length of the sprint. Daily Scrum is a 15-min event for the Developers of the Scrum Team. The primary purpose is to inspect progress within the sprint and adapt the sprint backlog, as necessary. Sprint Review is to examine the outcome of the sprint and determine future adaptations. The Scrum Team presents the work and progress to the stakeholders. The last event of each sprint, the Sprint Retrospective, is to plan ways to increase quality and effectiveness. The focus is on continuous process improvement to help Scrum Teams become great [16, 19].

2.2 The Scrum Master's Responsibilities

The overall responsibility of the Scrum Master has been defined by many researchers. Schwaber and Sutherland state that the Scrum Master is responsible for the Team's effectiveness while serving the Scrum Team and the larger organization [19]. Schwaber states that the Scrum Master makes sure that all the pieces of the Scrum process come together and work as a whole [17]. Schwaber and Beedle state that the Scrum Master conducts daily coordination meetings and removes any impediments that the team encounters [18].

Rubin states that the Scrum Master does this by helping everyone to understand and embrace the Scrum values, principles, and practices and is thereby responsible for supporting the team to gain that understanding [16].

Cohn describes the Scrum Master as both a Servant Leader and someone with no authority over the other Scrum Team members. However, he/she has authority over the process. That gives him/her the control to make decisions when the team does not decide independently. The Scrum Master is there to help the team in its use of Scrum. The attributes of a good Scrum Master are being responsible, humble, collaborative, committed, influential, and knowledgeable [6].

Sochova states that the Scrum Master has the responsibility to seek to build self-organized teams, make all people more active, and make the organization independent at every level [20].

We analyzed in more detail the Scrum Master's responsibilities described in four core publications on the responsibilities of the Scrum Master from Cohn [6]; Rubin [16]; Schwaber & Sutherland [19] and Sochova [20].

The responsibilities of Scrum Masters described in these four papers can be summarized as:

1. *Being a Coach:* Involves coaching the team members in self-management and cross-functionality.
2. *Being a Servant Leader:* Involves being a leader for the Scrum Team who ensures the highest priority needs are met.
3. *Having Process Authority:* involves the Scrum Master ensuring that the team enacts and adheres to the Scrum values, principles, and practices, along with the team's specific approach.
4. *Acting as an Interference Shield:* Involves protecting the Scrum Team from outside interference to remain focused on delivering business value at every sprint
5. *Acting as an Impediment Remover:* Involves removing all impediments that inhibit the team's productivity.
6. *Being a Change Agent:* Involves helping others understand the need for change.
7. *Taking Care of Scrum Events:* Involves ensuring all Scrum Events occur and are positive, productive, and kept within the timeline.

There is some variation in the responsibilities that are described in these four papers. We list which responsibilities are listed in each paper in Table 1.

Table 1. Responsibilities of Scrum Masters listed in the literature

Category	Rubin	Schwaber & Sutherland	Cohn	Sochova
Coach	X	X	X	X
Servant Leader	X	X	X	X
Process authority	X	X	X	X
Inference shield	X			X
Impediment remover	X	X	X	X
Change agent	X			
Scrum events		X		X

The authors all agree that the Scrum Master's responsibilities include being a coach, being a servant leader, having process authority, and being an impediment remover. Rubin and Sochova describe additionally that the Scrum Master should act as an inference shield, and Rubin also includes that the SM should be a change agent. Sochova, Schwaber, and Sutherland state that the SM should be responsible for Scrum events.

2.3   The Effect of the Covid-19 Pandemic

At the time of this data gathering, in April 2021, the Covid-19 pandemic has been active for over a year. People in software development (among others) have had to work a lot more from home. There have only been a few studies about the effect of the pandemic on working according to Scrum methods, but there has been a lot of research done on using Scrum in distributed teams.

The most common challenges found while using Scrum in distributed teams have been issues with synchronous communication. Other issues have been collaboration difficulties, communication bandwidth, tool support, large teams, and office space [12]. In more recent years, the most common issue encountered by distributed Scrum Teams has been communication, especially among stakeholders [24]. Recent studies have shown that Scrum Teams can adopt to distributed software development projects [10]. The new circumstances caused by Covid-19 do not significantly impact the projects [14].

Work Environment and Procedures. Before the pandemic, distributed teams usually consisted of people from different countries or regions, whereas now, former co-located teams have had to work more hours from home than in the office. For teams that were co-located before the pandemic, it was easier to plan meetings when everyone was at the office. Some people stopped working 9–5 since they started working from home [8]. People tend to work more flexible hours, while some team members prefer to work from home because of those flexible hours, fewer interruptions, and having all the tools needed [2].

The reduction of social time during working hours is often passively factored into project and release plans. Therefore, the workday is closer to contracted hours while working from home, magnifying the intensity of the workday that workers have not experienced before. This increases the risk of fatigue and burnout, impacting the overall team, and the product may suffer [11].

The whiteboard is used by Scrum Team members while working co-located, for example during Sprint Retrospective meetings, solving issues, or planning a sprint. However, it has not effectively been transferred into a remote work setting [8].

Meetings and Scrum Events. A recent study revealed that since the pandemic started, more meetings are within teams, and they last longer than before [8]. The most common issues in meetings encountered by distributed Scrum Teams in the past were people going off-topic, together with lack of involvement or low enthusiasm for participation for some team members [24]. The solutions suggested by Wu & Wang are designed to control the rhythm to ensure that meetings do not deviate from the subject and, for participation issues, to consult colleagues or discuss in informal meetings.

There have been increased distractions from instant messaging since the pandemic, which leads to more challenging context switching [8]. The same also applies to emails that can be distracting when everybody is on their computer during meetings, resulting in a lack of focus within teams [11].

Some challenges can occur with Daily Scrums while working in a remote setting. When co-located, problem-solving after the meeting could contain a quick chat after the daily stand-up while remotely, everyone logs out after the meeting [8]. Extending the meeting from 15 min to 30 min with the second half blocked for problem-solving could solve such a problem [7]. Another suggestion for Daily Scrum to go smoothly in a remote setting is encouraging teams to use video to keep them engaged and focused [7]. Daily Scrum can also be performed through an instant messaging application for consumption by the team at their own pace to reduce waste [11].

Since Sprint Planning can go on for four to eight hours, it is easier to achieve engagement for a more prolonged period when held in person than when working from home. Griffin suggests breaking Sprint Planning down into smaller, consumable pieces (Griffin, 2021). Other suggestions are to encourage prep work ahead of time and agree on what to achieve offline [7].

For Sprint Review, there are suggestions to keep presentation content crisp and concise and to integrate content in one place with one person [7]. Griffin also suggested having pre-recorded demos so the team can consume their own time [11].

Communication and Social Interaction. Good communication in Scrum Teams is essential. The team members exchange valuable information that needs to be transparent to provide a clear understanding which avoids surprises and helps build trust among the team members [16]. In the literature review of challenges of distributed Scrum Teams by Wu & Wang [24], one of the most significant issues was a lack or difficulty of synchronous communication. Synchronous communication is necessary to improve mutual understanding. Other issues were inefficient or ineffective communication due to a lack of suitable communication tools and insufficient network bandwidth. However, the most common issue encountered by distributed Scrum Teams is communication with stakeholders [24].

When it comes to communication, body language can tell us a lot about people's feelings and behavior. Understanding body language and behavior changes during distributed working can be a challenge [8]. This challenge increases for those who do not have a web camera or have it turned off. The human aspect is absent, such as facial expression, body language, and tone of voice, which produces a loss of communication [2].

A recent study of distributed software development teams conducted that the Covid-19 pandemic influenced communication to some extent since the office interactions are not present [2]. For hybrid teams before the pandemic, the fully remote work improved communication since all communication was transferred online [14].

While working remotely, there is a reduction of social time with team members and other co-workers. There are no common coffee breaks, corridor chats, and watercooler conversations, resulting in issues not being revealed as quickly as before. There could be regular social meetings for Scrum Teams [8]. For instance, online virtual coffee breaks increase online communication and interactions [2]. Social meetings can also be hosted, such as virtual parties or games for distributed team members [12].

Productivity. There have been different results from studies on whether co-located teams or distributed teams are more productive. For example, Teasley et al. performed a study that resulted in co-located teams being more productive than distributed teams, even when distributed in the same building [22]. In contrast, Stanford professor Nicholas Bloom performed a study that showed that working in a remote setting can lead to around 14% performance increase [4].

A recent study since the pandemic has indicated that there has been increased response time between Scrum Teams which causes delays [8]. And some team members in a recent case study felt that the situation with the pandemic is affecting their availability and productivity to work [2].

3   Method

With this research, the aim was to explore the changes that distributed work entails for the Scrum Master's responsibility compared to working at the office. Especially we focused on changes in the themes analyzed from the literature: the working methods, Scrum Events, communication and meetings, and productivity in the first 12 months of the Covid-19 period (April 2020–March 2021) compared to the preceding 12 months (April 2019–March 2020).

A qualitative method was conducted in the research using semi-structured interviews with the opportunity to ask supplementary questions. The qualitative method was more suitable than the quantitative for data collection in this study to gain an in-depth and contextual understanding of the impact of working primarily from home during the pandemic in the Scrum environment.

We describe the background of the participants, the conduction of the interviews, and the data analysis.

3.1   Participants

The participants were selected from seven different types of companies to gather different views. The companies were selected according to if they worked according to the Scrum methodology. We chose companies focused on software development or had a relatively big software department.

Eight interviews took place with nine participants from eight companies, five of whom were men and four women. One interview was conducted with two interviewees at the same time from the same company since the participants preferred that. This resulted in two different views, since their teams are separate, and they work on different projects. They answered the questions in turn with different results.

The participants were all either active in the Scrum Master role or comparable roles with Scrum Master responsibilities. Seven of them had completed a Certified Scrum Master course. Six of them had other additional responsibilities: two were project managers, two were quality assurance testers, one was a director, and one was a CTO.

All the participants had years of experience working in the software industry, the average being 17 years. They also had years of experience working in Scrum before and during the pandemic, which was essential to get their views and expertise in shift changing to a distributed working environment. Each of them is responsible for one to three teams.

3.2 Interviews

The interviews were semi-structured and conducted according to guidance from Lazar et al. [13]. All the interviews took place online using Microsoft Teams since all the participants did work from home or in an empty office because of the Covid-19 pandemic. The interviews were all recorded and documented, and the scheduled timing of the interviews was based on the participant's available hours. Each interview lasted approximately 20–30 min. One exception was the interview with two participants together which took 55 min. The conduction of the interviews took place in early April 2021 (April 6th–14th). Before the interviews started, the participants were informed about confidentiality and anonymity in the information process.

The question list had 22 open questions that were asked during each interview for the answers to be comparable. The questions were divided into three categories, as seen in Table 2. The interview questions were designed to answer the research question on the changes that distributed work entails for the responsibilities of the Scrum Master role. Therefore, the focus of the questions was on the changes the Scrum Masters and their teams had experienced in the last 12 months since working in a distributed work environment (April 2020 to March 2021) compared to the situations during the 12 months before the Covid-19 period (April 2019 to March 2020).

Table 2. Overview of the questions in the interview guide for the interviews.

Category	Theme of the question	Number of questions
General	Job, experience, responsibilities, projects, teams	8
Changes in the last 12 months	Work environment, work procedures, Scrum events, communication, sprints, productivity	8
Scrum experience in distributed working	Challenges/obstacles, went well/badly, communication importance, learning outcome	6

3.3 Data Analysis

The data analysis was conducted with thematical analysis according to Clarke et al. [5] after all interviews had been taken. The first author did the theme analysis, which was reviewed by the second and third authors. After each interview, the researcher listened to each of the recordings and documented the answers quite thoroughly to ensure consistency. Then the researcher compared the responses to each question from all the participants to analyze the similarity between the answers.

The results were categorized into five themes: 1) Work environment and procedures, 2) meetings and Scrum events, 3) communication and social interaction, 4) productivity and 5) future. The themes contain the results from the corresponding interview questions as seen in Table 3.

Table 3. The themes of the results with corresponding question categories

Category	Changes in the last 12 months	Scrum experience in distributed working
Work environment and procedures	X	
Meetings and scrum events	X	
Communication and social interaction	X	X
Productivity	X	
Future		X

4 Results

In this section, we describe the results of the responsibilities described by our participants in the study and the effect of the Covid-19 period they describe on the work environment and procedures, meeting and Scrum events, communication and social interaction, and productivity. We conclude by describing briefly their visions for the future.

4.1 Responsibilities of Scrum Masters

All the participants that were in the Scrum Master role or in comparable roles marked which of the Scrum Master responsibilities were analyzed from the theory, they perceived as their responsibilities. An overview of the responsibilities reported is shown in Table 4. Five of the participants perceived that they had all the responsibilities listed to be included in the Scrum Master role. On the contrary, four interviewees had perceived their responsibilities differently. Participants C and E, who both regarded themselves as project managers, shared the same responsibilities. Neither of them is responsible for the Process Authority aspect nor the Scrum Events. Participants B and D are both in the Scrum Master role as well as being Quality Assurance Testers. Still, their responsibilities vary, except neither of them has the responsibility of being a Change Agent. Participant B declared that the Product Owner is responsible for what was lacking in her Scrum Master role responsibilities in her work. All the participants agreed that being an Impediment Remover was a part of their responsibilities. Eight of the informants also had the responsibilities of being a Coach, a Servant Leader, and an Interference Shield. Seven of the informants had the responsibilities of called: Process Authority, Change Agent, and Scrum Events.

Table 4. The Scrum Master's responsibilities in the study

Category	A	B	C	D	E	F	G	H	I
Coach	X		X	X	X	X	X	X	X
Servant Leader	X	X	X		X	X	X	X	X
Process authority	X	X		X		X	X	X	X
Inference shield	X		X	X	X	X	X	X	X
Impediment remover	X	X	X	X	X	X	X	X	X
Change agent	X		X		X	X	X	X	X
Scrum events	X	X		X		X	X	X	X

4.2 Work Environment and Procedures

All participants and their teams have had to work from home most of the time during the last 12 months (April 2020 to March 2021) or since the Covid-19 pandemic started. In some cases, a few of them have been able to work in the office with strict rules and few employees at a time for a short period. The effect is different between companies and even departments since there were hybrid teams before the pandemic started for four of the nine participants.

The experience of working from home can be different for different people, but four participants felt it had been successful with few challenges. Two participants said that distributed work suits people in different ways. The people in their teams have different circumstances at home that they must consider.

Most participants did not think that the work procedure had changed since they started working from home, or that there were only minor changes. Four participants noticed that the increasing number of remote meetings and meetings moved to a remote setting. The infrastructure for working in a distributed environment had already been implemented for participant F and his teams before the pandemic started, so there was no big adjustment. For participants B and C, they and their teams needed to make the working procedure better. For example, participant C and his team found a solution to deliver all their projects remotely.

Five participants moved their tablet drawings and post-its to a virtual tool like Miro. One participant made these remarks: "It went well to move things to Miro, and there can be a lot implemented online that is harder to perform in person. The overview is straightforward in tools like Miro."

4.3 Meetings and Scrum Events

Five participants had a team member or members from other regions in Iceland or other countries before the pandemic, so their meetings were already remote. Still, the change was that everybody started being online at the meetings, not just the team members from other locations. Before the pandemic, these participants all had their meetings in meeting rooms at the office with co-located members attending while members from different areas connected remotely. Two of the participants said that now that everybody is online during virtual meetings, it makes all team members more equal than before. One participant was happy that it was a lot easier to reschedule meetings since the necessity of finding a meeting room is not relevant while working distributed.

Two participants mentioned the importance of having the video camera turned on during meetings. They talked about wanting to see people's faces and know they are monitoring the discussion. The discussion about recording meetings also came up with two participants, which they felt was essential as absent team members could then view the meetings later.

The modifications of the Scrum Events in the last 12 months compared to the preceding 12 months were different between participants. For two of them, the Daily Scrums have lengthened since they started working from home, as they added extra time to get the opportunity to discuss things that they usually addressed in the office after the daily meetings before the pandemic. The opposite occurred for another participant: The Daily Scrum became shorter than before due to fewer social discussions. Two participants thought that the Daily Scrums were more efficient done remotely, both because the team members attend simultaneously and because attendance has increased when everyone is working from home.

As for the other Scrum Events, two participants felt that the meetings go on longer without being decided beforehand while being held online. Other participants did not mention the Sprint Review being any different, except for one who informed that the Review is more valuable than being presented online versus in a hall filled with people. The Sprint Retrospective has been valuable to three participants since they started to work from home as it highlights problems when working distributed that they can deal with, for example, when there are challenges with working from home or with communication.

According to all the interviewed participants, working from home has not affected sprints, their framework, or their length. One participant felt that she and her team had an easier time planning each sprint while working from home because of their improved work procedure. One participant described how the Scrum layout is helpful in distributed work, while others felt it was impressive how well Scrum fitted distributed working environments.

4.4 Communication and Social Interaction

The communication since working from home has changed so that the Scrum Teams do not have the same opportunity to discuss issues that come up as effortlessly as sitting near each other in the office. According to four participants, the information is not flowing between team members as much as before. If they get stuck, they try for a longer time than when co-located before asking another team member.

A few participants described their solutions to this problem:

- "There is a bigger need now to ask the team if there is something that stops their work."
- "Everybody can communicate through chat and video calls, but there was much more silence through those channels at the beginning."

- "When a problem occurs that multiple team members need to solve together, they have an open virtual meeting where they can ask or give information if they need to. In the meantime, they work at their computer in silence."

On the other hand, three participants said that their teams were as active in communication as before. Participant H even stated that the communication was better while working from home. However, like participant E, that participant was in a hybrid team before the pandemic. Both experienced that team members showed more understanding of the original distributed team members since they all had to work distributed.

Communication with the stakeholders seems to be more challenging than within the teams during distributed working. Three of the participants even felt that this was the most significant effect of the pandemic. All the participants except one reported less contact with stakeholders in the last 12 months than in the preceding 12 months. But even one participant declared that communication was less when first starting to work from home. He stated that now they are using more online tools, so the stakeholders have become more active. According to seven participants, the decreased communication was primarily due to not meeting face-to-face as they could before.

Two of them could even walk to their stakeholder's desk to discuss matters while working at the office. Some participants had resourceful solutions. One participant mentioned: "The communication has improved after holding workshops." Another one said: "When the need for changes appeared, we held workshops for one to two days with the stakeholders."

One of the most discussed challenges for the participants and their teams while working from home is the lack of social interaction. Seven of them talked about how they missed meeting each other and other co-workers in person, either at the workplace or during social events outside the workplace. One participant said: "People want to get together. It's a challenge not being able to meet and do something fun." Another participant said: "The hardest thing in the last 12 months is not being able to celebrate anything. It's sad not to go out to dinner together or reward the team with a cake when they do a good job."

Participant G informed that a survey in his company showed that loneliness has increased among his co-workers since the pandemic started. That seems to be recurring in other companies too. Participant, I felt like it is harder to maintain the team's morale, and participant C felt there appears to be a momentum that needs rebuilding within his company.

The participants discussed various solutions that they or their company had done to minimize the social distance while working from home. Almost half have had successful social meetings (coffee breaks) once a week up to once a day with their team. These meetings contain either chatting or playing online games. The solution for one team was to have a social chat channel. Four participants also talked about attending virtual parties held by the company or the department.

4.5 Productivity

The participants' opinions varied when asked whether there were any productivity changes while working more distributed. Two participants felt the productivity had decreased, three thought it had increased, three thought it was similar to before, and one participant could not make a judgment. One participant discussed a survey done by his company that showed that people felt they were accomplishing more work while working from home. Three participants felt like they get more privacy at home to focus better on their work. And three others said their teams had a longer workday from home than in the office, especially at the beginning of the pandemic.

4.6 Future

Four participants felt like work should be in a more hybrid environment in the future, with people having the freedom to choose their work location. Two participants hoped to work less in a remote setting in the future. The participants had a few comments about their take on how they hoped meetings will evolve after the pandemic. One participant said: "I would like to keep on having remote meetings even if part of the team is in a meeting room. Then those people can have the video camera turned on and only one microphone." Another one said: "I would like to keep the meeting culture in a remote setting, so everybody is equal." The third participant stated: "I hope that after the pandemic, we can bring back face-to-face meetings with the customers."

5 Discussion

Since the Covid-19 pandemic began reaching people worldwide (around March 2020), many have had to work from home for the last year or even longer. The effect that working distributed could have on the Scrum Master's responsibilities was the aim of this research. The changes that affect working distributed according to Scrum the most are that all Scrum Events and meetings were moved to a remote setting.

The results in this study are based on interviews with nine participants who either have the role of Scrum Master or have similar responsibilities. It is not easy to generalize results based on interviews. Still, the results give reasonable indications for the changes for Scrum Masters and their teams when moving to a distributed environment from co-located.

The participants' responsibilities seem to be similar to what the literature suggests as the responsibilities for Scrum Masters, where authors agree that responsibilities consist of coaching, being a Servant Leader, Process Authority, and removing impediments. All participants are responsible for removing impediments, eight of the nine are Coaches and Servant Leaders, while seven are Process Authority.

Previous research on working with Scrum in a distributed setting claims that the most common issue is communication with stakeholders [24]. This is in line with the results from this study that indicate that the main issue for Scrum Teams since the participants started working from home is less communication with stakeholders. The reason behind that was that they could not meet their customers face-to-face as they did before the pandemic. Few participants felt it was more formal to email the stakeholders than walk to their desks as they could while working at the office. The possible effect for Scrum Masters and their teams of less contact with stakeholders could be a decrease in the quality of their product or an increase in waiting time, leading to less productivity. However, that needs to be researched further. According to Ahmad et al., customer communication and close collaboration are crucial for the development team and project success, but this becomes more complex in distributed teams [1].

The results show that the communication within the Scrum Teams has decreased for half of the participants. So, the effect of less communication is not as crucial as with the stakeholders. However, those participants informed that their team members were not as quick to ask for assistance or discuss issues as they did while sitting near each other in the office. As a result, they tend to try solving issues by themselves before asking other team members. Thus, the possible effect on the Scrum team can halter the project's success, which could be researched further. A recent study done a few months into the pandemic showed that communication was influenced by working from home since office interactions are not present [2]. As for teams that were hybrid before the pandemic, the communication improved [14]. This corresponds with the view of the participants in this study who were in hybrid teams before the whole team became distributed.

In their study, Connor et al. pointed out that one of the challenges while working in a distributed Scrum Team is the failure to incorporate co-located social constructions of time into Covid-19 distributed working [8]. In this study, most participants felt social interaction was a big challenge. They had various solutions, for example, taking virtual coffee breaks, playing online games, and having virtual parties.

Since distributed working began in earnest, all meetings that were at the office before the pandemic are now virtual. Hybrid teams usually had virtual meetings even though co-located team members attended meeting rooms. Connor et al. said that since the pandemic started, there have been more meetings, and they lasted longer than before (Connor et al., 2021). Only one participant in this study had that experience, but he was unsure if it had to do with working from home or the changes in his company.

Since this shift in the working environment, Scrum Team members tend to work more flexible hours and even have a longer workday than before [2, 8]. Few of the participants in this study mentioned that this was the case, especially early on. Connor et al. also discussed that the whiteboard had not been effectively transferred to a remote work setting [8]. That issue seems to be resolved by using a tool like Miro, which is done by just over half of the participants in this study.

The results indicate that working from home does not seem to affect the Scrum Events for most of the participants. The Daily Scrum is now longer for two of the participants for the team to discuss issues that they previously addressed in the office. Comella-Dorda et al. suggested extending the Daily Scrum from 15 min to 30 min, with the second half blocked for problem-solving [7]. The sprints tended to stay the same for all the participants in this study while working from the office.

There seems to be a difference in the productivity changes for Scrum Teams since they started to work from home, but participants had different opinions on that. However, Badiale and Connor et al. indicate that there has been a decrease in productivity for Scrum Teams since the pandemic started [2, 8].

This situation has revealed that some people like working from home and would like to continue to do so, especially for one or a few days a week. And the meeting culture might be here to stay since so many are happy with the setting.

The results in this study are based on interviews with nine participants in the Scrum Master role or having Scrum Master responsibilities even though the informants did not all have that title. One of the limitations of the study is that not all participants worked entirely as Scrum Masters. Future studies might include more Scrum Masters or include looking at perspectives of other Scrum Team members, like the Product Owner role or the Developers. Future research studies could also include studying the effect of less communication on the project and productivity, especially with stakeholders while working distributed after the Scrum methodology. It would also be useful to study the long-term effect of following the Scrum process in a distributed work environment since this research took place only a year into the Covid-19 pandemic.

6 Lessons Learned

In this project, we have studied what changes are reported on the responsibilities included in the Scrum Master role in distributed work in the last year (April 2020 to March 2021). The results show that the main changes are that all the Scrum Events are now (April 2021) virtual along with all communication and meetings. Some of them have been demanding for the Scrum Masters while others became easier.

Previous studies on working on Scrum projects since the Covid-19 pandemic started (March 2020) have shown that there is an indication of a decrease in productivity, longer workdays, and more and longer meetings. These studies were conducted only a few months into the pandemic. In contrast to previous studies, this research was conducted after the participants had been working from home for over a year.

The results from this study do not show that productivity has decreased. Only a few participants tended to have longer workdays but only in the first months of the pandemic. In addition, there was no change reported in the number and duration of meetings during the period of the study except for one participant.

Additionally, the results indicate that the main issue for Scrum Masters and their teams when moving from co-located to a distributed work environment is less communication with stakeholders. The lack of communication within the teams did not seem to be as much of a problem, though half the participants said the flow of information between team members was not as much as before. Another issue that most of the participants discussed were the lack of social interaction within the teams. Some of them felt that the most challenging thing about working from home was not meeting each other.

Moreover, the results show that working from home does not seem to affect the Scrum Events for most of the participants. It would mainly be the Daily Scrum that was in a changed format for some of the informants. But the sprints stayed the same in length for everyone. Most of the participants felt that following the Scrum process while working from home was easy.

Acknowledgement. First and foremost, the authors gratefully thank the participants for their time, interest, and valuable answers to the research questions.

References

1. Ahmad, M.O., Lenarduzzi, V., Oivo, M., Taibi, D.: Lessons learned on communication channels and practices in Agile Software Development. In: 2018 Federated Conference on Computer Science and Information Systems, pp. 929–938 (2018)
2. Badiale, M.E.: The dynamics of communication in global virtual software development teams: a case study in the agile context during the Covid-19 pandemic. Dissertation (2020). http://urn.kb.se/resolve?urn=urn:nbn:se:uu:diva-413832
3. Bass, J.M.: Scrum Master activities: process tailoring in large enterprise projects. In: 2014 IEEE 9th International Conference on Global Software Engineering, pp. 6–15 (2014)
4. Bloom, N.: To raise productivity, let more employees work from home. Harvard Bus. Rev. **92**, 28–30 (2014)
5. Clarke, V., Braun, V., Hayfield, N.: Thematic analysis. In: Qualitative Psychology: A Practical Guide to Research Methods, pp. 222–248 (2015)
6. Cohn, M.: Succeeding with Agile: Software Development Using Scrum. Pearson Education (2009)
7. Comella-Dorda, S., Garg, L., Thareja, S., Vasquez-McCall, B.: Revisiting agile teams after an abrupt shift to remote. McKinsey & Company (2020). https://www.mckinsey.com/business-functions/organization/our-insights/revisiting-agile-teams-after-an-abrupt-shift-to-remote
8. Connor, M.O., Conboy, K., Dennehy, D.: COVID-19 affected remote workers: a temporal analysis of information system development during the pandemic. J. Decis. Syst. **31**, 1–27 (2021)
9. Ereiz, Z., Mušić, D.: Scrum without a Scrum Master. In: 2019 IEEE International Conference on Computer Science and Educational Informatization (CSEI), pp. 325–328 (2019)
10. Faniran, V.T., Badru, A., Ajayi, N.: Adopting Scrum as an Agile approach in distributed software development: a review of literature. In: 2017 1st International Conference on Next Generation Computing Applications (NextComp), pp. 36–40 (2017)
11. Griffin, L.: Implementing lean principles in scrum to adapt to remote work in a Covid-19 impacted software team. In: Przybyłek, A., Miler, J., Poth, A., Riel, A. (eds.) LASD 2021. LNBIP, vol. 408, pp. 177–184. Springer, Cham (2021). https://doi.org/10.1007/978-3-030-67084-9_11
12. Hossain, E., Babar, M.A., Paik, H.: Using Scrum in global software development: a systematic literature review. In: 2009 Fourth IEEE International Conference on Global Software Engineering, pp. 175–184 (2009)
13. Lazar, J., Feng, J.H., Hochheiser, H.: Research Methods in Human-Computer Interaction. Morgan Kaufmann, Burlington (2017)
14. Marek, K., Wińska, E., Dąbrowski, W.: The state of agile software development teams during the Covid-19 pandemic. In: Przybyłek, A., Miler, J., Poth, A., Riel, A. (eds.) LASD 2021. LNBIP, vol. 408, pp. 24–39. Springer, Cham (2021). https://doi.org/10.1007/978-3-030-67084-9_2
15. Noll, J., Razzak, M., Bass, J., Beecham, S.: A study of the Scrum Master's role. In: Felderer, M., Méndez Fernández, D., Turhan, B., Kalinowski, M., Sarro, F., Winkler, D. (eds.) PROFES 2017. LNCS, vol. 10611, pp. 307–323. Springer, Cham (2017). https://doi.org/10.1007/978-3-319-69926-4_22
16. Rubin, K.S.: Essential Scrum: A Practical Guide to the Most Popular Agile Process. Addison-Wesley, Boston (2017)
17. Schwaber, K.: Agile Project Management with Scrum. Microsoft Press, Redmond (2004)
18. Schwaber, K., Beedle, M.: Agile Software Development with Scrum. Prentice Hall. Upper Saddle River (2002)

19. Schwaber, K., Sutherland, J.: The 2020 Scrum Guide. The Scrum Guide (2020). https://scr umguides.org/scrum-guide.html
20. Sochova, Z.: The Great ScrumMaster: #ScrumMasterWay. Addison-Wesley Professional, Boston (2016)
21. Takeuchi, H., Nonaka, I.: The new new product development game. Harv. Bus. Rev. **64**(1), 137–146 (1986)
22. Teasley, S., Covi, L., Krishnan, M., Olson, J.: How does radical collocation help a team succeed? pp. 339–346. Association for Computing Machinery (2000)
23. VersionOne: State of Agile Survey. The 15th Annual State of Agile Survey (2020). https://sta teofagile.com/
24. Wu, L., Wang, Z.: Understanding and managing the challenges of distributed scrum teams. Dissertation (2020). http://urn.kb.se/resolve?urn=urn:nbn:se:bth-20622

Late-Breaking Results

Considering Users' Personal Values in User-Centered Design Processes for Media and Entertainment Services

Melanie Berger[1,2]([✉]) [iD], Guillaume Pottier[2], Bastian Pfleging[3] [iD],
and Regina Bernhaupt[1,2] [iD]

[1] Department of Industrial Design, Eindhoven University of Technology, Eindhoven,
The Netherlands
{m.berger,r.bernhaupt}@tue.nl
[2] ruwido Austria GmbH, Neumarkt, Austria
[3] TU Bergakademie Freiberg, Freiberg, Germany

Abstract. The way users consume media is defined and influenced by users' values. Methods in User-Centered Design (UCD) processes typically do not address users' values adequately to enable designers to understand the impact values have when it comes to the design of long-term user experience. This work presents two contributions (1) the relationship between users' values and entertainment behavior based on a web survey study, and (2) a proposed set of long-term oriented value-based persona that can be used as guidance for the design of future TV and entertainment services and systems.

Keywords: Human values · User-centered design · Media · Entertainment · Long-term user experience · Persona

1 Introduction

For the design of TV and entertainment user interfaces (UI) the key to success currently is a design that focuses on flexibility, adding components or content similar to what people experience on their smartphones [7, 11] to the TV. New content is provided in an app-oriented portal that is typically represented via the main TV UI [3]. Especially latest developments of services from over-the-top providers like *Netflix*[1] or *Amazon Prime*[2] show that supporting long-term user experience (UX) e.g., personalized recommendations [13, 16, 19, 23] is at the center of the development of the next generation of entertainment services [2, 6, 24]. Besides that, additional features are accessible by using secondary devices like smartphones or tablets, which allow users to enjoy content on different platforms [9, 11] or enable them to share experiences via social media [14].

The original version of this chapter was revised: a second affiliation was added to the first author and Fig. 3 and Table 1 were revised. The correction to this chapter is available at
https://doi.org/10.1007/978-3-031-14785-2_14

[1] Netflix: https://www.netflix.com/, last accessed: 2022/05/28.

[2] Amazon Prime: https://www.amazon.com/Prime-Video, last accessed: 2022/05/28.

© IFIP International Federation for Information Processing 2022
Published by Springer Nature Switzerland AG 2022, corrected publication 2022
R. Bernhaupt et al. (Eds.): HCSE 2022, LNCS 13482, pp. 129–139, 2022.
https://doi.org/10.1007/978-3-031-14785-2_8

The main practice in this industry of IPTV providers is to neglect recent design and development trends including the focus on UX [15] and developments towards more user-centered approaches [15] and rather established plan-driven (waterfall) development processes [5, 21]. A key aspect consequently is the ability to understand long-term usage of entertainment systems and services and what aspects, or factors influence long-term usage for time spans like years and not only for several months/days. While in the past 50 years, the design to enhance media experience has primarily focused on users' needs - the need to be entertained, informed, distracted, or relaxed [11, 18], key aspects of how peoples' behavior changes over time and what they strive in their lives on a longer-term, defined as values [25, 26], has been neglected [6].

Values are overall life principles of individuals which guide beliefs, convictions, and daily activities [25] and, in comparison to needs, they are long-term oriented, explain the motivational bases of attitudes [26], are motivating, and provide directions for decisions as well as the emotional intensity of experiences [25, 26]. Consequently, values implicitly define goals that reflect the interest of individuals but also of social communities.

Thus, in this work, we explore if values can be a useful, psychological concept to understand users' long-term usage of media products (e.g., smart speakers, remote controls) and services. Based on insight into the relationship between users' values and media consumption, we aim to tailor the User-Centered Design (UCD) approach toward more value-orientation to better support long-term UX by proposing a set of value-based personas.

2   Related Work

2.1   User-Centered Design, System Development, and User Experience

Designing with a focus on the end-user by following the UCD approach facilitates the creation of highly usable and accessible products [20]. Iteratively integrating and reflecting on users' needs, expectations, traits, and motivations support designing for a higher experience [20]. Today's software engineering in the media sector tends to incorporate UX as a central aspect of design decisions. We define UX (momentary UX) as "how people have experienced a period of encountering a system" [24] with their aspects of emotions, personal beliefs, and preferences [15]. Even though the momentary UX refers to the actual usage of a product or service, it is influenced indirectly by the experience before a first encounter (anticipated UX) such as related systems, advertisements, or others' opinions [24]. Besides that, UX extends after every usage through reflection on the actual usage or opinions raised (episodic UX) and can also change when having used a product for a long(er) time (cumulative or long-term UX) [24].

For the field of IPTV, key factors for UX that have been identified [8, 22] include "Aesthetic visual impression (beauty and classic aesthetics); Emotion; Stimulation; Identification; Relatedness; and Meaning and Value" [22] as well as the form of interaction technique, and the relation between UX and basic usability [8, 22]. While personal attitudes in terms of needs have been included in such evaluation methods for the UX of IPTV services to support momentary UX, values had not been considered to our knowledge as an opportunity to especially enhance long-term UX.

2.2 Basic Human Values

Basic human values are defined as "concepts or beliefs about desirable end states or behaviors, that transcend specific situations, guide selection or evaluation of behavior and events" [25] and are used to "explain the motivational bases of attitudes and behavior" [26]. Thus, human values are goals that arise from different desires and situations and are guiding principles in a person's life. Values define different goals that reflect the interests of an individual. They are motivating and provide directions, as well as emotional intensity. Values also act as judgments and justifications of actions and are acquired through both social groups and unique learning experiences [27]. Overall, values are critical motivators of behaviors and attitudes [26]. The theory of basic human values from Schwartz et al. [26] reports four main value groups with two up to five values per group (see Fig. 1):

- *Openness to Change*: people who are highly into openness to change strive for the independence of thought and actions and are ready for changes [26]. Values: self-direction, stimulation, hedonism.
- *Self-Enhancement*: people highly into self-enhancement emphasize the pursuit of one's interests and strive for success and dominance over others [26]. Values: hedonism, achievement, power, face.
- *Conservation*: people highly into conservation emphasize order, self-restriction, preservation of the past, and resistance to change [26]. Values: face, security, tradition, conformity, humanity.
- *Self-Transcendence*: people highly into self-transcendence emphasize concern for the welfare and interests of others [26]. Values: humanity, benevolence, universalism.

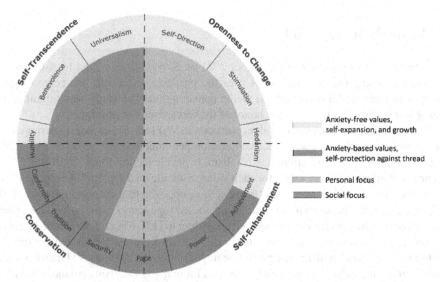

Fig. 1. The four different value groups (quadrants) and their underlying values (gray cycle) - are adapted from [26].

Overall, there are 12 values (for value group alignment see Fig. 1) that are unique to one another as they underlie different motivational factors and therefore represent different overall life goals. The more apart values are presented in Fig. 1. the more different the underlying motivational factors are (e.g., values opposite to each other like Achievement vs. Benevolence). Overall, these values and their representative groups apply to all humans, independent of their religion or culture [26].

3   Problem Description

The design and development of TV and entertainment services are typically driven by technological developments and the importance to evolve systems. Due to the legacy of the technology in the field, a key aspect in the design of such services is to understand the long-term usage of entertainment systems [6]. While Allen et al. report that users' values can impact buying decisions [4], little is known about how those values affect media consumption and how users' values can be integrated into UCD approaches for supporting long-term UX. We believe that if designers and IPTV providers consider users' values, and tailor their products to support one or several values better, their products can enhance users' overall experience.

However, as of now, little is known about how values (1) are connected to users' media behavior, (2) shift over time, and (3) how this can be considered in the design of future media-related products. In this paper, we answer the following research questions:

- *How do values impact users' media behavior and consumption?*
- *How can we design future products that take the value changes and their effect on media behavior into consideration?*

4   Method: Survey Study

We conducted a web survey in December 2021 on *SurveyMonkey*[3] and focused on the assessment of the user's value shifts over the past five years and its accompanying changes in their media behavior and media consumption. The study was submitted to and approved by the ethical review board of the researcher's institution.

We used the Short Schwartz Values Survey (SSVS) [10, 17] to assess participants' values with ten validated questions, one question per value (power, achievement, hedonism, stimulation, self-direction, universalism, benevolence, tradition, conformity, and security). Participants were asked for each value to decide on a 9-point Likert scale if the value is of supreme importance for them ($= 8$) or opposed to their principle ($= 0$) [10, 17]. To determine a person's main value group, the average scores of the individual values questions per value group were processed according to [17]. For entertainment-oriented features, we asked three questions based on a 7-point Likert scale (extremely important to not important at all) referring to five important media categories [1]: audio (e.g., music streaming, radio, and podcast), video (traditional TV, video on demand, and video

---

[3] SurveyMonkey: https://www.surveymonkey.com/dashboard/, last accessed: 2022/05/28.

sharing platforms), news, social media (e.g., Facebook, Instagram), and digital communities (e.g., Reddit). To assess the values-shift over the past five years each participant answered the SSVS and entertainment-oriented questions twice. Besides that, the survey also included demographic questions (age, gender, home country) and questions related to technological equipment owned and entertainment services used.

5   Results: Media Consumption and User's Values

The recruitment of participants was outsourced to a professional agency. Overall, 144 people from German-speaking households (Germany $= 93$, Austria $= 39$, Switzerland $= 11$, Other $= 1$) participated in the survey study. Participants' average age was 38.15 years (SD $= 7.42$ years), ranging from 23 to 61.65 participants identified as women and 79 as men. Filling out the survey took on average 17 min and participants received compensation of 2.5 Euros. Overall, 103 out of 144 participants use free or cable TV, 94 video-on-demand services, and 106 indicated using social media.

5.1   Value-Shift

Comparing the changes in media behavior and the related value changes - based on the four value groups, between now and five years ago, we performed non-parametric Wilcoxon tests due to the ordinal nature of the data. Investigating the value shift, our data outlines that participants are today significantly more into universalism ($Z = 2.79$, $p = .005$) and benevolence ($Z = -2.64$, $p = .008$) than 5 years ago. Overall, we found that participants are nowadays significantly more into the value group of *Self-Transcendence* ($Z = -3.25$, $p = .001$) compared to five years ago. Even though participants value security today more ($Z = -2.99$, $p = .003$), a value shift towards the group of *Conservation* could not be observed ($Z = -1.56$, $p = .119$). In addition, there is a slight increase in the importance of self-direction ($Z = -2.99$, $p = .052$). However, the overall value group of *Openness to Change* does not show any difference between now and then ($Z = -.188$, $p = .851$). Besides that, there was also no difference observed for any values connected to the group of *Self-Enhancement* or the group itself ($Z = -.311$, $p = .756$).

5.2   Media Consumption Change

About media consumption and usage, our data outlines that having a big screen for watching media content ($Z = -2.108$, $p = .035$), having access to content at any time ($Z = -3.145$, $p = .002$), and watching videos without interruption (e.g., advertisements) ($Z = -3.159$, $p = .002$) is nowadays more important than it was five years ago. In addition, users strive significantly stronger for the content of their interests ($Z = -5.445$, $p < .001$), access to both local ($Z = -4.284$, $p < .001$) and global news ($Z = -2.865$, $p = .004$), and the possibility to listen to music at any time ($Z = -2.161$, $p = .031$). However, watching shows or content directly from live TV broadcasts is nowadays less important than it was in the past ($Z = 2.980$, $p = .003$). Apart from these changes, users report that accessing online libraries and being able to select from a variety of different content is still as important as it was in the past. This also holds for having access to social media to stay informed about other people and to connect with friends. In addition, it is important that media is relaxing, inspiring, fun, entertaining, and enables to gain knowledge. Besides that, we observed dependencies of features and functions (correlation). For instance, when users use an online video library, they want to be able to select from a variety of different content (r(142) = .710, p < .001). Users also prefer a big screen in combination with different content (r(142) = .717, p < .001). In addition, when having access to a variety of content, users seek access at any time at any place (r(142) = .718, p < .001). When it comes to making a buying decision, a product that provides additional features (e.g., voice control, 3D, or virtual reality) should be compatible with different devices (e.g., smart home) (r(142) = .748, p < .001). In addition, a product out of renewable resources should also be produced sustainably (r(142) = .905 p < .001).

5.3 Media Consumption Based on Users' Values

To understand the media consumption based on users' values, we looked detailed into those answers from n = 99 participants that could be attributed unambiguously to one of the value groups as their most important one. We excluded cases that reported having two or more value groups of similar importance. We investigated how important the assessed media characteristics are for certain value groups.

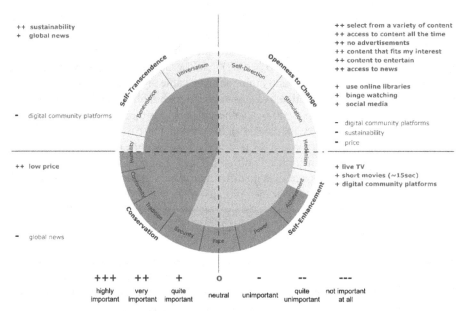

Fig. 2. Importance of media characteristics depending on users' main value group. Importance ranges from highly important (+++) to not important at all (---).

In Fig. 2, we outline the main characteristics for each value group ranging from highly important (+++) to not important at all (---) (also a 7-point Likert scale as used in the survey). We report in the following only statistically significant differences between value groups.

Survey participants reported *Self-Transcendence* as their most important value group (42.4%), showed a higher interest in sustainability-oriented offers and products, and would be interested in entertainment services supporting their behaviors and choices to support sustainable lifestyles. Their main interest lies in global news, while they perceive digital community platforms (e.g., *Facebook*) as one of the services they would not value long-term. *Openness to change* is a key value for 18.2% of the participants. They are eager to have access to content at all times, want to select from a broad variety of content, value services where content fits their interest (to be entertained, to receive news as key categories), and in general prefer advertisement-free services. They are the group that is into binge-watching the most and value social media as an information source. Global news is least important to participants who self-reported *Conservation* as their central value (32.3%). This group has only one key indicator when it comes to media entertainment: price. They are the least likely to spend money, to accept ideas on how to support a more sustainable lifestyle, and their local environment and surroundings are key for the media entertainment-related choices. With only 7,1% of participants who identify with *Self-Enhancement* as a key value for life, this is the smallest group in terms of representation in the overall survey sample. This group values live-TV, and short movies, and not surprisingly wants to use community platforms the most.

6 Value-Based Personas

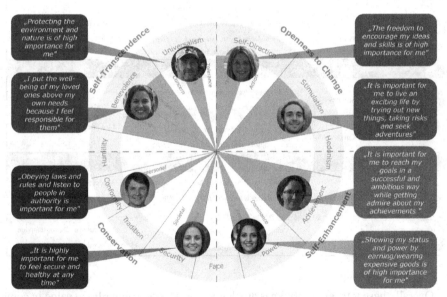

Fig. 3. The defined eight personas, aligned with their underlying main value of the Schwartz value theory [26].

To best support long-term UX and customer satisfaction, we defined eight typical, differential persona types depending on key values, associated with media behavior as well as media service affinities. Figure 3 shows how the eight personas are distributed over the different values, based on the original description of the Schwartz values theory [26]. Overall, a persona should be bold and represent unique characteristics [12]. Since every value group consists of two or more values with a unique motivational background [25, 26], we created only two personas per value group. This allowed us to cover every value group as best as possible with bold personas while not involving too many personas, which might make design decisions impossible [12].

Table 1. Detailed overview of the name, underlying value, quote, and media behavior of the eight defined personas

Persona	Value	Quote	Media Behavior
Openness to Change			
Marie	Self-Direction	*"The freedom to encourage my ideas and skills is of high importance for me"*	• Access to media all the time • Knowledge gain through media
Luke	Stimulation	*„It is important for me to live an exciting life by trying out new things, taking risks, and seeking adventures"*	• Variety of content • Binge-watching
Self-Enhancement			
Simone	Achievement	*„It is important for me to reach my goals in a successful and ambitious way while getting admired for my achievements "*	• Quick information via short movies and clips
Sylvia	Power	*„Showing my status and power by earning/wearing expensive goods is of high importance for me"*	• Connection with others via digital community platforms
Conservation			
Anna	Security	*„It is highly important for me to feel secure and healthy at any time"*	• No changes
Mark	Conformity	*„Obeying laws and rules and listening to people in authority is important for me"*	• Low price
Self-Transcendence			
Diana	Benevolence	*„I put the well-being of my loved ones above my own needs because I feel responsible for them"*	• Access to global and local news
Anton	Universalism	*„Protecting the environment and nature is of high importance for me"*	• Sustainable media consumption • Sustainable media products

Overall, these total eight personas are defined by a unique, underlying value in combination with the associated media behavior investigated through our media survey. Since values are long-term oriented guiding principles, these specific types of persona support designers in making decisions beyond what normal need-oriented personas would enable. Thus, they enable implicitly to design for long-term values instead of short-term needs which helps the design to already initially lay the focus towards long-term UX and customer loyalty in addition to instant gratification. Table 1 provides an overview of all personas and their main characteristics derived from the values and their media behavior.

7 Discussion

The personas in this work represent the values and media behavior of users from middle Europe, with a focus on German-speaking audiences. These type of personas describe users differently allowing to segment users into value groups and enabling service design to be focusing on long-term oriented users' values [25, 26] when it comes to understanding key moments for long-term UX.

To maximize their application, designers, producers, and marketers must take into account as many of these life-defining values as possible when conceiving products, content, and marketing pieces. To do so, they have to identify how users' values interfere with their product or service. As an example, a new streaming platform offering social network features will please the "benevolence" (sharing experiences with others, staying in touch) and "power" (displaying wealth, themselves) value groups the most, while displeasing the "security" group who might have concerns about the use of their personal data when using the system. The personas can help identify every group's apprehensions about a feature, positive or negative.

This methodological approach is also valuable when looking into communication between stakeholders. They can serve as means to discuss different properties that might be contradicting and can help to align requirements like the business handling aspects (e.g., payment processes), security requirements, technical requirements (bandwidth when it comes to streaming, infrastructure like set-top-boxes, etc.) and user-oriented properties like UX or usability. For instance, when designing for services it is difficult to discuss which key software qualities or features should be most important. It might seem tempting to improve UX with high-definition videos, but for the users who value sustainability, this might be a negative aspect in the long term, as higher resolution means (in the end) more use of electricity [28].

Even though values are independent of cultures [27], the relationship between values and media behavior might not be transferable to other cultures, and regions. To use this approach, it will be necessary to redo the media studies as well as the set-up of the persona for non-German-speaking regions. This is effective when it comes to large-scale developments of media infrastructures with a design and development team that (in the IPTV domain) comprises at least 50 if not up to several hundreds of designers and developers involved.

8 Conclusion

Is there a relationship between which values people self-identify and the media that they consume? Is it beyond the simple fact that it would affect the buying decision [4]? And if there is a relation, how could we benefit from this knowledge when it comes to UCD processes? Motivated by these questions, we have been demonstrating in this work how human values, in general, define the way users consume media and how they influence users' media behavior. We further used these insights to enhance UCD processes to support long-term UX. Therefore, we developed a set of eight value-based personas to guide future designers toward the generation of long-term UX impacts and higher customer satisfaction with entertainment services. Thus, the contribution of this article is two-fold: first, we investigated the relation between users' values and their media behavior and outline that human values affect not only users' buying decisions [4], instead, they also influence what and which type of media users consume. Second, we made a methodological contribution by developing long-term oriented value-based personas that can help in a UCD process of entertainment services to better design for the long-term UX due to the ability to focus on values.

As a next step, we see the application of such types of design support in a large-scale TV and entertainment service development in Europe as a case study to validate the effectiveness of our personas. When adapting and adopting methods, the key challenge is to show the usefulness of such an approach, investigating how to apply this approach cross-domains, for example when it comes to entertainment in more untraditional environments like cars or inside an aircraft.

References

1. 12 Types of Media, Simplicable. https://simplicable.com/new/media. Accessed 28 May 2022
2. A guide to Content Personalization for Publishers, Automated (2022). https://headerbidding.co/content-personalization/. Accessed 3 June 2021
3. Abreu, J., Almeida, P., Varsori, E., Sílvia, F.: Interactive television UI: industry trends and disruptive design approaches. In: Proceedings of the XIX International Conference on Human Computer Interaction (Interacción 2018), pp. 1–8. Association for Computing Machinery, New York (2018). https://doi.org/10.1145/3233824.3233851
4. Allen, M.W., Ng, S.H.: The direct and indirect influences of human values on product ownership. J. Econ. Psychol. **20**(1), 5–39 (1999). https://doi.org/10.1016/S0167-4870(98)00041-5
5. Benington, H.D.: Production of large computer programs. In: Proceedings of the 9th International Conference on Software Engineering (ICSE 1987), vol. 9, pp. 299–310. IEEE Computer Society Press, Washington, DC (1987)
6. Bernhaupt, R., Murko, C., Pirker, M.: The future of media consumption: results from a comparative study of consumer behaviour changes in the living rom. In: Proceedings of IBC 2018. IBC (2018)
7. Bernhaupt, R., Guenon, R., Mancient, F., Desnos. A.: More is more: investigating attention distribution between the television and second screen applications – a case study with a synchronised second screen video game. In: Proceedings of IBC 2017, IBC (2017)
8. Bernhaupt, R., Pirker, M.: Evaluating user experience for interactive television: towards the development of a domain-specific user experience questionnaire. In: Kotzé, P., Marsden, G., Lindgaard, G., Wesson, J., Winckler, M. (eds.) INTERACT 2013. LNCS, vol. 8118, pp. 642–659. Springer, Heidelberg (2013). https://doi.org/10.1007/978-3-642-40480-1_45
9. Blake, J.: Television and the Second Screen: Interactive TV in the Age of Social Participation, 1st edn. Routledge (2016). https://doi.org/10.4324/9781315690902
10. Boer, D.: SSVS-G. Short Schwartz's value survey - German. In: Kemper, C., Zenger, M., Brähler, E. (eds.) Psychologische und sozialwissenschaftliche Kurzskalen, pp. 299–302. Medizinisch-Wissenschaftliche Verlagsgesellschaft, Berlin (2014)

11. Cesar, P., Geerts, D.: Social interaction design for online video and television. In: Nakatsu, R., Rauterberg, M., Ciancarini, P. (eds.) Handbook of Digital Games and Entertainment Technologies, pp. 1157–1193. Springer, Singapore (2017). https://doi.org/10.1007/978-981-4560-50-4_39

12. Cooper, A., Saffo, P.: The Inmates Are Running the Asylum. Sams Publishing, Carmel (2004)

13. De Vriendt, J., Degrande, N., Verhoeyen, M.: Video content recommendation: an overview and discussion on technologies and business models. Bell Labs Tech. J. **16**(2), 235–250 (2011). https://doi.org/10.1002/bltj.20513

14. Hu, H., Huang, J., Zhao, H., Wen, Y., Chen, C., Chua, T.: Social TV analytics: a novel paradigm to transform TV watching experience. In: Proceedings of the 5th ACM Multimedia Systems Conference (MMSys 2014), pp. 172–175. Association for Computing Machinery, New York (2014). https://doi.org/10.1145/2557642.2579373

15. International Organization for Standardization: Ergonomics of human-system interaction—Part 210: Human-centred design for interactive systems (ISO 9241-210:2019) (2019)

16. Jain, S., Grover, A., Thakur, P., Choudhary, S.: Trends, problems and solutions of recommender system. In: International Conference on Computing, Communication & Automation, pp. 955–958 (2015). https://doi.org/10.1109/CCAA.2015.7148534

17. Lindeman, M., Verkasalo, M.: Measuring values with the short Schwartz's value survey. J. Pers. Assess. **85**(2), 170–178 (2015). https://doi.org/10.1207/s15327752jpa8502_09

18. Livaditi, J., Vassilopoulou, K., Lougos, C., Chorianopoulos, K.: Needs and gratifications for interactive TV applications: implications for designers. In: Proceedings of the 36th Annual Hawaii International Conference on System Sciences (HICSS 2003), vol. 4, no. 4. IEEE Computer Society (2003)

19. McInerney, J., Elahi, E., Basilico, J., Raimond, Y., Jebara, T.: Accordion: a trainable simulator for long-term interactive systems. In: Fifteenth ACM Conference on Recommender Systems, vol. 15, pp. 102–113. Association for Computing Machinery, New York (2021). https://doi.org/10.1145/3460231.3474259

20. Norman, D.A.: Human-centered design considered harmful. Interactions **12**(4), 14–19 (2005)

21. Petersen, K., Wohlin, C., Baca, D.: The waterfall model in large-scale development. In: Bomarius, F., Oivo, M., Jaring, P., Abrahamsson, P. (eds.) PROFES 2009. LNBIP, vol. 32, pp. 386–400. Springer, Heidelberg (2009). https://doi.org/10.1007/978-3-642-02152-7_29

22. Pirker, M., Bernhaupt, R.: Measuring user experience in the living room: results from an ethnographically oriented field study indicating major evaluation factors. In: Proceedings of the 9th European Conference on Interactive TV and Video (EuroITV 2011), pp. 79–82. Association for Computing Machinery, New York (2011). https://doi.org/10.1145/2000119.2000133

23. Recent Trends in Personalization at Netflix, Netflix. https://research.netflix.com/publication/Recent%20Trends%20in%20Personalization%20at%20Netflix. Accessed 28 May 2022

24. Roto, V., Law, E.L., Vermeeren, A., Hoonhout, J.: User Experience White Paper – Bringing clarity to the concept of user experience (2011)

25. Schwartz, S.H., Bilsky, W.: Toward a universal psychological structure of human values. J. Pers. Soc. Psychol. **53**(3), 550–562 (1987). https://doi.org/10.1037/0022-3514.53.3.550

26. Schwartz, S.H.: An overview of the Schwartz theory of basic values. Online Read. Psychol. Cult. **2**(1), 1–20 (2012). https://doi.org/10.9707/2307-0919.1116

27. Schwartz, S.H.: Are there universal aspects in the structure and contents of human values? J. Soc. Issues **50**(4), 19–45 (1994). https://doi.org/10.1111/j.1540-4560.1994.tb01196.x

28. The carbon footprint of streaming video: fact-checking the headlines, IEA.org. https://www.iea.org/commentaries/the-carbon-footprint-of-streaming-video-fact-checking-the-headlines. Accessed 30 May 2022

Automated UX Evaluation for User-Centered Design of VR Interfaces

Kadiray Karakaya[1] , Enes Yigitbas[2(✉)] , and Gregor Engels[2]

[1] Heinz Nixdorf Institute, Paderborn University, Paderborn, Germany
[2] Software Innovation Campus Paderborn, Paderborn University, Paderborn, Germany
{kadiray.karakaya,enes.yigitbas,gregor.engels}@uni-paderborn.de

Abstract. User-centered design (UCD) is a continuous product development process where user feedback shapes the final product. An initial product design is iteratively refined until it provides a satisfying user experience (UX). Applying this iterative process to the development of Virtual Reality (VR) applications using traditional evaluation techniques such as questionnaires and interviews following UX testing is time-consuming. Active feedback from the users needs to be manually evaluated before it can be reflected in the subsequent refinements. In this work, we propose a framework to speed up the UCD process of VR applications by utilizing automated UX evaluation. We demonstrate it on the UCD of a VR-assisted robot programming interface. We conduct a UX study with 14 participants and report that we achieve a final design that provides a better UX, which evolved in short iteration cycles.

Keywords: Virtual Reality · User-centered design · Automated user experience evaluation

1 Introduction

User-centered design (UCD) involves the users of a product in its development process. The idea is to get user feedback in the early development stages, where changes are easy to make. UCD is an iterative process that continues until the product provides a satisfying user experience (UX) to the users [1]. Iterative processes such as agile are employed intensively in software development practice. The idea of combining the philosophies of agile software development and UCD, as user-centered agile software development (UCASD), has been an active research subject [2]. In recent years, agile software development has evolved into DevOps with the goal of applying agile principles to cover also the operations of software [3]. DevOps aims for continuous delivery of software changes to the end-user as fast as possible by utilizing automation in every step of the software development life cycle (SDLC). Inspired by DevOps [4], we imagine a pipeline

R. Bernhaupt et al. (Eds.): HCSE 2022, LNCS 13482, pp. 140–149, 2022.
https://doi.org/10.1007/978-3-031-14785-2_9

approach to UCD with automated UX evaluation, which we name *DevUxOps*. DevUxOps aims to promote continuous UX improvement by utilizing automated UX evaluation in the early development phase. It can be applied to the UCD of digital products in general. However, its impact can be better highlighted in the domain of VR applications compared to the domain of web or mobile applications. VR devices are not yet as commonly accessible as PCs or smartphones, this causes two challenges. First, UX evaluation of VR applications usually requires users to be present to physically equip the devices. Second, because users need to take turns, evaluation sessions cannot be conducted in parallel. Therefore, in this work we report our experience during the UCD of a VR application, specifically a VR-assisted robot programming interface. To apply this approach in the VR domain, we use AutoQUEST [13], an automated UX evaluation tool for VR applications. We start with an initial VR interface design and improve its UX by applying the DevUxOps approach. We conduct a UX study with 14 participants to investigate whether the final design provides a better UX.

The rest of the paper is organized as follows. In Sect. 2, we describe the related approaches. Our DevUxOps solution approach is introduced in Sect. 3. In Sect. 4, we explain a concrete implementation of our approach. Section 5 presents the target application. We conclude with a discussion and future work in Sects. 6 and 7 respectively.

2   Background and Related Work

Virtual Reality (VR) has been a topic of intense research in the last decades. In the past few years, massive advances in affordable consumer hardware and accessible software frameworks are now bringing VR to the masses. VR interfaces support the interaction in an immersive computer-generated 3D world and have been used in different application domains such as training [27], education [28], healthcare [29], or even collaborative software modeling [30].

In the following, we consider the related work with regard to the combination of UCD and agile software development methods, usability evaluation of VR interfaces, and the application domain of VR-assisted robot interaction. The combination of UCD and agile methods has been studied intensively over the past years [6,7]. Barambones et al. [5] introduced a lightweight agile user-centered design (AUCD) process to address the challenges of integrating UCD and agile. Klemets et al. [8] investigated a user-centered continuous delivery process, where super-users influenced the system iterations. Continuous delivery is an integral part of DevOps, which relies on a high degree of automation [4]. Automation of usability evaluation has also been studied extensively [9].

Usability evaluation of VR interfaces has been classified by Bowman et al. [12] into three binary groups regarding the user involvement, context of evaluation, and type of results. The methods that require user involvement aim to retrieve direct user feedback in the form of questionnaires [14] or interviews [15]. The context of the evaluation can be application-specific or generic. Regarding the type of results, evaluation methods can be quantitative or qualitative.

Quantitative methods deal with the objective assessment of the system, e.g. performance models like Fitts' law or GOMS [16]. Qualitative methods depend on expert evaluation techniques such as heuristic evaluation [26] or cognitive walkthrough [25]. A more recent approach, AutoQUEST [13] has been introduced by Harms et al. for the automated UX evaluation of VR interfaces. AutoQUEST [11] was initially developed as a generic evaluation framework for event-driven software. It was extended to detect usability smells of VR interfaces by monitoring user activities. We use AutoQUEST as the automation tool to demonstrate the DevUxOps conceptual framework which requires automated UX evaluation. The term DevUxOps has previously been mentioned by Siau et al. [10] as a mere potential extension to DevOps. However, to the best of our knowledge, it has not been studied in the literature.

We apply DevUxOps in the field of VR-assisted robot programming. Robot teleoperation and robot programming are promising application domains for VR applications. The works by Whitney et al. [19] and Lipton et al. [24] allow controlling robots from a remote location by using VR interfaces. The works by Burghardt et al. [20], and Yigitbas et al. [23] enabled non-programmers to program robotic systems through VR interfaces to perform a diverse set of tasks in industrial settings or assembly lines. None of these applications have utilized automated UX evaluation. However, it has been investigated for websites [21], mobile applications [22], and other VR application domains [13].

3   DevUxOps

In this section, we explain the DevUxOps approach in the example domain of VR-assisted robot programming. Engineering a user interface is a complex task. In UCD, an initial design often undergoes a series of refinements until it passes an extended UX evaluation with real users. When testing the UX of a VR-assisted robot programming interface, the traditional approach would be the following: integration of the VR interface with the real-world robotic system, extended UX evaluation including questionnaires and interviews, and refinement of the VR application until it fulfills the evaluation criteria. Since the whole system is evaluated, if a design does not get approved, the same process loop will be applied to the subsequent versions of the application. Depending on the strictness of the application domain and the evaluation criteria, this process can easily become time-consuming. Instead, we propose the DevUxOps conceptual framework shown in Fig. 1.

DevUxOps makes use of automated UX evaluation, requires refinement of the VR application until it fulfills the evaluation criteria, only then allows the integration of the VR application with the real-world robotic system and an extended UX evaluation of the system as a whole. With DevUxOps, usability issues can be detected early on, leading to a faster iteration of refined application versions. Automated UX evaluation is the core of DevUxOps. The iterative design process is applied until a subject application fulfills the usability criteria. The criteria can differ depending on the requirements, expectations of the users, and the application domain.

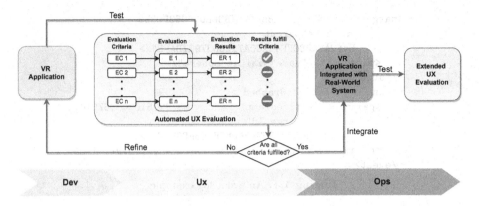

Fig. 1. DevUxOps applied to UCD of a VR-assisted robot programming interface

4 Implementation

When integrating AutoQUEST as the automated UX evaluation tool in the DevUxOps pipeline, we define the automated UX evaluation criteria based on *efficiency* and *usability smells*. Efficiency is measured by the time taken to complete a task, and usability smells are user behavior that indicates usability issues [13]. Figure 2, shows the integration of the automated UX evaluation with the VR application. AutoQUEST provides components that can be directly imported into the Unity game engine [17]. AutoQUESTMonitor continuously listens to the events created by interactable elements. The listened events are aggregated and sent to a remote AutoQUESTServer for logging. The logs are then used for detecting usability smells.

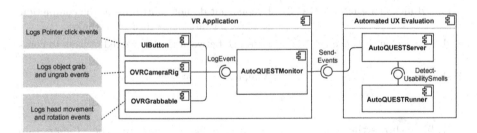

Fig. 2. Integration of the VR application with the automated UX evaluation

With the AutoQUEST integration we were able to monitor the following VR events: pointer click, object grab and ungrab, head movement, and rotation. AutoQUESTMonitor detects and identifies each interacted game object in the VR scene with a unique id. Events are registered with the type of the event, the id of the target object, and timestamp. Listing 1.1 shows an example log with a target sphere object and an object grabbed event.

```
<target id="F4B52179E8B84267B36BD96953FB3BBF">
    <param name="parent" value="
        E442AE5B8CFF4E2C0A722CD37927BAFE"/>
    <param name="name" value="Sphere"/>
</target>
<event type="objectGrabbed">
    <param name="timestamp" value="637320510800067510"/>
    <param name="targetId" value="
        F4B52179E8B84267B36BD96953FB3BBF"/>
    <param name="targetPosition" value="(1, 0.97, 1.21)"/>
</event>
```

Listing 1.1. An event log example

4.1 Evaluation Criteria

As shown in Fig. 1, DevUxOps requires the definition of evaluation criteria for the automated UX evaluation. Since the application domain is VR-assisted robot programming, we define the first evaluation criterion as the efficiency of programming, i.e. time taken to program the robot. As we use AutoQUEST as the concrete evaluation method, we choose the rest of the evaluation criteria from the usability smells that AutoQUEST can detect.

Table 1. Automated UX evaluation criteria

Criteria	Description
Efficiency (EC 1)	Time taken to program the robot
Important tasks (EC 2)	An event sequence that is executed frequently
Required inefficient actions (EC 3)	Events that do not contribute to the completion of tasks but are performed nevertheless
High interaction distance (EC 4)	Distance between the interacted objects to complete a task
Task retried (EC 5)	A repeated event sequence

Table 1 shows the defined evaluation criteria. We measure the *efficiency* in seconds, the rest of the criteria are measured in counts. *Important tasks* correspond to frequently executed event sequences, these events are good candidates for improving the overall efficiency. *Required inefficient actions* correspond to head movements and rotations, their counts should also be minimized. *High interaction distance* can be tiring for the users, the smaller the distance the better. *Task retried* occurs when users fail to achieve their goal and retry the task, which should also be minimized.

5   Target Application

To demonstrate the conceptual framework on the UCD of a target application, we design and iteratively improve the UX of a VR-assisted robot programming interface. The interface allows users the program a real robotic arm by providing interaction mechanisms in the virtual environment. We have first started with an initial design of the target VR application, and evaluated its UX according to the evaluation criteria shown in Table 1. We have refined its design until we have fulfilled the defined criteria. After that, we conducted an extended UX evaluation study with real users who have performed a predefined task with the initial and the final versions of the VR application. In the extended UX evaluation, the VR interface is integrated with the real-world robotic system. In the initial design, shown in Fig. 3a, the interface allows the recording of the robot arm's movements. It is possible to activate suction to pick up cube objects and deactivate it to release them. The goal is to program the robot so that the cubes on the left of the robot are placed in squares that match their colors.

Table 2. Important usability smells of the initial design

Criteria	Logged events	Description
Important tasks (EC 2)	PointerClick =>ReplayButton PointerClick =>RecordButton	Time spent mostly on clicking the replay and record buttons
High interact. distance (EC 4)	SuctionButton =>Hints	Suction button and hints pane are too distant
Task retried (EC 5)	ObjectGrabbed =>Arm ObjectUngrabbed =>Arm PointerClick =>SuctionButton	Moving the robot arm and starting suction failed often

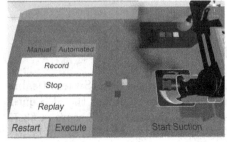 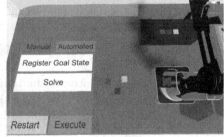

(a) Initial Design   (b) Final Design

Fig. 3. Initial and final design of the VR interface

Table 2 shows the important usability smells of the initial design. Note that we only list the smells with significant occurrences. When refining the VR interface, we focus on minimizing these smells to improve the overall efficiency. We omit to present the design and usability smells of the subsequent versions for brevity. Figure 3b, shows the final design. It has been guided by the usability smells listed in Table 2. Therefore, in this design, we aimed to reduce the number of buttons and replaced the logic of recording the arm movements with the possibility to let the users directly put cube objects to their target positions. For example, the start suction button is no longer required, because the users can directly pick up the cubes. The robot will automatically start suction when it touches a cube.

After reaching a design that satisfies the automated UX evaluation criteria, we have finally moved on to the extended UX evaluation step in the conceptual framework. In this step, we aimed to find out whether we were able to improve the UX of the initial design with the final design. Therefore, we performed a UX evaluation study with 14 participants. The participants had a diverse age group ranging between 23 and 64, where the mean age was 27. Almost all of the participants have completed a higher education degree. Half of the participants never used a VR headset before. We asked them to program the robot to move the cube objects to the target positions, first by using the initial design and then by using the final design. To compare the two designs, first, we applied the automated UX evaluation once more during the user test sessions. Second, we asked the participants to fill out the SUS questionnaire. Table 3, shows the results of the automated UX evaluation for the initial and final design. Usability smells for all the evaluation criteria have been reduced, improving the overall mean efficiency.

Table 3. Automated evaluation results comparison for the initial vs the final design

	Initial design	Final design
Efficiency (EC 1)	325.14 s	186.57 s
Important tasks (EC 2)	57	39
Required inefficient actions (EC 3)	40	29
High interaction distance (EC 4)	46	31
Task retried (EC 5)	9	3

As part of the comparative evaluation, we have used the SUS (System Usability Score) questionnaire [18]. We asked the participants to fill out the SUS questionnaire separately for each design. From this, we derived a SUS score of 63,75 for the initial design and 80,54 for the final design. A higher SUS score indicates better usability.

6 Discussion

Overall, we report that by applying the DevUxOps approach, we were able to obtain a better final design. The final design of the target application provides a better UX to the users based on the UX evaluation criteria of efficiency and number of usability smells. Compared to the initial design, it enables the users to perform the same task more efficiently and it contains fewer usability smells. Applying a traditional UCD approach could have led to a similar UX improvement, however, we report that DevUxOps enabled short iteration cycles by not having to conduct an extensive UX evaluation study after each design iteration.

It can be challenging to decide when to stop improving the design of the target application and start with an extended UX evaluation. It can be guided by a simple heuristic, where a design will be accepted after none of the acceptance criteria improve significantly.

DevUxOps as a conceptual framework can be applied in diverse application domains, where user-centered design can be applied. The key requirement of this framework is the automation of the UX evaluation. Application of the framework can be limited depending on the application domain, e.g. where it is difficult to measure the usability of the product. Since the UCD process can be practically applied to the design of non-digital products too, automated UX evaluation in the context of such products needs to be investigated. We have applied the framework in a rather complex application domain, VR-assisted robot programming. However, it should generally be easily applicable for the design of digital products such as web and mobile applications. The success of the framework is highly dependent on the capabilities of the underlying automated UX evaluation tools. Since our demonstration was based on AutoQUEST, the UX evaluation criteria were limited to the usability smells that AutoQUEST can detect.

7 Conclusion and Future Work

In this work, we have presented a conceptual framework for the UCD process of VR applications by utilizing automated UX evaluation. We have implemented it concretely by using AutoQUEST as the automated evaluation tool. We have demonstrated it on the UCD of a target application, where we iteratively refine a VR-assisted robot programming interface. We have reevaluated the subsequent refinements only with the automated UX evaluation, which enabled a faster overall UCD process. Finally, we have performed an extended UX evaluation to compare the initial design of the interface to its final design. The extended evaluation results show that the final design is more efficient, has fewer usability issues, and provides a better UX than the initial design. We have considered the efficiency of the user interface and the number of usability smells as an approximate indicator of the overall UX. In future work, further evaluation criteria can be considered and integrated into the automated UX evaluation. Currently, the refinement process is done manually based on the gained results, the refinement process itself can also be (semi-)automatized.

References

1. Abras, C., Maloney-Krichmar, D., Preece, J., Bainbridge, W.: Encyclopedia of Human-Computer Interaction. Sage Publications, Thousand Oaks **37**, 445–456 (2004)
2. Brhel, M., Meth, H., Maedche, A., Werder, K.: Exploring principles of user-centered agile software development: a literature review. Inf. Softw. Technol. **61**, 163–181 (2015)
3. Lwakatare, L.E., Kuvaja, P., Oivo, M.: Relationship of DevOps to agile, lean and continuous deployment. In: Abrahamsson, P., Jedlitschka, A., Nguyen Duc, A., Felderer, M., Amasaki, S., Mikkonen, T. (eds.) PROFES 2016. LNCS, vol. 10027, pp. 399–415. Springer, Cham (2016). https://doi.org/10.1007/978-3-319-49094-6_27
4. Ebert, C., Gallardo, G., Hernantes, J., Serrano, N.: DevOps. IEEE Softw. **33**(3), 94–100 (2016)
5. Barambones, J., Moral, C., Ferre, X., Villalba-Mora, E.: A scrum-based development process to support co-creation with elders in the ehealth domain. In: Bernhaupt, R., Ardito, C., Sauer, S. (eds.) HCSE 2020. LNCS, vol. 12481, pp. 105–117. Springer, Cham (2020). https://doi.org/10.1007/978-3-030-64266-2_6
6. Silva, T., Martin, A., Maurer, F., Silveira, M.: User-centered design and agile methods: a systematic review. In: 2011 Agile Conference, pp. 77–86 (2011)
7. Sohaib, O., Khan, K.: Integrating usability engineering and agile software development: a literature review. In: 2010 International Conference on Computer Design and Applications, vol. 2, pp. V2-32–V2-38 (2010)
8. Klemets, J., Storholmen, T.C.B.: Towards super user-centred continuous delivery: a case study. In: Bernhaupt, R., Ardito, C., Sauer, S. (eds.) HCSE 2020. LNCS, vol. 12481, pp. 152–165. Springer, Cham (2020). https://doi.org/10.1007/978-3-030-64266-2_9
9. Ivory, M., Hearst, M.: The state of the art in automating usability evaluation of user interfaces. ACM Comput. Surv. **33**, 470–516 (2001). https://doi.org/10.1145/503112.503114
10. Siau, K., Woo, C., Storey, V., Chiang, R., Chua, C., Beard, J.: Information systems analysis and design: past revolutions, present challenges, and future research directions. Commun. Assoc. Inf. Syst. **50**(1), 33 (2021)
11. Herbold, S., Harms, P.: AutoQUEST–automated quality engineering of event-driven software. In: Proceedings of the 2013 IEEE Sixth International Conference on Software Testing, Verification and Validation Workshops, pp. 134–139 (2013). https://doi.org/10.1109/ICSTW.2013.23
12. Bowman, D., Gabbard, J., Hix, D.: A survey of usability evaluation in virtual environments: classification and comparison of methods. Presence: Teleoper. Virtual Environ. **11**, 404–424 (2002). https://doi.org/10.1162/105474602760204309
13. Harms, P.: Automated usability evaluation of virtual reality applications. ACM Trans. Comput.-Hum. Interact. **26**(3), 1–36 (2019). https://doi.org/10.1145/3301423
14. Darken, R., Sibert, J.: Wayfinding strategies and behaviors in large virtual worlds. In: Proceedings of the SIGCHI Conference on Human Factors in Computing Systems, pp. 142–149 (1996). https://doi.org/10.1145/238386.238459
15. Bowman, D., Hodges, L.: Formalizing the design, evaluation, and application of interaction techniques for immersive virtual environments. J. Vis. Lang. Comput. **10**, 37–53 (1999)

16. John, B., Kieras, D.: The GOMS family of user interface analysis techniques: comparison and contrast. ACM Trans. Comput.-Hum. Interact. **3**, 320–351 (1996). https://doi.org/10.1145/235833.236054
17. Unity Unity Real-Time Development Platform | 3D, 2D VR & AR Engine (2022). https://unity.com/
18. Brooke, J.: SUS-a quick and dirty usability scale. Usability Eval. Ind. **189**(194), 4–7 (1996)
19. Whitney, D., Rosen, E., Ullman, D., Phillips, E., Tellex, S.: ROS reality: a virtual reality framework using consumer-grade hardware for ROS-enabled robots. In: 2018 IEEE/RSJ International Conference on Intelligent Robots and Systems (IROS), pp. 1–9 (2018)
20. Burghardt, A., Szybicki, D., Gierlak, P., Kurc, K., Pietruś, P., Cygan, R.: Programming of industrial robots using virtual reality and digital twins. Appl. Sci. **10**, 486 (2020)
21. Harms, P., Grabowski, J.: Usage-based automatic detection of usability smells. In: Sauer, S., Bogdan, C., Forbrig, P., Bernhaupt, R., Winckler, M. (eds.) HCSE 2014. LNCS, vol. 8742, pp. 217–234. Springer, Heidelberg (2014). https://doi.org/10.1007/978-3-662-44811-3_13
22. Yigitbas, E., Jovanovikj, I., Josifovska, K., Sauer, S., Engels, G.: On-the-fly usability evaluation of mobile adaptive UIs through instant user feedback. In: Lamas, D., Loizides, F., Nacke, L., Petrie, H., Winckler, M., Zaphiris, P. (eds.) INTERACT 2019. LNCS, vol. 11749, pp. 563–567. Springer, Cham (2019). https://doi.org/10.1007/978-3-030-29390-1_38
23. Yigitbas, E., Karakaya, K., Jovanovikj, I., Engels, G.: Enhancing human-in-the-loop adaptive systems through digital twins and VR interfaces. In: 2021 International Symposium on Software Engineering for Adaptive and Self-Managing Systems (SEAMS), pp. 30–40 (2021)
24. Lipton, J., Fay, A., Rus, D.: Baxter's homunculus: virtual reality spaces for teleoperation in manufacturing. IEEE Robot. Autom. Lett. **3**, 179–186 (2018)
25. Polson, P., Lewis, C., Rieman, J., Wharton, C.: Cognitive walkthroughs: a method for theory-based evaluation of user interfaces. Int. J. Man-Mach. Stud. **36**, 741–773 (1992)
26. Nielsen, J.: Heuristic Evaluation. Usability Inspection Methods, pp. 25–62 (1994)
27. Yigitbas, E., Jovanovikj, I., Scholand, J., Engels, G.: VR training for warehouse management. In: VRST 2020: 26th ACM Symposium on Virtual Reality Software and Technology, pp. 78:1–78:3 (2020)
28. Yigitbas, E., Tejedor, C., Engels, G.: Experiencing and programming the ENIAC in VR. Mensch Comput. **2020**, 505–506 (2020)
29. Yigitbas, E., Heindörfer, J., Engels, G.: A context-aware virtual reality first aid training application. Proc. Mensch Comput. **2019**, 885–888 (2019)
30. Yigitbas, E., Gorissen, S., Weidmann, N., Engels, G.: Collaborative software modeling in virtual reality. In: 24th International Conference on Model Driven Engineering Languages and Systems, MODELS 2021, Fukuoka, 10–15 October 2021, pp. 261–272 (2021). https://doi.org/10.1109/MODELS50736.2021.00034

Requirements-Based Composition
of Tailored Decision Support Systems

Jonas Kirchhoff[✉][iD], Christoph Weskamp[iD], and Gregor Engels[iD]

Software Innovation Lab, Paderborn University, Paderborn, Germany
{jonas.kirchhoff,christoph.weskamp,engels}@upb.de

Abstract. Corporate decision makers have individual requirements for decision support influenced by business goals, regulatory restrictions or access to resources such as data. Ideally, decision makers could quickly create tailored decision support systems (DSS) themselves which optimally address their individual requirements for decision support. Although service-oriented architectures have been proposed for DSS customization, they are primarily targeting trained software developers and cannot immediately be adapted by decision makers or domain experts with little to no software development knowledge. In this paper, we therefore motivate an assisted process-based service composition approach which can be used by non-developers to create tailored DSS. For assistance during service composition, we contribute a meta-model for the formalization of both decision support requirements and functionality of decision support services. Models created according to the meta-model can be used to detect mismatches between a decision maker's requirements for decision support and services selected in the service composition representing a DSS. Furthermore, the formalizations may even be used for automated service composition given a decision maker's decision support requirements. We demonstrate the expressiveness of our meta-model in the domain of regional energy distribution network planning.

Keywords: Service-oriented DSS · End-user programming · Automated service composition · Decision support system generator

1 Introduction

Business environments are increasingly volatile, uncertain, complex and ambiguous (VUCA). As a result, decision makers must consider many influencing factors with frequent, unpredictable change and unknown cause-effect relationships when making a decision [2,14]. More and more decision makers therefore rely

Partially supported by the North Rhine Westphalian Ministry of Economic Affairs, Innovation, Digitalisation and Energy (MWIDE) through grant 005-2011-0022 and the European Regional Development Fund (ERDF) through grant EFRE-0801186.

on interactive computer-based decision support systems (DSS) to assist them in the identification of optimal decisions [18].

As observed during an interdisciplinary research project with industry partners for decision support in the domain of regional energy distribution network planning [10], decision makers traditionally turn to established DSS developers to obtain an "off-the-shelf DSS" for their decision problem. Due to the fact that these DSS frequently come with limited to no customization capabilities, the decision support provided by an off-the-shelf DSS must immediately align with the requirements for decision support of an individual decision maker. Requirements for decision support however are situational in the sense that they vary based on the context in which an individual decision maker operates. For instance, in the domain of regional energy distribution network planning, decision makers can only leverage a cross-sectoral planning approach when managing distribution networks for multiple energy sectors. Decision makers may furthermore prioritize metrics such as network reliability and network reinforcements costs differently, or have different access to resources such as data or time available to identify an optimal decision. Similar situations can be observed in the domain of business model development [8] and supply chain management [4,21]. With respect to these situational factors, it is unlikely that the decision support provided by a non-customizable DSS fully addresses the individual requirements for decision support of a concrete decision maker.

A misalignment of DSS functionality and requirements for decision support leaves decision makers with two alternatives: The first alternative is to use the DSS anyway, thereby potentially basing decisions on suboptimal recommendations computed by the DSS. Suboptimal decisions however endanger the success of a company and – in case the company manages critical infrastructure such as a regional energy distribution network – might even negatively affect society as a whole. The second alternative is working with the DSS developer to extend the decision support provided by the DSS according to the situational requirements of the decision maker. This however is a cost- and time-intensive undertake, which again limits competitiveness in VUCA business environments.

In order to ensure the quick availability of optimal decision support, decision makers should ideally be able to create tailored DSS by themselves. Figure 1 shows how this could work: After selecting an application domain (here: energy distribution network planning), a decision maker can specify their requirements for decision support, e.g., to minimize investment costs (CAPEX) of an electricity network with 2.5 h available to identify an optimal decision. Next, the decision maker can model their decision making process as a business process using the *Business Process Model and Notation* (BPMN) [17]. BPMN seems suitable due to its widespread use and familiarity among many stakeholders [1,13], regardless of their background. Each activity of the decision support process corresponds to an interoperable decision support service provided by a DSS developer. In the example shown in Fig. 1, a demand forecast is generated before the associated network is optimized. Data can be produced at runtime by the decision maker (e.g., `currentDemand`) or as a result of service execution (`electricityDemand`). Out-

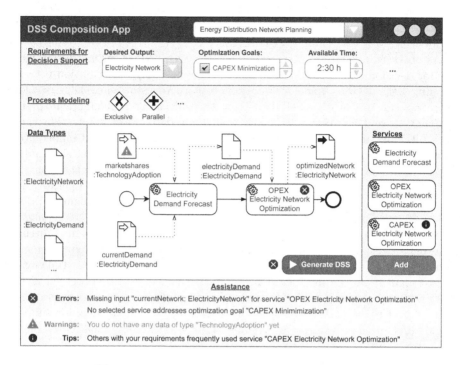

Fig. 1. Mockup for a *DSS composition application*

put data (`optimizedNetwork`) will be returned to the decision maker. An assistance highlights errors, warnings and tips regarding the composition. These can regard service interfaces (e.g., missing or unsuitable input data types), requirements for decision support (e.g., optimizing for a wrong metric), or resource availability (e.g., having no suitable data instances to be used at runtime). After the service composition is completed, the corresponding DSS can be generated and executed. During execution, the decision maker can interact with the DSS as usual. In the background, a workflow engine invokes services with the data provided by the decision maker or generated by other services as described by the underlying process model.

The suitability of BPMN for service composition in service-oriented architectures has already been proven with process-driven applications [20]. This includes assistance in the form of dataflow validation between application services based on service interfaces (e.g., [11] for DSS). In this paper, we therefore focus on laying the foundations for assisting decision makers in selecting services during process composition that align with their decision support requirements. For this purpose, we contribute a meta-model for the formalization of both decision support requirements and service functionality in the context of a software platform for DSS generation shown in Fig. 1. Models created according to the meta-model can be used to detect mismatches between a decision maker's requirements for decision support and services selected by decision makers in the composition representing a DSS. The formalizations may even be used for automated service composition given a decision maker's requirements for decision support.

The remainder of the paper is structured as follows: We first discuss related work with a focus on service-oriented DSS and service composition in Sect. 2 to support explanations throughout the paper. In Sect. 3, we present requirements for the meta-model which is subsequently explained in Sect. 4. We demonstrate our model in Sect. 5 and conclude the paper with a summary and outlook on future work in Sect. 6.

2   Research Background

In this section, we first present background information on service-oriented DSS (Sect. 2.1) which supports the subsequent explanations throughout the paper. Afterwards, we discuss existing work for automated service composition in service-oriented DSS (Sect. 2.2) which also utilizes formalizations for required/provided service functionality and therefore relates to our approach.

2.1   Service-Oriented DSS

Demirkan and Delen [5] define a *service-oriented DSS* as a DSS with a service-oriented architecture which supports the cross-enterprise design, development, identification, and consumption of reusable services. There are multiple motivations to choose a service-oriented architecture for a DSS. While Demirkan and Delen mention agility in response to change in the context of definition, Figueira et al. [7] mention maintainability in the context of a Software-as-a-Service deployment model, and Horita et al. [9] as well as Stănescu et al. [19] mention the need for cloud platforms' scalability to handle big data sources – an aspect which also plays an important role in Demirkan and Delen's paper. In this context, it is comprehensible that many works (e.g., [9,19,22]) primarily focus on replacement of DSS data sources by decision makers. This is however not sufficient with respect to our project experience presented in the previous Sect. 1, which demonstrates that even computation methods and other decision support functionality must be exchanged based on the situational requirements of decision makers. However, service-oriented architectures are designed for trained software engineers and cannot be immediately adapted by non-developers which prevents the quick availability of an individualized DSS. The same applies for DSS generators without a service-oriented architecture which use mathematical modeling [3] or software frameworks [4] to abstract from concrete programming tasks – skills that decision makers usually do not display [18].

2.2   Automated Service Composition

Automated service composition may be used to account for the lack of programming knowledge by decision makers. Approaches using automated service composition in a DSS context include the work by Kwon [12], Dzemydienė et al. [6], and Mustafin et al. [16]. They are based on using a similar formalization for both service functionality and a decision maker's requirements for decision support. Based on these formalizations, a service composition can be identified which matches the requirements.

The approach by Mustafin et al. [16] comes closest to the meta-model for requirements and functionality formalization presented in this paper. The approach is based on the OWL-S [15] specification to formalize service functionality (and requirements for decision support). A provided/required service profile includes information about input and output (process) parameters as well as preconditions and side-effects. Non-functional service characteristics such as resource consumption can be specified as service parameters (cf. [15, Fig. 2] and associated explanation). However, this approach lacks some specificity: With respect to functional decision support service characteristics/requirements, it is not possible to specify optimization goals, i.e., which metrics should be minimized and maximized, or which computation method is used. The latter is for instance relevant in energy distribution network planning to be conformant with regulatory constraints. With respect to non-functional service characteristics/requirements, the approach does not provide any guidelines how for instance the consumption of monetary or temporal resources can be specified as a service parameter. These shortcomings will become more evident throughout the next section in which we explain the requirements for the formalization of provided and required decision support service functionality in more detail.

3   Formalization Requirements

In the following, we describe characteristics of decision making which are prerequisites for the formalization of decision support requirements and decision support services. The requirements are derived from the aforementioned research project for decision support in the domain of energy distribution network planning with partners from academia and industry [10].

FR1 – *Data Constraints.* Decision support software, independent of whether it is provided in form of a holistic DSS or a modular decision support service, has certain data requirements which must be fulfilled by the decision maker using the software. An individual decision maker however has only limited data access. It is possible to differentiate between constraints on data types (e.g., the required input is an electricity network) and data instances (e.g., the electricity network provided at runtime may not exceed a certain size).

FR2 – *Method Constraints.* A method in this context refers to how the value of a metric or the overall decision recommendation is computed. For instance, when assessing the reliability of an electricity network, there might be multiple standards on how this reliability is computed. Regulatory constraints however may only allow a specific standard to be used. If a decision should be optimized with respect to one or multiple metrics such as the investment costs for reinforcement of an electricity network, the considered metrics need to be documented with an associated goal, i.e., minimization or maximization.

FR3 – *Decision Constraints.* Especially in presence of decisions which should optimize a metric, it is useful to define constraints on other metrics of the provided decision recommendation. For instance, when minimizing investment costs during electricity network reinforcement, a lower bound for network reliability should be provided from a decision maker's perspective to avoid the recommendation of doing nothing to avoid any investment costs.

FR4 – *Resource Constraints.* In addition to data, other limited resources such as money or time are consumed to compute a decision recommendation.

FR5 – *Execution Constraints.* The execution mode of a decision support service may also decide whether or not a service can be included in a tailored DSS. For instance, for time-critical decisions, it is important that the selected services have a high availability so that the decision support is actually available if needed. Additionally, the place of service execution, i.e., on-premises or remote, can be relevant when dealing with sensitive data such as clients' energy demands.

FR6 – *Domain Ontology.* An ontology is needed to document which entities are present in the application domain under consideration. Furthermore, parameterizing the formalization with respect to an ontology of the application domain makes it extensible to support multiple application domains.

4   Formalization Meta-Model

Our meta-model to address the requirements defined in the preceding Sect. 3 is documented as a UML class diagram and split over multiple packages which are shown in Figs. 2 to 5 and subsequently explained.

The **Types-package** shown in Fig. 2 allows the definition of entity types with respect to their `Attributes` which may be of qualitative or quantitative nature. A `QuantitativeAttribute` can optionally specify a `minValue`, `maxValue` and a `measurementUnit`. A `QualitativeAttribute` may specify a `range` of valid values. `SingleValueQualitativeAttribute` and `MultiValueQualitativeAttribute` document how many of these values may be specified for an `Instance` of the `Type`. Instances of a `Type` are described using the **Instances-package**. The `Attribute`-values of an `Instance` are defined via fulfilled `Assertions`. There is one subclass of `Assertion` for each of the `Attribute`-subclasses. The explanation of the **Types-** and **Instances-**packages is deliberately kept short as they are not useful on their own. Instead, they serve as a base for the other packages.

The **Data-package** shown in Fig. 3 defines `DataTypes` and associated `DataInstances` of an application domain. An example for a `DataType` in the example domain of electricity distribution network planning is an *Electricity Network* with a `QuantitativeDataAttribute` *Investment Costs* and a `MultiValueQualitativeAttribute` *Reliability Design* specifying which types of network assets such as "cables" or "transformers" may fail without impacting network functionality. A `DataType` can be expressed by a nonzero amount of `DataFormats`. A `DataInstance` is a certain data document available at runtime, e.g., a concrete file in a specific `format` describing a concrete *Electricity Network* such as *"my-network.en"*. The `DataInstance` furthermore documents

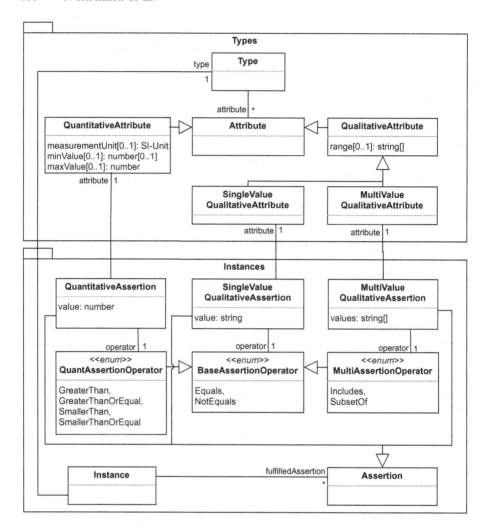

Fig. 2. Meta-model for types and instances

Attribute-values via Assertions, e.g., that the *Investment Costs* equal 3.14 million Euro.

Information on how data was or can be computed is documented using the Computation Methods package also shown in Fig. 3. Again, the Types- and Instances-package enable the definition of ComputationMethodTypes and ComputationMethodInstances respectively. An example for a ComputationMethodType would be *Electricity Network Optimization*. Associated ComputationMethodInstances could be optimization approaches such as *Mathematical Exact Network Optimization* or *Heuristic Network Optimization*. In case of optimization, the optimization target is documented as an Objective. The Objective documents the QuantitativeDataAttribute which is optimized

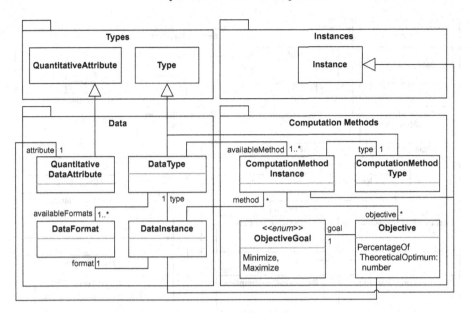

Fig. 3. Meta-model for data and computation methods

and the goal of the optimization, e.g., *Minimize Investment Costs* in case of an *Electricity Network*. Furthermore, the gap to a theoretical optimum can be specified, e.g., to document that a heuristic approach only achieves 80% of the theoretically achievable optimum. The available ComputationMethodInstances are documented for each DataType. Each DataInstance documents the actually used ComputationMethodInstance. The design choice to document the used computation method at data-level instead of service-level is that decision makers may reuse data computed during a previous interaction with a tailored DSS. In this case, the information about how the data was computed should not get lost.

The Service Interface-package shown in Fig. 4 describes the input and output of a Decision Support Service as a Slot. Each Slot specifies the data it consumes/produces with an associated DataQuantity documenting the minimum and maximum quantity of DataInstances that are consumed/produced. Constraints on the consumed and produced data as well as the used computation method for the produced data can be annotated using the previously discussed packages of Fig. 3. In the context of electricity network planning, a Decision Support Service might be a service encapsulating a concrete linear optimization model which minimizes investment costs given the current state of the network and expected future electricity demands.

The execution of a Decision Support Service such as *Remote* or *On-Premises* is specified using the Service Execution-package (cf. Fig. 4). Execution consumes resources as described using the Resource Consumption-package. A ResourceConsumption is specified as a combi-

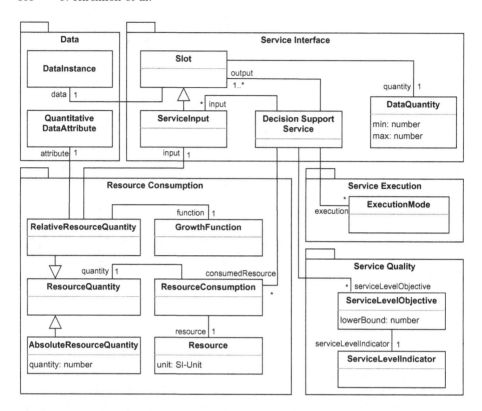

Fig. 4. Meta-model for the formalization of decision support services

nation of a `Resource` such as *time in seconds* or *money in Euro* and a `ResourceQuantity`. The quantity of the resource can either be specified "statically" as an `AbsoluteResourceQuantity` or "dynamically" as a `RelativeResourceQuantity`, i.e., relative to a `QuantitativeDataAttribute` of a `ServiceInput` given a mathematical `GrowthFunction`. For instance, the previously mentioned service for electricity network optimization using a mathematical optimization model may specify a runtime which is *exponential* in the *size* of the *electricity network* provided as input.

Lastly, a `Decision Support Service` exhibits certain quality characteristics as described by the `Service Quality-package` (cf. Fig. 4). Each quality characteristic is described using a `ServiceLevelObjective` which specifies a `lowerBound` with respect to a `ServiceLevelIndicator`. For instance, a service may specify an *availability of 99% or higher*.

Another package provides the capabilities to model decision makers' requirements for decision support. It builds upon the previously explained packages by introducing a `DecisionMaker` class to document desired output and available input `DataInstance`s, available `Resource`s and acceptable service qualities. Due

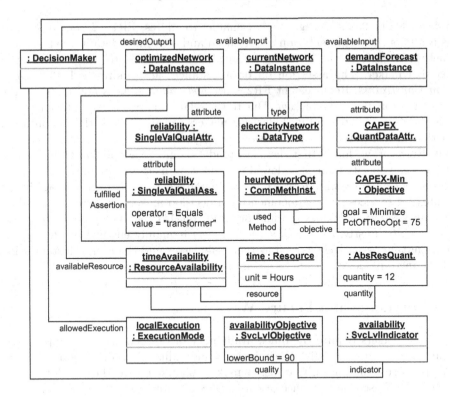

Fig. 5. Example model for decision support requirements

to its simplicity, we do not explain the package here but use it for the demonstration in the upcoming section.

5   Demonstration and Discussion

We instantiated our meta-model in the domain of energy distribution network planning [10] to demonstrate its applicability. An excerpt documenting a decision maker's requirements for electricity network planning is given by the UML object diagram depicted in Fig. 5: The desired output of a decision maker is an electricity network which minimizes investment costs (CAPEX) while ensuring network reliability with respect to transformers. For this purpose, the decision maker can provide the current electricity network and a demand forecast (whose data type is not shown in the diagram for simplification purposes). The decision maker prefers the use of a heuristic optimization method which guarantees at least 75% of the theoretical optimum. The execution may take up to 12 h and can only be performed on local hardware with 90% service availability.

Other excerpts of the case study were given as textual examples throughout the previous explanations of meta-model packages. Our case study confirmed that the meta-model addresses the formalization requirements presented in Sect. 3. The `Data`-package is a key enabler to address FR1 – *Data Constraints* as it allows the documentation of produced and consumed data in the `Service`-package as well as the documentation of data available to and desired by a decision maker. The assertion on data instances also addresses FR3 – *Decision Constraints*. Requirement FR2 – *Method Constraints* is addressed by the `Computation Methods`-package. Due to the relation between computation methods and data depicted in Fig. 3, decision makers can also include the computation method as a requirements for decision support when specifying their desired output. However, we found that the meta-model should be adapted so that decision makers can specify multiple allowed computation methods. Requirement FR4 – *Resource Constraints* is addressed by the `Resource Consumption`-package in the context of services and by documenting a decision maker's resource availability. Packages `Service Execution` and `Service Quality` address FR5 – *Execution Constraints*. Lastly, FR6 – *Domain Ontology* is mainly enabled by the `Types`-and `Instances`-package as well as their subclasses and the overall instantiation of the meta-model classes for a given application domain.

6 Summary and Future Work

Decision makers require the quick availability of tailored decision support systems that optimally assist them in their individual decision making process. We proposed that, ideally, decision makers should create these tailored DSS themselves based on a service-oriented DSS architecture. However, since decision makers often have no software development knowledge, they either need to be assisted during the composition of decision support services, or service composition must happen automatically based on requirements for decision support specified by a decision maker. Both approaches require a formalization of decision support functionality requested by decision makers and provided by decision support services in order to match those two together. In this paper, we therefore contributed a meta-model for the formalization of decision support functionality. It can be used both for the formalization of decision support service functionality and decision makers' requirements for decision support. The meta-model extends on existing approaches by increasing expressiveness with respect to functional and non-functional decision support characteristics. In particular, these extensions include the method and metrics used for optimization as well as service-level objectives. We demonstrated the expressiveness of our meta-model by applying it to an example in the application domain of regional energy distribution network planning.

As stated before, the presented meta-model is only the foundation for matching decision support requirements and functionality. Naturally, a next step in future work is to develop a validation algorithm which checks whether a service composition described according to our meta-model addresses all (or some) of the modeled requirements for decision support of an individual decision maker. On the one hand, this approach can be used for validating that a service composition assembled by a decision maker addresses all requirements for decision support (cf. assistance in Fig. 1). On the other hand, given a formalization of requirements for decision support, the approach can be used to match decision support services and service compositions in context of an automated service composition approach. Before implementing and utilizing this validation algorithm, we may try to merge our meta-model with OWL-S to leverage existing service matching and composition functionality based on the W3C recommendation. The mapping onto OWL-S would also immediately give us an XML-based concrete syntax, which otherwise would need to be defined before the models can be algorithmically processed.

References

1. Awad, A., Decker, G., Lohmann, N.: Diagnosing and repairing data anomalies in process models. In: Rinderle-Ma, S., Sadiq, S., Leymann, F. (eds.) BPM 2009. LNBIP, vol. 43, pp. 5–16. Springer, Heidelberg (2010). https://doi.org/10.1007/978-3-642-12186-9_2
2. Bennett, N., Lemoine, G.J.: What a difference a word makes: understanding threats to performance in a VUCA world. Bus. Horiz. **57**(3), 311–317 (2014)
3. Bhargava, H., Sridhar, S., Herrick, C.: Beyond spreadsheets: tools for building decision support systems. Computer **32**(3), 31–39 (1999)
4. Brodsky, A., Al-Nory, M., Nash, H.: SC-CoJava: a service composition language to unify simulation and optimization of supply chains. In: Dolk, D., Granat, J. (eds.) Modeling for Decision Support in Network-Based Services. LNBIP, vol. 42, pp. 118–142. Springer, Heidelberg (2012). https://doi.org/10.1007/978-3-642-27612-5_6
5. Demirkan, H., Delen, D.: Leveraging the capabilities of service-oriented decision support systems: putting analytics and big data in cloud. Decis. Support Syst. **55**(1), 412–421 (2013)
6. Dzemydienė, D., Maskeliūnas, S., Miliauskas, A., Naujikienė, R., Dzemydaitė, G.: E-service composition for decision support, based on monitoring of contamination processes and analysis of water resource data. Technol. Econ. Dev. Econ. **21**(6), 869–884 (2015)
7. Figueira, G., Amorim, P., Guimarães, L., Amorim-Lopes, M., Neves-Moreira, F., Almada-Lobo, B.: A decision support system for the operational production planning and scheduling of an integrated pulp and paper mill. Comput. Chem. Eng. **77**, 85–104 (2015)
8. Gottschalk, S., Yigitbas, E., Nowosad, A., Engels, G.: Situation- and domain-specific composition and enactment of business model development methods. In: Ardito, L., Jedlitschka, A., Morisio, M., Torchiano, M. (eds.) PROFES 2021. LNCS, vol. 13126, pp. 103–118. Springer, Cham (2021). https://doi.org/10.1007/978-3-030-91452-3_7
9. Horita, F.E., de Albuquerque, J.P., Marchezini, V., Mendiondo, E.M.: Bridging the gap between decision-making and emerging big data sources: an application of a model-based framework to disaster management in Brazil. Decis. Support Syst. **97**, 12–22 (2017)
10. Kirchhoff, J., Burmeister, S.C., Weskamp, C., Engels, G.: Towards a decision support system for cross-sectoral energy distribution network planning. In: Breitner, M.H., et al. (eds) Energy Informatics and Electro Mobility ICT (2021)

11. Kirchhoff, J., Gottschalk, S., Engels, G.: Detecting data incompatibilities in process-driven decision support systems. In: Business Modeling and Software Design. Springer (2022, to appear)
12. Kwon, O.B.: Meta web service: building web-based open decision support system based on web services. Expert Syst. Appl. **24**(4), 375–389 (2003)
13. Lohmann, N., Nyolt, M.: Artifact-centric modeling using BPMN. In: Pallis, G., Jmaiel, M., Charfi, A., Graupner, S., Karabulut, Y., Guinea, S., Rosenberg, F., Sheng, Q.Z., Pautasso, C., Ben Mokhtar, S. (eds.) ICSOC 2011. LNCS, vol. 7221, pp. 54–65. Springer, Heidelberg (2012). https://doi.org/10.1007/978-3-642-31875-7_7
14. Mack, O., Khare, A.: Perspectives on a VUCA world. In: Mack, O., Khare, A., Krämer, A., Burgartz, T. (eds.) Managing in a VUCA World, pp. 3–19. Springer, Cham (2016). https://doi.org/10.1007/978-3-319-16889-0_1
15. Martin, D., et al.: OWL-S: semantic markup for web services. W3C Member Submission (2004). https://www.w3.org/Submission/2004/SUBM-OWL-S-20041122/
16. Mustafin, N., Kopylov, P., Ponomarev, A.: Knowledge-based automated service composition for decision support systems configuration. In: Silhavy, R., Silhavy, P., Prokopova, Z. (eds.) CoMeSySo 2021. LNNS, vol. 231, pp. 780–788. Springer, Cham (2021). https://doi.org/10.1007/978-3-030-90321-3_63
17. Object Management Group: Business process model and notation (2014). https://www.omg.org/spec/BPMN/. Accessed 21 June 2022
18. Savić, D.A., Bicik, J., Morley, M.S.: A DSS generator for multiobjective optimisation of spreadsheet-based models. Environ. Modell. Softw. **26**(5), 551–561 (2011)
19. Stănescu, I.A., Ştefan, A., Filip, F.G.: Cloud-based decision support ecosystem for renewable energy providers. In: Camarinha-Matos, L.M., Baldissera, T.A., Di Orio, G., Marques, F. (eds.) DoCEIS 2015. IAICT, vol. 450, pp. 405–412. Springer, Cham (2015). https://doi.org/10.1007/978-3-319-16766-4_43
20. Stiehl, V.: Definition of process-driven applications. In: Process-Driven Applications with BPMN, pp. 13–41. Springer, Cham (2014). https://doi.org/10.1007/978-3-319-07218-0_2
21. Weskamp, C., Koberstein, A., Schwartz, F., Suhl, L., Voß, S.: A two-stage stochastic programming approach for identifying optimal postponement strategies in supply chains with uncertain demand. Omega **83**, 123–138 (2019)
22. Zhang, C., Zhao, T., Li, W.: The framework of a geospatial semantic web-based spatial decision support system for digital earth. Int. J. Digit. Earth **3**(2), 111–134 (2010)

Towards Collaborative Vision Video Production: How to Integrate Different Stakeholders

Lukas Nagel[1]([⊠])[iD], Jil Klünder[1][iD], Christoph Hausmann[2],
and Kurt Schneider[1][iD]

[1] Software Engineering Group, Leibniz Universität Hannover, Hanover, Germany
{lukas.nagel,jil.kluender,kurt.schneider}@inf.uni-hannover.de
[2] Leibniz Universität Hannover, Hanover, Germany

Abstract. Differing mental models of stakeholders can lead to conflicting requirements which can threaten the success of the software project if they are not resolved. Therefore, producing a shared understanding of the project vision among stakeholders is crucial. Vision videos are one possible method to produce such a shared understanding by allowing stakeholders to identify and resolve discrepancies between their mental models. However, stakeholders often mistakenly expect a high effort being required for the production of vision videos and therefore refrain from using them. In this paper we present concepts that are designed to aid stakeholders in a collaborative production of vision videos by enabling them to produce vision videos using their personal smartphones. The concepts reduce an individual stakeholder's workload by distributing the necessary tasks amongst all relevant stakeholders.

Preliminary sessions of an experiment comparing a prototype of our concepts with existing methods have resulted in the discovery of promising tendencies. Participants using the prototype were only required to actively work on the vision video for little over half the time. We expect these tendencies to be strengthened by further experiment sessions. Nevertheless, our results indicate that the concepts presented in this paper are a meaningful step towards a collaborative vision video production.

Keywords: Requirements engineering · Vision video · Collaboration

1 Introduction

Eliciting correct and comprehensive requirements is an important part of the requirements engineering process [15]. However, gathering incorrect or qualitatively insufficient requirements is one of the main reasons for a software project's failure [6]. The elicitation process is made even more difficult by the existence

R. Bernhaupt et al. (Eds.): HCSE 2022, LNCS 13482, pp. 163–176, 2022.
https://doi.org/10.1007/978-3-031-14785-2_11

of differing mental models of stakeholders, which can lead to conflicting requirements [13]. Therefore, the mental models of stakeholders must be aligned by producing a shared understanding [5]. One way to produce such a shared understanding is the use of so-called vision videos that present concrete visions of a system's functionality [10,17,20]. Once they are produced, these videos present an effective way to detect and resolve discrepancies in mental models [10].

Problem Statement. The common use of vision videos is inhibited by stakeholders' missing knowledge regarding their production [7]. Gaining such knowledge requires an effort that is seen as too costly. While research on vision videos has resulted in the "Affordable Video Approach" [17], missing knowledge might still lead to the assumption of a costly production effort [7]. Therefore, vision videos are seldomly used. Additionally, the specific research field of a collaborative production of videos with stakeholders that are dispersed among different countries has not been discussed in existing literature.

Objective. The concepts described in this paper look to fill this research gap by enabling the use of personal smartphones for contributions to vision videos. This allows a diverse spectrum of stakeholders to participate in the production process. The concepts also attempt to reduce the workload of the individual by distributing and parallelizing the workload among the participating stakeholders. Thereby, we look to enable a more widespread production and use of vision videos. We also seek to minimize the barrier of entry that stakeholders face when starting to produce vision videos. Therefore, the cognitive load that users experience while working with our concepts should be kept to a minimum [19]. Ideally, users only need a short time to get used to their work with the concepts and are able to focus their mental effort on the vision video production.

Contribution. In this paper, we present concepts that are designed to fulfill these criteria. The concepts are demonstrated with screenshots from a prototypical smartphone application. This prototype is also used to evaluate the concepts in two preliminary experiment sessions. Over the course of these sessions, two simulated workshops were conducted in which vision videos were produced collaboratively. One group used the prototype to produce their vision video, while the other utilized a preinstalled video editing application on their computers. The results of these sessions present promising tendencies regarding the value of a collaborative production of vision videos. We expect that further experiment sessions will validate some of these tendencies and reveal statistically significant evidence for the positive impact of our concepts. Such evidence would prove that the concepts can majorly reduce the video production effort that is required from individual stakeholders. Thereby, vision videos should find a wider application and help more stakeholders achieve a shared understanding.

Outline. The rest of the paper is structured as follows: Section 2 discusses other work that is related to this paper. We present our own concepts in Sect. 3. An evaluation is laid out in Sect. 4 before the results of two initial experiment sessions are described in Sect. 5 and discussed in Sect. 6. Section 7 concludes the paper and provides information regarding planned future work.

2   Related Work

The idea of integrating vision videos in software projects to allow shared understanding and to facilitate requirements communication is not new. Several
authors propose the use of vision videos. For example, Creighton and Bruegge
use videos to visualize scenarios [2]. Xu et al. [22] introduce the idea of *Evolutionary Scenario Based Design* in which parts of the software system, that are
not yet implemented, are presented as a video recording in order to be always
able to present the system as a whole (despite missing functionalities).

However, despite the frequent proposals to use (vision) videos in software
projects, the production of the like is only partially covered by researchers. In
order to support the collection of information in workshops, Karras et al. [8]
developed ReqViDa which allows to annotate and, thus, structure a workshop
video. Quality aspects that should be considered when producing a vision video
have been subject to Karras et al.'s work [10] in which they present a quality
model for vision videos. According to the affordable video approach [17], vision
videos can to be produced at low cost and effort.

To support the production of vision videos, Karras et al. [11] present an
approach of producing videos from digital prototyping. A walk-through of these
digital prototypes, can be recorded as a demonstration of interaction sequences.

Leaving the step of the production behind, there is some research focusing
the joint viewing of vision videos [12]. The authors compare synchronous and
asynchronous viewing of vision videos in online settings and point to advantages
and disadvantages of both settings – depending on the context.

In contrast to these existing papers, our approach focuses on the collaborative
production of vision videos in order to reduce the effort for a single producer.

3   Concepts

Our concepts are based on the idea of using smartphones for the production of
vision videos. According to the most recent Ericsson Mobility Report[1], 6.3 billion
smartphone subscriptions were active in 2021. Smartphones are therefore likely
to be owned by most relevant stakeholders. Most smartphones include cameras
capable of recording videos [17].

Karras et al. [10] define the phases for a successful production of vision videos
as *preproduction, shooting and postproduction*. Our concepts are designed to
support stakeholders during all three phases:

3.1   Concepts Supporting the Preproduction Phase

In the *preproduction* phase, the vision video is planned [10]. Among other aspects,
the story, single scenes and relevant contents of the video are defined [10]. We
look to support stakeholders with their preproduction efforts by enforcing the

---

[1] https://www.ericsson.com/en/reports-and-papers/mobility-report.

definition of initial scenes to be the first step of any new vision video production project. Scenes are defined by simply naming them. Our approach ensures that stakeholders begin their process by thinking about what to portray in the video in a broader sense. Figure 1 presents an example of what a prototype implementing this concept could look like.

Fig. 1. Initial definition of scenes.

Fig. 2. Template selection screen.

Envisioning the individual steps of a vision video can be a daunting task, especially when there is no prior experience with vision videos. Similar to Bartindale et al.'s work [1], we propose offering templates as is visible at the bottom of Fig. 1. An example of these templates can be seen in Fig. 2. Our concept defines templates to have a name (1) and a short description (2). The main purpose of templates, however, is providing a predefined number of scenes that ease the initial creation of the vision video's structure. Scenes are defined by name and length and can also include preexisting media (3). Templates can only be created by experienced vision video producers. One example for a template could be a set of scenes representing elements that every vision video should include like a problem statement, a solution and a presentation of how the solution improves the state-of-the-art [9].

Another part of our concepts is an overview of the defined scenes. An example of this idea is visualized in Fig. 3. An overview realizing our concepts consists of a timeline (1) and more information (2) regarding a selected element.

The timeline of our overview concept presents the different scenes, their length in seconds and thumbnails that give a visual clue for their content. In

Fig. 3. Overview screen.   **Fig. 4.** "Editor-View".

order to keep the timeline's elements at a recognizable size, not all elements should be visible at the same time. This design also lessens the likelihood of users being overwhelmed by a large number of objects. We propose the use of finger gestures like the scrolling that is implemented in Google's Play Store[2].

Furthermore, our overview concept presents more detailed information like the name of the selected scene and an interactive video player. It also displays the current length of the full video, as well as the maximum length according to guidelines defined by Karras and Schneider [9].

3.2 Concepts Supporting the Shooting Phase

The *shooting* phase consists of the recording of the vision video's scenes [10]. To support stakeholders during this phase we conceptualized an "Editor-View" that clearly divides the overview from the availability of editing options. This requires less elements on screen at the same time and lowers the cognitive load experienced by users [18]. Figure 4 presents an example of what this view could look like. Our concept of the "Editor-View" includes an option to change the name of the scene (1) and the same information that is available in the overview (2). Most importantly, options for changes to the scene (3) are available in this view, including a "change media" option that enables the shooting of new video clips. This "change media" option should adhere to Rupp et al.'s [16] findings by also enabling the import of existing media files.

---

[2] https://play.google.com/store.

Another aspect is the automatic application of guidelines during the shooting process. We make use of the vision video guidelines by Karras and Schneider [9]. This automatic application is included to increase the quality of the produced vision video while requiring less prior knowledge from stakeholders. For example, we require video clips to be recorded in the landscape ratio format with an aspect ratio of 16:9 and in resolutions of 720p or 1080p.

3.3   Concepts Supporting the Postproduction Phase

A finalization of the vision video takes place in the *postproduction* phase [10]. Our concept of an "Editor-View" also offers options for an edit of the recorded video clips. Clips can be trimmed to keep within time constraints defined by Karras and Schneider's guidelines [9]. Other editing functionality from work by Rupp et al. [16] like the annotation video clips with texts should also be included.

For a collaborative production of vision videos, our concepts allow a marking of scenes as finished. Finished scenes are indicated as such on the overview. Users can focus on other scenes when contributing to the vision video.

During the *postproduction*, our concepts also include a preview of the current video. This preview plays all recorded video clips as defined during the *preproduction* phase. It also offers a way of watching scenes individually to enable stakeholders to discuss any scene-specific questions.

The final concept relevant to the *postproduction* phase is an automatic joining of the produced scenes to a full vision video without any further user input. The edit can be performed simultaneously to the export of the video due to the planning during the *preproduction*. This export can therefore happen in the background while stakeholders shift their attention to other tasks or take a break.

3.4   Concepts Supporting All Phases

According to Ellis et al. [3] coordination is necessary, since its absence makes a collaborative work more difficult and enables conflicts to arise. Conflicts that arise in asynchronous environments are harder to resolve than when working synchronously, as it is harder to find suitable times to hold meetings. To enable stakeholders to achieve a "good-enough" coordination in asynchronous settings, we propose an issue system similar to the one used in github[3]. Tasks can be created and assigned to scenes and individual members of the vision video project. They consist of a title, a status like "to do" or "in progress" and comments that can be added by team members. These comments support stakeholders in their reflection of the vision and can lead to the creation of explicit knowledge [4]. A summary of all issues and their current statuses in a Kanban-Board enables project members to coordinate with their peers and to gain an overview of their progress. Additionally, users should be provided with a summary of any issues and scenes that are currently assigned to them.

---

[3] https://github.com/features/issues.

4   Evaluation

To evaluate the concepts described in this paper we designed an evaluation that simulated an application of the concepts in a workshop scenario. This evaluation has thus far been conducted in two small preliminary sessions. The main goal of the evaluation is to answer our research question of *can a collaborative android application support stakeholders in their production of vision videos?*.

4.1   Material

During the experiment, BigBlueButton[4] was used to communicate with the participants and the experimenter moderating the session. A document was prepared that contained an outline of the vision that participants were asked to visualize in a vision video. The vision concerned a smart file cabinet that supported users with storing and finding of documents. The experimental group of participants were asked to install a prototypical implementation of our concepts presented on their personal smartphones. The control group made use of Nextcloud[5] to share their video files and the "Video Editor" application that was built into their windows installation. No new software needed to be installed. Lastly, an online questionnaire was handed out. This questionnaire included questions regarding the demographics of participants and inquired about their experience in the study, all of which were answered on 5-point Likert scales. Test subjects were asked to provide comments on positive or negative aspects that they encountered. Additionally, the questionnaire also asked them to give a self-report on their cognitive load on the 9-point Paas-Scale [14].

4.2   Population

Suitable participants for this experiment are all potential stakeholders for software projects who own a smartphone. They are not required to fill any specific stakeholder role since vision videos are used to create a shared understanding among all stakeholders. Any prior knowledge regarding requirements engineering processes is also not needed as our concepts are designed to support stakeholders who are new to the production of vision videos.

Thus far, eight test subjects have taken part in the study. Two of them were female, six identified as male. All but one participant indicated that they have some background in computer science. The participants were split into two groups of four, one of which – the experimental group – used the prototype implementing our concepts, while the other – the control group – made use of tools that were already installed on their desktop computers.

---

[4] https://bigbluebutton.org/.
[5] https://nextcloud.com/.

4.3 Experiment Procedure

At the beginning of an experiment session an experimenter, who also took part in the workshop as the role of a moderator, gave a quick introduction regarding the goal of the evaluation and to the concept of vision videos. Then, participants were asked to give information regarding their demographic data in a questionnaire, before both groups were allowed to familiarize themselves with the tools that they were supposed to use over the course of the session. This familiarization lasted a total of five minutes for both groups.

As a next step, the task that participants worked on in the study was handed out. Participants started by starting to plan their vision video. This consisted of the initial planning of scenes. The experimenter posing as a moderator of the simulated workshop provided advice regarding the structure of the video and the content of the scenes to ensure that the results of both groups were comparable.

A stopwatch was started once all scenes were defined by the participants and the shooting phase began. Both groups shot their video media using their smartphones. Members of the experimental group were able to directly add the recorded media to the scenes within the prototype. Members of the control group had to upload their files to the Nextcloud. The stopwatch was stopped for the experimental group as soon as all scenes had been filmed and the automatic export had been started. For the control group, the stopwatch was paused once all scenes were shot and uploaded to the cloud. The time measurement was then resumed for the time required to edit the final video. This meant that times for both the *shooting* and the *postproduction* phases were measured. This second measurement was not applicable to the experimental group as the final edit of the vision video was performed during the export. Edits of individual scenes were performed by stakeholders before the upload to the cloud.

To edit the final video of the control group, a single participant that had some prior experience working with the "Video Editor" application downloaded all media files produced by the group. In a continuous exchange with the remaining participants of the control group, the final vision video was edited. Once all test subjects were satisfied, the experimenter stopped the stopwatch.

Lastly, the experimenter measured the time that was required for the final export of the vision videos. Simultaneously, participants were asked to answer the rest of the questionnaire which consisted of questions regarding their experience over the course of the experiment.

5 Results

The preliminary study sessions conducted thus far have yielded some interesting results regarding the effort that is required to produce vision videos using existing methods or using the concepts laid out in this paper.

The times that were measured by the experimenter presented a number of differences between the vision video production processes of the two groups. The control group spent 27 min and 29 s filming their scenes. They then edited the video files for 18 min and 50 s before starting an export of the finalized video that took 18 s. In total, the control group took 46 min and 37 s to produce a vision video. The group using the prototypical implementation of our concepts took 23 min and 47 s to shoot their scenes and perform initial edits on the individual scenes using the "Editor-View". The export of the final video that included the automatic addition of transitions between scenes took 12 min and 28 s. In total, the experimental group took 36 min and 15 s to produce their vision video after the *preproduction* phase was finished. An important result to recognize is that there is a large difference in the time that stakeholders were required to actively work on the vision video production project. While the control group spent 27 min and 29 s shooting their scenes and an additional 18 min and 50 s editing the video, the majority of the editing tasks were performed automatically in the prototype used by the experimental group. Members of the control group had to be active for a total of 46 min and 37 s. In contrast, the experimental group only took 23 min and 47 s to shoot and edit their scenes before being able to take a break while the prototype exported the video. An overview of the measured times including differences in percentages can be found in Table 1.

Table 1. Time measurements in MM:SS.

	Shooting	Editing	Export	Total	Active time
Control group	27:29	18:50	00:18	46:37	46:19
Change	−13.5%	−100%	+4,155%	−22.2%	−48.7%
Experimental group	23:47	00:00	12:28	36:15	23:47

One aspect of the questionnaire was the subjective effort required to operate the tools. This question was answered on a 5-point Likert scale with the values of 1 and 5 indicating a very low and a very high effort respectively. The four participants of both two groups answered with the same values, namely 2, 2, 3 and 3. Therefore, the data obtained in the preliminary sessions of our study did not present any differences regarding the effort required to operate the tools.

Another part of the questionnaire asked test subjects to report on the effort that they experienced while distributing the resources produced during the session. Once again a 5-point Likert scale was used to answer this question. In line with the previous question, values of 1 and 5 indicate a very low effort and very high effort. Participants of the control group answered with values of 2, 3, 3 and 4. Members of the experimental group indicated the values 1, 2, 2 and 2. The results of a Mann-Whitney U test indicated that the difference is not statistically significant ($U = 3$, $p = 0{,}19 > 0{,}05$).

The questionnaire also included a question regarding the subjectively rated quality of the produced vision video. This question was answered using a 5-point Likert scale. Values of 1 and 5 represented a very low or very high quality of the produced vision video. The control group answered this question with values of 3, 3, 3 and 4. Slightly higher values were indicated by the experimental group with ratings of 3, 4, 4 and 4. The Mann-Whitney U test revealed that this difference is not statistically significant (U = 3, p = 0,19 > 0,05).

The final aspect of the questionnaire was the cognitive load measured on the Paas scale [14]. This scale ranges from values of 1 indicating a very low mental effort that is for example experienced when riding a bike, to very high mental effort that would for example be experienced when taking an exam. The control group responded with values of 3, 4, 4 and 6. Slightly lower values of 3, 3, 4 and 5 were reported by the experimental group. The Mann-Whitney U test did not find a statistically significant difference (U = 6, p = 0,56 > 0,05).

Lastly, the test subjects were asked to give positive and negative comments. Three participants of the experimental group expressed that the user interface of the prototype was easy to use. Additionally, one participant expressed that a tutorial was missing in the prototype. A tutorial could further reduce the effort experienced while operating the tool.

6   Discussion

The results of our evaluation offer some insights regarding our research question of *can a collaborative android application support stakeholders in their production of vision videos?*. Further evaluation sessions are still required to validate the tendencies that could be observed in our data. However, these tendencies offer some preliminary information regarding the impact of our concepts.

One of the main findings of the preliminary experiment sessions were the times taken by the groups to finish their videos. Participants using the concepts described in this paper were able to finish the *shooting* and *postproduction* phases of their video production in 10 min and 22 s less than the control group. An even larger difference could be found in the active working times. The experimental group needed to be active for 22 min and 50 s less than the control group. Therefore, a smaller time commitment is required from stakeholders who use our concepts. The main reason for this advantage of our concepts is the absence of a dedicated editing step. A large part of the editing is performed automatically. However, further evaluations with further groups of potential stakeholders and other visions are required to validate this finding.

Two questions of the questionnaire asked the participants of the experiment about the subjective effort that they perceived during the simulated workshops. Regarding the effort of operating the tools, both groups indicated the exact same values and that they did not perceive a high or very high required effort. Test subjects were able to focus most of their mental effort on the task of producing a vision video despite working with unfamiliar tools. The results therefore indicate that the concepts were sufficiently easy to use. In contrast, a difference was found in the answers regarding the effort required to share the produced resources. Participants working with the prototype indicated that they perceived a smaller amount of effort than their peers working preexisting methods. While the difference is not statistically significant, the results present an initial indication that the prototype helped the participants distribute their resources. We expect to find statistically significant results once the sample size is increased.

The results also show a slight difference in the subjectively rated quality of the produced vision videos that is not statistically significant. However, no participant indicated a low quality of the produced videos. Both groups were able to produce vision videos that the participants were satisfied with.

The final aspect of the questionnaire regarded the cognitive load as indicated on the Paas scale [14]. We found no statistically significant difference. A slight tendency is evident indicating that participants using the concepts perceived a slightly lower cognitive load. Additionally, the highest value indicated by a participant of the experimental group was a 5, indicating a cognitive load of medium strength. This means that no participant was overwhelmed by the prototype.

The results of the two preliminary sessions have not revealed any statistically significant results. However, some promising tendencies are visible. These tendencies could theoretically be caused by statistical noise, but might also be reinforced with an increase of the sample size. Based on the positive comments made by participants of the experimental group, we expect the results of further experiment sessions to confirm the tendencies found thus far.

All in all, we believe that the concepts are a promising start regarding our research question of *can a collaborative android application support stakeholders in their production of vision videos?*. The concepts laid out in this paper are a meaningful step towards a collaborative android app that can support stakeholders in their production of vision videos.

6.1   Threats to Validity

The results of our study are subject to some threats that limit their validity. We discuss these threats to validity according to Wohlin et al. [21].

Conclusion Validity. The main threat to validity is the missing statistical significance of our results. Analyzing the data descriptively points to some tendencies that are not supported by the quantitative analysis. This missing significance of the results can be due to the small sample size. Future studies are required to strengthen our results. The small sample size increases the risk of outliers having a strong influence. However, the collected data was rather stringent than diverse which is why we do not expect any influence of outliers. Our conclusions emerge from a preliminary study and must not be overinterpreted. We plan to conduct further studies with a more diverse group of participants and with a larger sample size.

Internal Validity. Our study and data analysis was mainly conducted by a single person. This introduces the risk of misinterpretations and systematic errors. However, each step of the experiment was reviewed by two other researchers.

Construct Validity. The main threat to the construct validity is the strong focus of the experiment on the video production. Consequently, we did not consider other aspects of the collaboration such as the task system.

In addition, due to the Covid19-pandemic, we conducted the experiment remotely. This introduced different threats: Each participant conducted the tasks with their own devices and at different locations. This influenced for example the time required to download, upload or export a video. However, we did not observe such an influence and expect similar hardware as most participants (computer scientists) use them for gaming, software development, and similar purposes. Besides the used hardware, other random irrelevancies could also have influenced the results. The remote setting introduced the risk of background noise (the risk of a ringing door or incoming phone calls). Nevertheless, we do not expect a huge influence of this threat, as we did not observe any of these aspects during the experiment.

External Validity. As typical for experiments, the participants knew that they participated in an artificial setting. An evaluation of our approach in a real project is required in order to prove its usefulness and applicability in practice.

6.2   Future Work

The threats to validity of our results show the need for further research efforts, especially the continuation of the experiment. We plan on performing a comprehensive user study with a much larger amount of participants. A concrete idea is to make use of a large scale software project course taken by university students. The production of vision videos is a vital part of the course. We plan an application of the evaluation defined in this paper by splitting the software project teams into two sets. One set of groups will be asked to work with the prototype used for the experiments of this paper, while the other uses the same existing methods as the control group. We hope to find more evidence for the tendencies found in the two preliminary sessions in this comprehensive study.

Additionally, the presented concepts require an evaluation in more asynchronous scenarios. Our concepts have only been tested with a simulated workshop. Their applicability for asynchronous scenarios still needs to be evaluated.

7   Conclusion

In this paper, we have described concepts that enable stakeholders to produce vision videos collaboratively using their personal smartphones. We look to reduce the effort that is required for the production of vision videos from each participating stakeholder. The concepts were implemented in a prototype which in turn was used to test their impact in a user study. Thus far, two preliminary sessions of the experiment have been completed. Their results provide initial insights into the differences between a prototype implementing the presented concepts and existing methods. While the results do not present any statistically significant results, a number of tendencies could be observed indicating the value of the described concepts. For example, participants of the experimental group were working actively for only a little over half the time that was required of the control group. This reduction of effort did not lead to a lower satisfaction with the resulting vision videos' quality. While further evaluation efforts are required to validate these tendencies, our results are a promising start.

Acknowledgment. This work was supported by the German Research Foundation (DFG) (project *ViViUse*, grant No. *289386339*).

References

1. Bartindale, T., Schofield, G., Wright, P.: Scaffolding community documentary film making using commissioning templates. In: Proceedings of the 2016 CHI Conference on Human Factors in Computing Systems, pp. 2705–2716 (2016)
2. Creighton, O., Ott, M., Bruegge, B.: Software cinema-video-based requirements engineering. In: 14th IEEE International Requirements Engineering Conference (RE 2006), pp. 109–118. IEEE (2006)
3. Ellis, C.A., Gibbs, S.J., Rein, G.: Groupware: some issues and experiences. Commun. ACM **34**(1), 39–58 (1991)
4. Fayard, A.L., Metiu, A.: The role of writing in distributed collaboration. Organ. Sci. **25**(5), 1391–1413 (2014)
5. Glinz, M., Fricker, S.A.: On shared understanding in software engineering: an essay. Comput. Sci. Res. Dev., 363–376 (2014). https://doi.org/10.1007/s00450-014-0256-x
6. Hussain, A., Mkpojiogu, E.O.: Requirements: towards an understanding on why software projects fail. In: AIP Conference Proceedings, vol. 1761, p. 020046. AIP Publishing LLC (2016)
7. Karras, O.: Software professionals' attitudes towards video as a medium in requirements engineering. In: Kuhrmann, M., et al. (eds.) PROFES 2018. LNCS, vol. 11271, pp. 150–158. Springer, Cham (2018). https://doi.org/10.1007/978-3-030-03673-7_11
8. Karras, O., Kiesling, S., Schneider, K.: Supporting requirements elicitation by tool-supported video analysis. In: 2016 IEEE 24th International Requirements Engineering Conference (RE), pp. 146–155. IEEE (2016)
9. Karras, O., Schneider, K.: An interdisciplinary guideline for the production of videos and vision videos by software professionals. Technical report. arXiv:2001.06675 (2020)
10. Karras, O., Schneider, K., Fricker, S.A.: Representing software project vision by means of video: a quality model for vision videos. J. Syst. Softw. **162**, 110479 (2020)
11. Karras, O., Unger-Windeler, C., Glauer, L., Schneider, K.: Video as a by-product of digital prototyping: capturing the dynamic aspect of interaction. In: 2017 IEEE 25th International Requirements Engineering Conference Workshops (REW), pp. 118–124. IEEE (2017)
12. Nagel, L., Shi, J., Busch, M.: Viewing vision videos online: opportunities for distributed stakeholders. In: 2021 IEEE 29th International Requirements Engineering Conference Workshops (REW), pp. 306–312. IEEE (2021)
13. Norman, D.A.: The Design of Everyday Things. Basic Books Inc., New York (2002)
14. Paas, F.G.: Training strategies for attaining transfer of problem-solving skill in statistics: a cognitive-load approach. J. Educ. Psychol. **84**(4), 429 (1992)

15. Pohl, K.: Requirements Engineering: Fundamentals, Principles, and Techniques. Springer, Heidelberg (2010)
16. Rupp, C., et al.: Requirements-Engineering und -Management: Das Handbuch für Anforderungen in jeder Situation. Carl Hanser Verlag GmbH Co KG (2020)
17. Schneider, K., Busch, M., Karras, O., Schrapel, M., Rohs, M.: Refining vision videos. In: Knauss, E., Goedicke, M. (eds.) REFSQ 2019. LNCS, vol. 11412, pp. 135–150. Springer, Cham (2019). https://doi.org/10.1007/978-3-030-15538-4_10
18. Shneiderman, B.: The eyes have it: a task by data type taxonomy for information visualizations. In: The Craft of Information Visualization, pp. 364–371. Elsevier (2003)
19. Sweller, J., Ayres, P., Kalyuga, S.: Measuring cognitive load. In: Cognitive Load Theory, vol. 1, pp. 71–85. Springer, New York (2011). https://doi.org/10.1007/978-1-4419-8126-4_6
20. Vistisen, P., Poulsen, S.B.: Return of the vision video: can corporate vision videos serve as setting for participation? Nordes **7**(1) (2017)
21. Wohlin, C., Runeson, P., Höst, M., Ohlsson, M.C., Regnell, B., Wesslén, A.: Experimentation in Software Engineering. Springer, Heidelberg (2012). https://doi.org/10.1007/978-3-642-29044-2
22. Xu, H., Creighton, O., Boulila, N., Bruegge, B.: From pixels to bytes: evolutionary scenario based design with video. In: Proceedings of the ACM SIGSOFT 20th International Symposium on the Foundations of Software Engineering, pp. 1–4 (2012)

Posters and Demos

Development of a Conversational Dietary Assessment Tool for Cardiovascular Patients

Yunjie Liu(✉) ⓘ, W. F. Goevaerts, Max V. Birk, Hareld Kemps, and Yuan Lu

Department of Industrial Design, Eindhoven University of Technology,
PO Box 513, 5600 MB Eindhoven, The Netherlands
{y.liu12,w.f.goevaerts,m.v.birk,h.m.c.kemps,y.lu}@tue.nl

Abstract. Cardiovascular diseases (CVDs) are currently the leading cause of death worldwide. Accumulated evidence indicates that a healthy diet contributes significantly to health promotion and an increase in quality of life for those living with CVDs. While dietary intake management plays an integral part in cardiac rehabilitation (CR), tracking dietary intake is burdensome, resulting in measurement errors caused by the burden of manual food logging, low adherence, incomplete data, or erroneous information.

In this paper, we present a chatbot, as a conversational dietary assessment tool to help users capture their dietary intake and provide feedback to support users in understanding their dietary choices. With this chatbot, we conducted a preliminary evaluation study with 9 experts specializing in the field of CR programs or dietary behavior management, who were asked to use the chatbot to self-report their dietary intake for one week. The results show that the chatbot is easy to interact with and experts praised its simplicity and flexibility. Besides, the chatbot has shown the potential to contribute to dietary intake management.

Keywords: Chatbot · Conversational dietary assessment tool · Cardiovascular patients · Cardiac rehabilitation · Dietary behavior management

1 Introduction

Cardiovascular diseases (CVDs) are currently the major cause of morbidity and the leading cause of death worldwide [1]. With studies showing that 80% of CVDs can be preventable by obtaining a healthy lifestyle [2], medical experts created a multidisciplinary cardiac rehabilitation (CR) program as a standard outpatient treatment, in which patients will be treated for up to 12 weeks depending on their risk profiles and personal needs [3, 4]. This program has proven to be cost-effective [5, 6] and has a positive impact on reducing the recurrence and risk of cardiovascular diseases [7].

Accumulated evidence indicates that a healthy diet contributes significantly to health promotion and reducing cardiovascular risk factors [8]. Dietary interventions have been recommended to be included in the CR program, which incorporate dietary education and healthy dietary guidance [9]. Studies prove that self-reporting can raise self-awareness and facilitate dietary intake self-management [10]. Meanwhile, dietary assessment is

© IFIP International Federation for Information Processing 2022
Published by Springer Nature Switzerland AG 2022
R. Bernhaupt et al. (Eds.): HCSE 2022, LNCS 13482, pp. 179–190, 2022.
https://doi.org/10.1007/978-3-031-14785-2_12

important for health professionals to assess patients' dietary behavior [11] and deliver personalized dietary interventions. However, despite the proven benefits, the referral rate to dieticians remains low [12, 13]. It's believed to be caused by the program capacity and the fact that providing personalized dietary advice is cost and labor intensive [12, 14]. Digital interventions, with the implementation of mHealth and eHealth technologies [15], offer great potential to deliver cost-effective dietary interventions by enabling dietary intake self-tracking and providing personalized advice [16].

Traditional dietary assessment tools, such as the 24-h Dietary Recall (24 h) or the Food Frequency Questionnaire (FFQ), are the most commonly used methods of recall [17]. Nevertheless, the workload related to these methods results in measurement errors caused by high labor of manual food logging, low adherence, incomplete data, or erroneous information. To address the aforementioned issues, conversational agents, i.e., chatbots, promise to improve the self-tracking experience by increasing flexibility and reliability of dietary intake reports [18], as well as alleviating the burden of manual input [19] and promoting self-reflection on dietary behavior [20, 21].

In this paper, we proposed a chatbot-based conversational dietary assessment tool to facilitate food logging and provide real-time feedback for self-reflection. The chatbot is an internet-based service that runs on a web-based/mobile-based platform. With the pre-determined recall schedule, it can proactively initiate inquiries about dietary intake in the form of a dialogue. With the chatbot, we conducted a preliminary evaluation study with 9 experts specializing in cardiac rehabilitation or dietary behavior management. The results are promising and experts praised its simplicity and flexibility. They rated its positive impact on promoting healthy dietary behavior through the chatbot by delivering nutrition education and bridging the cognitive gap between how patients perceive their dietary habits and their actual habitual intake.

2   Related Work

2.1   Food Tracking

Evidence indicates that self-tracking could raise the awareness of food consumption behaviors [22] and nudge individuals to adopt a healthier eating habit [23, 24]. Self-reported methods of recall and real-time recording are developed for dietary assessment. The food records method [25] requires real-time recording, whereas the recall methods highly depend on individuals' memory. The 24-h Dietary Recall (24 h) method [26] tracks actual dietary intake within the previous 24-h period, while the Food Frequency Questionnaire (FFQ) [27] attempts to capture the habitual intake by querying the consumption frequency of food items based on a predefined food list.

However, tracking detailed dietary intake manually can be time-consuming and burdensome, which leads to underreporting and low adherence. Besides, the workload is high for the dieticians to assess the dietary behavior. In recent years, the development of technology-based interventions has aimed at reducing the burden of food tracking and increasing the accuracy of self-reporting. In particular, the proliferation of smartphones has made the implementation of mobile-based food tracking applications popular among nutrition researchers, designers and commercial application developers. Online dietary assessment tools such as INTAKE24 [28] and ASA24 [29] claimed to offer a convenient and low-cost alternative to traditional dietary assessment methods. However, the dependence on the users' memory remains high and research shows that users are frustrated by high labor of manual data entry [30]. Prior HCI studies have focused on addressing these issues [30–32], by increasing the frequency of dietary intake logging, as well as developing an extensive food database [30] and a variety of input methods, such as food scanners [33], photography recognition [34–36], and natural language processing [37]. At the same time, the particular food intake related to nutritional risk factors for cardiovascular patients (e.g., salt, fatty acids, sugar) should be carefully assessed, as the consumption of which would be related to hypertension, high cholesterol, obesity and diabetes.

2.2 Chatbots

A chatbot is a computer program designed to stimulate conversation with users, which converses through text or voice, while understanding and responding like a smart entity [38]. With the fast-growing popularity of chatbot development, an increasing number of studies in the field of interaction design emerged, investigating the potential of applying this natural-language-based technology [39].

Within the health-related domain, many recent applications have demonstrated chatbots as an effective way to get users engaged in their own health management and promote their healthy wellbeing. Chatbots have been integrated and researched in various areas, such as providing information regarding cancer [40], monitoring sleep patterns [19], enabling asthma self-management [41], promoting smoking cessation [42, 43] and weight loss [44], as well as mental health and phycological wellbeing [45]. The evaluation revealed that chatbots have several advantages in proactively triggering users for self-monitoring in a form of a dialogue [20], as well as promoting the users' self-care and self-reflection regarding the dialogue content [18, 21]. Participants argued that the chatbot can be a good listener without the feeling of being judged [46]. In addition, a literature review conducted by Vaidyam et al. [47] revealed the potential benefits of chatbots in health-related self-education and higher adherence to lifestyle changes.

Moreover, there are a growing number of studies design chatbots to track food consumption and promote healthy eating behavior. Fadhil & Gabrielli [48] proposed a chatbot system to promote the long-term adherence to the healthy dietary behavior change by delivering support to nutrition education. Prasetyo [49] presented the Foodbot which delivers the goal-oriented healthy eating interventions via notification prompts and personalized recommendations. Besides, Casas et al. [50] presented the design of a food diary coaching chatbot, which allows users to set their goals from pre-defined options and track their goal achievements. Improved consumption was found in some participants, and they argued that self-reporting increased their awareness. Evidence shows promising contribution towards promoting healthy dietary behavior by supporting goal setting and delivering personalized dietary behavior change interventions accordingly. Few studies have focused on reducing the burden on both food composition self-logging from patients and efforts on dietary assessment for healthcare professionals.

3   Chatbot Design

We design a chatbot-based conversational dietary assessment tool to help users manage their food intake. The chatbot is built on top of the MiBida-platform [51], which enables communication and data storing, in the form of a web-based/mobile-based application. The chatbot aims at offering a flexible and reliable way of food tracking, as well as providing real-time feedback to support users in understanding and self-reflecting on their food choices. In addition, the target population of the chatbot is cardiovascular patients in the Netherlands. To ensure the chatbot could be used among this population, we firstly developed a chatbot food composition database. In this part, we will present and describe the development of its database and the chatbot design.

3.1   Food Database

We develop a chatbot food composition database to enable the dietary intake logging on a food group level, specifically investigating users' adherence to the healthy eating guidelines and facilitating the goal achievement tracking.

Food group classification is based on the Dutch Food Composition Database (NEVO) [52], in which the basic 27 food categories are used as a starting point. From there, decisions are made on the in/exclusion of each food category based on the dietary requirements and guidelines for the target group, proposed in the Dutch food-based dietary guidelines (RGV-2015) [53]. Subsequently, several groups are combined in an attempt to simplify the recording process of similar items. This results in a total of 17 food categories (see Fig. 1). Moreover, the larger food categories are further divided into 71 subgroups with a total of 132 food items to specify the actual food item consumed. In addition, to specifically investigate the intake of the target group-related nutritional risk factors (e.g., salt, fatty acids, and sugar) and associated foods added to meals, additional details regarding certain food items are required (e.g., salted/unsalted nuts, full/semi-skimmed/skimmed milk, etc.). Moreover, emojis are selected to represent the food groups, facilitating an intuitive interaction for recording.

When selecting a food item, users are simultaneously prompted to insert the corresponding portion size. To ease the portion size estimation, consumed amounts are quantified either in household measures (e.g., glasses, bowls, teaspoons, tablespoons, and serving spoons), standard portions (e.g., pieces, packages), or handfuls. The provided options are based on the portion-online database [54] which enables the portion size inputs to be converted and stored in grams to the back-end for further analysis. Meanwhile, to aid in the estimation, explanations are provided. For example, the chatbot asks how many tablespoons of butter are spread on the bread to quantify the consumed amount, while the average amount on one slice of bread is given as a reference. For complex items such as salt intake, its portion size can be estimated with certain food choices (e.g., low-salt/normal version of bread), and eating habits, i.e., using bouillon blocks while making the soup, adding salt while cooking (yes/no) and/or to the dish (yes/no). At the moment, this simple approach is good enough for general behavior monitoring since the chatbot does not currently consider precise nutritional values, e.g., calories and nutrients.

3.2   Chatbot Development

To track dietary intake and provide feedback accordingly in an intuitive and flexible manner, a chatbot-based conversational dietary assessment tool is developed and built on top of the MiBida-platform [51], programmed to facilitate communication and data storing. This chatbot offers a low-burden way for a variety of users to track their food consumption. Interactions between users and the chatbot include three modules, namely the conversation module, the goal-setting module and the reflection module.

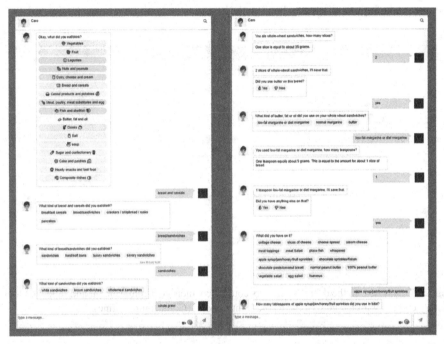

Fig. 1. Screenshots of the dialogue in the chatbot. This chatbot was named Caro by the researcher, which could be personalized by the users.

The chatbot can be used as a recall method and offers users the flexibility of pre-defining their recall schedule. To reduce the tracking burden, the chatbot asks about the food intake three times per week, including two working days and one weekend day. During the measurement day, the chatbot proactively makes dietary intake inquiries based on the tailored recall periods through push notifications. In the conversation module (see Fig. 1), we design the chatbot dialogue with a defined set of consecutively related questions to collect food intake. When initiating the chatbot, the conversation starts by asking whether the user ate or drank anything (i.e., Heb je wat gegeten/gedronken?, in English, Did you eat/drink anything?). Users can start reporting by clicking buttons to choose from different food categories, which will lead to the input inquiries from the food item level. Afterward, the chatbot asks follow-up questions regarding its type and corresponding portion size. In addition, related questions regarding the possible associated foods (e.g., spreads, sugar, fat, or salt) added on/to the reported food item are initiated accordingly. After adding each food item, the chatbot reports back to the users in the chat and checks if they need to alter their input in case of misreporting. Once recorded, the reported food intake will show in the dashboard, and users are not allowed to make further changes.

Meanwhile, to reduce the overall selection time, the chatbot allows text entry. We applied the Fuzzy Terminology Recognition, which is responsible for processing natural-language inputs. Given an input text (e.g., a consumed food item), the system infers the belonging food item groups in the food database that approximately matches users' dietary intake input and checks back with the users, reducing overall selection time.

Fig. 2. Dashboard. In the dashboard, users could view their goal achievement and reflect on their dietary choices with the help of the traffic light system. (Color figure online)

In the goal-setting module, users can set goals based on their risk profiles and personal needs. They could view their goal achievements in the dashboard and the goal-tracking period differs from the types of goals. For example, one can set a goal as eating 200 g of vegetables daily. The chatbot checks their goal achievement daily and the amount of vegetable input attributes to closing the ring by achieving the goal.

Meanwhile, in the reflection module (see Fig. 2), users can look into the real-time data regarding their dietary intake. Besides showing all the food intake inputs, we create the reflection module with the implementation of a traffic light system to help them understand and reflect on their food choices. The traffic light system is developed based on the Dutch Nutrition Guidelines [53]. The specific type of food item and the consumption amount are the main determinants when applying the color-coding labels. To be specific, the green label (e.g., vegetables, legumes) stands for healthy choices, while the red label (e.g., deep-fried snacks) suggests that users should avoid these choices which would have a negative impact on their wellbeing. The yellow label (e.g., unfiltered coffee) suggests to reduce the overall consumption amount of those food items.

Furthermore, dieticians and caregivers can access patients' dashboards and provide personalized dietary interventions accordingly, while checking the patients' compliance rate with the food consumption self-logging as requested.

4 Preliminary Study

We carried out a preliminary study to evaluate the chatbot in terms of usability and overall self-tracking experience, as well as to examine if the chatbot could be applied to enable patients' self-tracking and support dietary assessment for the dieticians. We included experts in cardiology, including cardiologists ($N = 1$) and dieticians ($N = 2$), and researchers on dietary behavior management ($N = 6$) and conducted a one-week study.

During the onboarding session, participants explored the function and the conversation flow of the chatbot by following and completing the task of self-reporting all food and beverages consumed within the previous 3 h. Afterward, in the one-week study, participants tracked their dietary intake via the chatbot, with three non-consecutive full days, including two working days and one weekend day. For each measurement day, participants received notifications for food logging three times per day and once in the morning the day after. In the end, participants joined a semi-structured interview, where we asked about their experience with the chatbot (e.g., things they like/dislike/expected about the system, potential for food tracking and aiding for dietary assessment, etc.). In addition, the list of food categories and the food items in the chatbot were shown to the participants, to discuss the possible missing food items in the chatbot.

Feedback from the experts was transcribed and coded by different themes (e.g., user experience, dietary assessment, behavior change, etc.), and further analyzed by the researcher. Overall, experts confirmed the idea that there's a need for an innovative dietary assessment tool to help the patients with food tracking and self-reflecting. In addition, by asking the patients to track their dietary intake, dieticians could assess their dietary behavior and provide personalized dietary prescriptions accordingly.

4.1 Results and Discussion

Impacts on User Engagement. The results from the expert reviews show that the chatbot is easy to interact with and experts praised its simplicity and flexibility. According to the experts, the chatbot created an intuitive conversation flow and enabled users to register their food intake simply by clicking and typing. In addition, the feature of quick-reply with predefined follow-up questions simplifies the food logging. Moreover, they rated the proactive feature of the chatbot in initializing the conversation accordingly to the users' dining schedule, could remind them to stick to their self-reporting timeline, and reduce the memory bias compared to the 24-h dietary recall.

However, they presented their concerns that it may be burdensome for the users, who have a regular recipe for a certain meal if they have to constantly repeat their data entry. For the future work of design, we will add a new function for the users to create their own recipes or regular food composition (e.g., a daily breakfast) and they only have to report the total quantity consumed.

Meanwhile, they questioned the limits of chatbot food database. To address this issue, we will include the function of reporting missing items, allowing users to register missing food items by text entry and report the portion size by choosing from measurement methods. This will be stored both in food logging and missing item categories.

Impacts on Dietary Behavior Management and Self-reflection. Experts highly rated the potential benefits of applying the chatbot to enable dietary behavior management both from the patients' perspective and the dieticians' perspective. From the patients' perspective, with the function of the dashboard and the traffic light system, the chatbot could bridge the cognitive gap between how patients perceive their dietary habits and their actual habitual intake. They pointed out that self-reporting and feedback on the dietary choices could potentially raise awareness, and may have a positive influence on promoting their self-reflection and making them mindful of their food choices.

As for the dieticians, they were positive about applying the chatbot to assess the dietary behavior of the patients, as it could aid as a reference for the personalized dietary prescription. With access to the patients' dashboard, dieticians could track their adherence to the Dutch Food Guideline and dietary interventions in general. Besides, they mentioned that, for certain cardiovascular patients, the chatbot helps them to specifically investigate the food intake related to nutritional risk factors (e.g., salt, fat, sugar, and fluid for certain patients). The goal-setting module not only promotes the patients to become more aware of their food intake, but also helps the dieticians to track and provide suggestions accordingly.

Experts highly praised the potential of the chatbot implementation and proposed that for further encouragement of dietary behavior change, personalized dietary advice can be delivered to the patients via the chatbot. However, the development of the personalized recommendations generating system and how patients react to different kinds of interventions require further research. To aid in generating personalized food recommendations, corresponding contextual inquires, e.g., food choice motives, will be added to the chatbot dialogue. This helps the system to understand users' food choice determinants and contributes to the personalized just-in-time (JIT) intervention services.

5 Conclusion and Future Work

In this paper, we presented the design of a chatbot-based conversational dietary assessment tool for cardiovascular patients in the Netherlands. This chatbot aims to help the patients track their dietary behavior, as well as understand and reflect on their food choices. Our preliminary study with the 9 experts was quite promising and has shown the potential of applying the chatbot to track the food intake of the patients and help dieticians to provide personalized dietary prescriptions.

For future work, we plan to conduct a user study within a 3-month clinal trial among cardiovascular patients presenting in the cardiac rehabilitation program. Participants will join an onboarding interview and use the chatbot to self-report their food intake for three months. Questionnaires including System Usability Scale (SUS) and Chatbot Usability Questionnaire (CUQ), as well as a semi-structured interview, will be conducted in the end for chatbot evaluation, in terms of usability, and user experience on the user interface and the conversation flow. Next, the chatbot food composition database can be enriched by enabling users to add to the missing food category. Lastly, we want to apply food choice inquiries and utilize the generation models to enable the automatic generation of personalized food recommendations.

References

1. Word Health Organization: Cardiovascular disease (CVDs), May 2017. https://www.who.int/en/news-room/fact-sheets/detail/cardiovascular-diseases-(cvds)
2. Virani, S.S., et al.: Heart disease and stroke statistics—2020 update: a report from the American Heart Association. Circulation 141(9), e139–e596 (2020)
3. Knuuti, J., et al.: 2019 ESC guidelines for the diagnosis and management of chronic coronary syndromes. Eur. Heart J., 1–71 (2019). https://doi.org/10.1093/eurheartj/ehz425
4. NVVC-CCPH, & LMDO-H: Beslisboom poliklinische indicatiestelling hartrevalidatie 2010. Kwaliteitskoepel (2010). http://www.kwaliteitskoepel.nl/assets/structured-files/OVERIG/
5. Shields, G.E., Wells, A., Doherty, P., Heagerty, A., Buck, D., Davies, L.M.: Cost effectiveness of cardiac rehabilitation: a systematic review. Heart 104(17), 1403–1410 (2018)
6. Edwards, K., et al.: The cost-effectiveness of exercise-based cardiac rehabilitation: a systematic review of the characteristics and methodological quality of published literature. Heal. Econ. Rev. 7(1), 1–23 (2017). https://doi.org/10.1186/s13561-017-0173-3
7. Rauch, B., et al.: The prognostic effect of cardiac rehabilitation in the era of acute revascularisation and statin therapy: a systematic review and meta-analysis of randomized and non-randomized studies—The Cardiac Rehabilitation Outcome Study (CROS). Eur. J. Prev. Cardiol. 23, 1914–1939 (2016). https://doi.org/10.1177/2047487316671181
8. Engelfriet, P., Hoekstra, J., Hoogenveen, R., Büchner, F., Rossum, C.V., Verschuren, M.: Food and vessels: the importance of a healthy diet to prevent cardiovascular disease. Eur. J. Cardiovasc. Prev. Rehabil. 17(1), 50–55 (2010)
9. Ambrosetti, M., et al.: Secondary prevention through comprehensive cardiovascular rehabilitation: from knowledge to implementation. 2020 update. A position paper from the Secondary Prevention and Rehabilitation Section of the European Association of Preventive Cardiology. Eur. J. Prev. Cardiol. 28(5), 460–495 (2021)
10. du Pon, E., Kleefstra, N., Cleveringa, F., van Dooren, A., Heerdink, E.R., van Dulmen, S.: Effects of the proactive interdisciplinary self-management (PRISMA) program on self-reported and clinical outcomes in type 2 diabetes: a pragmatic randomized controlled trial. BMC Endocr. Disord. 19(1), 1–9 (2019)
11. England, C.Y., Andrews, R.C., Jago, R., Thompson, J.L.: A systematic review of brief dietary questionnaires suitable for clinical use in the prevention and management of obesity, cardiovascular disease and type 2 diabetes. Eur. J. Clin. Nutr. 69(9), 977–1003 (2015)
12. Zullo, M.D., Jackson, L.W., Whalen, C.C., Dolansky, M.A.: Evaluation of the recommended core components of cardiac rehabilitation practice: an opportunity for quality improvement. J. Cardiopulm. Rehabil. Prev. 32(1), 32–40 (2012)
13. Brouwers, R.W.M., Houben, V.J.G., Kraal, J.J., Spee, R.F., Kemps, H.M.C.: Predictors of cardiac rehabilitation referral, enrolment and completion after acute myocardial infarction: an exploratory study. Neth. Heart J. 29(3), 151–157 (2020). https://doi.org/10.1007/s12471-020-01492-0
14. Lacroix, S., Cantin, J., Nigam, A.: Contemporary issues regarding nutrition in cardiovascular rehabilitation. Ann. Phys. Rehabil. Med. 60(1), 36–42 (2017)
15. Neutelings, I., Levy, P., Djajadiningrat, T., Hummels, C.: Enhancing co-responsibility for patient engagement. Des. J. 20(sup1), S2273–S2283 (2017)

16. Cho, S.M.J., et al.: Effect of smartphone-based lifestyle coaching app on community-dwelling population with moderate metabolic abnormalities: randomized controlled trial. J. Med. Internet Res. **22**(10), e17435 (2020). https://doi.org/10.2196/17435. PMID: 33034564; PMCID: PMC7584978

17. Brouwer-Brolsma, E., et al.: Dietary intake assessment: from traditional paper-pencil questionnaires to technology-based tools. In: Athanasiadis, I.N., Frysinger, S.P., Schimak, G., Knibbe, W.J. (eds.) ISESS 2020. IAICT, vol. 554, pp. 7–23. Springer, Cham (2020). https://doi.org/10.1007/978-3-030-39815-6_2

18. Fadhil, A.: Can a chatbot determine my diet? Addressing challenges of chatbot application for meal recommendation (2018). arXiv preprint arXiv:1802.09100

19. Rick, S.R., Goldberg, A.P., Weibel, N.: SleepBot: encouraging sleep hygiene using an intelligent chatbot. In: Proceedings of the 24th International Conference on Intelligent User Interfaces: Companion, pp. 107–108, March 2019

20. Schulman, D., Bickmore, T.W., Sidner, C.L.: An intelligent conversational agent for promoting long-term health behavior change using motivational interviewing. In: AAAI Spring Symposium: AI and Health Communication, March 2011

21. Kocielnik, R., Xiao, L., Avrahami, D., Hsieh, G.: Reflection companion: a conversational system for engaging users in reflection on physical activity. Proc. ACM Interact. Mob. Wearable Ubiquit. Technol. **2**(2), 1–26 (2018)

22. Burke, L.E., et al.: The effect of electronic self-monitoring on weight loss and dietary intake: a randomized behavioral weight loss trial. Obesity **19**(2), 338–344 (2011)

23. Nahum-Shani, I., et al.: Just-in-time adaptive interventions (JITAIs) in mobile health: key components and design principles for ongoing health behavior support. Ann. Behav. Med. **52**(6), 446–462 (2018)

24. Thomas, J.G., Bond, D.S.: Behavioral response to a just-in-time adaptive intervention (JITAI) to reduce sedentary behavior in obese adults: implications for JITAI optimization. Health Psychol. **34**(S), 1261 (2015)

25. Ortega, R.M., Pérez-Rodrigo, C., López-Sobaler, A.M.: Dietary assessment methods: dietary records. Nutr. Hosp. **31**(3), 38–45 (2015)

26. Gibson, R.S., Ferguson, E.L.: An Interactive 24-Hour Recall for Assessing the Adequacy of Iron and Zinc Intakes in Developing Countries (No. BOOK). ILSI Press, Washington, DC (1999)

27. Thompson, F.E., Subar, A.F.: Dietary assessment methodology. In: Nutrition in the Prevention and Treatment of Disease, pp. 5–48 (2017)

28. Bradley, J., et al.: Comparison of INTAKE24 (an online 24-h dietary recall tool) with interviewer-led 24-h recall in 11–24 year-old. Nutrients **8**(6), 358 (2016)

29. Subar, A.F., et al.: The automated self-administered 24-hour dietary recall (ASA24): a resource for researchers, clinicians and educators from the National Cancer Institute. J. Acad. Nutr. Diet. **112**(8), 1134 (2012)

30. Cordeiro, F., et al.: Barriers and negative nudges: exploring challenges in food journaling. In: Proceedings of the 33rd Annual ACM Conference on Human Factors in Computing Systems, pp. 1159–1162, April 2015

31. Epstein, D.A., Cordeiro, F., Fogarty, J., Hsieh, G., Munson, S.A.: Crumbs: lightweight daily food challenges to promote engagement and mindfulness. In: Proceedings of the 2016 CHI Conference on Human Factors in Computing Systems, pp. 5632–5644, May 2016

32. Noronha, J., Hysen, E., Zhang, H., Gajos, K.Z.: PlateMate: crowdsourcing nutritional analysis from food photographs. In: Proceedings of the 24th Annual ACM Symposium on User Interface Software and Technology, pp. 1–12, October 2011

33. Andrew, A.H., Borriello, G., Fogarty, J.: Simplifying mobile phone food diaries. In: 2013 7th International Conference on Pervasive Computing Technologies for Healthcare and Workshops, pp. 260–263. IEEE, May 2013

34. Almaghrabi, R., Villalobos, G., Pouladzadeh, P., Shirmohammadi, S.: A novel method for measuring nutrition intake based on food image. In: IEEE Instrumentation and Measurement Technology Conference (J2MTC), pp. 366–370 (2012)
35. Kong, F., Tan, J.: DietCam: regular shape food recognition with a camera phone. In: IEEE International Conference on Body Sensor Networks (BSN), pp. 127–132 (2011)
36. Wang, D.-H., Kogashiwa, M., Kira, S.: Development of a new instrument for evaluating individuals' dietary intakes. J. Am. Diet. Assoc. **106**(10), 1588–1593 (2006)
37. Oh, H., Nguyen, J., Soundararajan, S., Jain, R.: Multimodal food journaling. In: Proceedings of the 3rd International Workshop on Multimedia for Personal Health and Health Care, pp. 39–47, October 2018
38. Adamopoulou, E., Moussiades, L.: An overview of chatbot technology. In: Maglogiannis, I., Iliadis, L., Pimenidis, E. (eds.) AIAI 2020. IAICT, vol. 584, pp. 373–383. Springer, Cham (2020). https://doi.org/10.1007/978-3-030-49186-4_31
39. Piccolo, L.S.G., Troullinou, P., Alani, H.: Chatbots to support children in coping with online threats: socio-technical requirements. In: Designing Interactive Systems Conference 2021, pp. 1504–1517, June 2021
40. Belfin, R.V., Shobana, A.J., Manilal, M., Mathew, A.A., Babu, B.: A graph based chatbot for cancer patients. In: 2019 5th International Conference on Advanced Computing & Communication Systems (ICACCS), pp. 717–721. IEEE, March 2019
41. Kadariya, D., Venkataramanan, R., Yip, H.Y., Kalra, M., Thirunarayanan, K., Sheth, A.: KBot: knowledge-enabled personalized chatbot for asthma self-management. In: 2019 IEEE International Conference on Smart Computing (SMARTCOMP), pp. 138–143. IEEE, June 2019
42. Calvaresi, D., Calbimonte, J.P., Dubosson, F., Najjar, A., Schumacher, M.: Social network chatbots for smoking cessation: agent and multi-agent frameworks. In: 2019 IEEE/WIC/ACM International Conference on Web Intelligence (WI), pp. 286–292. IEEE, October 2019
43. Wang, H., Zhang, Q., Ip, M., Lau, J.T.F.: Social media–based conversational agents for health management and interventions. Computer **51**(8), 26–33 (2018)
44. Holmes, S., Moorhead, A., Bond, R., Zheng, H., Coates, V., McTear, M.: WeightMentor: a new automated chatbot for weight loss maintenance. In: Proceedings of the 32nd International BCS Human Computer Interaction Conference, vol. 32, pp. 1–5, July 2018
45. Elmasri, D., Maeder, A.: A conversational agent for an online mental health intervention. In: Ascoli, G.A., Hawrylycz, M., Ali, H., Khazanchi, D., Shi, Y. (eds.) BIH 2016. LNCS (LNAI), vol. 9919, pp. 243–251. Springer, Cham (2016). https://doi.org/10.1007/978-3-319-47103-7_24
46. Lee, Y.-C., Yamashita, N., Huang, Y., Fu, W.: "I Hear You, I Feel You": encouraging deep self-disclosure through a chatbot. In: Proceedings of the 2020 CHI Conference on Human Factors in Computing Systems, Honolulu, HI, USA, CHI 2020, pp. 1–12. Association for Computing Machinery, New York (2020). https://doi.org/10.1145/3313831.3376175
47. Vaidyam, A.N., Wisniewski, H., Halamka, J.D., Kashavan, M.S., Torous, J.B.: Chatbots and conversational agents in mental health: a review of the psychiatric landscape. Can. J. Psychiatry **64**(7), 456–464 (2019)
48. Fadhil, A., Gabrielli, S.: Addressing challenges in promoting healthy lifestyles: the al-chatbot approach. In: Proceedings of the 11th EAI International Conference on Pervasive Computing Technologies for Healthcare, pp. 261–265, May 2017
49. Prasetyo, P.K., Achananuparp, P., Lim, E.P.: Foodbot: a goal-oriented just-in-time healthy eating interventions chatbot. In: Proceedings of the 14th EAI International Conference on Pervasive Computing Technologies for Healthcare, pp. 436–439, May 2020
50. Casas, J., Mugellini, E., Khaled, O.A.: Food diary coaching chatbot. In: Proceedings of the 2018 ACM International Joint Conference and 2018 International Symposium on Pervasive and Ubiquitous Computing and Wearable Computers, pp. 1676–1680, October 2018

51. MiBida. https://mibida.nl/. Accessed 23 June 2022
52. Dutch Food Composition Database. https://www.rivm.nl/en/dutch-food-composition-dat abase. Accessed 29 July 2021
53. Kromhout, D., Spaaij, C.J.K., de Goede, J., Weggemans, R.M.: The 2015 Dutch food-based dietary guidelines. Eur. J. Clin. Nutr. **70**(8), 869–878 (2016)
54. Portie-Online. https://portie-online.rivm.nl/. Accessed 22 Apr 2022

Emoti-Office, Using Emotional and Contextual Data to Improve Employees' Working Needs in the Office

Rutger Verstegen$^{(\boxtimes)}$ (iD) and Regina Bernhaupt (iD)

Eindhoven University of Technology, Het Eeuwsel 53, 5612 AZ Eindhoven, Netherlands
`r.verstegen@student.tue.nl`, `r.bernhaupt@tue.nl`

Abstract. In a world of connected smart devices where data is easily available, there is an opportunity to enhance existing technology to better adapt towards office workers' needs. In this work, we explore the idea of how emotion can be one of many data points to be taken into account in a room planning calendar environment. We present Emoti-Office, a system that (1) collects emotional and contextual data in an office setting, (2) considers how to use this data and (3) how to link emotions with the desired output of a room suggestion or work environment to be reserved and used. Emoti-Office contributes to the field of office working research and development by proposing a context-aware and adaptive design which uses emotions to improve office workers' environment by adapting to their needs.

Keywords: Office · Emotions · Workers · Needs

1 Introduction

One of the key aspects when it comes to the productivity of people in an office environment is the emotional state. With current technological advancements, measuring data and controlling elements of office environments already gives many opportunities, on how to support people in the office environment. Nevertheless, the domain still seems underexplored when it comes to how emotions can be taken as data input for certain types of decisions and recommendations in office software and systems.

With the Internet of Things (IoT), everyday objects can have networked interconnections, allowing for communication with other devices or humans [1]. However, using these data and technologies to improve office settings is not a trivial task. It requires understanding what the user(s) needs and their desires are, in a wide range of situations where locations, participants, emotions and other variables might differ. The research question that this paper focuses on, is

© IFIP International Federation for Information Processing 2022
Published by Springer Nature Switzerland AG 2022
R. Bernhaupt et al. (Eds.): HCSE 2022, LNCS 13482, pp. 191–200, 2022.
https://doi.org/10.1007/978-3-031-14785-2_13

the following: "How can emotional- and contextual data be gathered and used with existing technology to adapt office environments to support employees' working needs?". This paper explores this design space and proposes a design concept called Emoti-Office.

Emoti-Office uses self-reported emotional state and calendar data as input. With this data, office situations can adapt accordingly for both individuals and groups of employees. This design is relevant because it researches the usage of existing IoT hardware with emotional input. In a workplace setting, this could allow for better adaptation of the workplace towards users' needs. Differentiating on workplace design has been identified as one of the three major factors that could improve the performance of knowledge workers [6].

The contribution of this work lays in the field of smart industry, exploring emotion as a possible element and proposing an initial design for such a system.

2   Related Work

Computers might benefit from knowing the situation of a user during interaction to adapt the environment more accurately to the user's needs [11]. More specifically, emotions have vital roles in background processes (such as decision-making, perception and creativity), and some subsets of emotions could improve systems [26]. Traditional inputs for computer interaction ignore the implicit emotional indicators, which is why they do not provide human-like natural interactions [29]. Expanding the area of Human-Computer Interaction with the inclusion of emotional communication and handling of the data is called Affective computing [24]. The literature there is vast and goes beyond this contribution to be detailed.

A key fact is that emotions and mental state can influence productivity. Previous studies show that happiness of employees is positively related to employee productiveness [3,15,23]. On the other hand, negative emotions are positively associated with counter-productive work behavior [2]. Emotions can change our attitude towards our current and next actions [25]. Emoti-Office measures emotions to better understand users, their needs and to let the workplace adapt to these needs.

For categorizing human emotions, there are two conventional methods: the discrete basic emotion description and the dimension approaches [18]. With the basic emotion description, are set numbers of basic emotions, such as research by Izard, which found 12 basic emotions [12] and more recently Jack et al. who argue for four basic emotions [13]. With the dimension approach, several dimensions organize emotional responses. Most often valence, arousal and approach-avoidance (urge towards or away from something) are used [20].

Understanding what people's emotions are, can be done by deriving these emotions from the body or by asking participants to self-report. Deriving emotions can be done using facial video and audio [21], heart rate variability [27], blood volume pressure [16] and head movements [29]. For self-reporting emotions, a wide range of designs have been already proposed in research, with a 2016 meta-review analyzing 40 interfaces from the past 11 years [9].

Bernhaupt et al. [4] have been doing seminal work in the early 2000s on how emotions can be integrated in a work environment, asking users to improve their emotion by smiling to control a game. While such a behavior change might not always be welcomed by users, a more neutral way to allow to self-identify emotions to influence for example room booking selection seems appropriate.

For understanding emotions in the office, some work already exists. For instance, the Mood Squeezer which allowed employees to set emotions to allow for discussion on emotion [10]. Next to that a system has been proposed to detect emotions using sensors and then regulate negative emotions in an office to improve productivity [22].

Both in scholarly writings and in everyday language, the words mood and emotion are often used interchangeably [7]. However, there are slight differences between mood and emotion, which will be described in the table below.

Table 1. Comparing Emotion and Mood on different properties [7].

	Emotion	Mood
Relative duration	Short	Long
Intensity	High	Low
Antedencents	Identifiable antecedents	Gradual onset with cumulative antecedents
Directed to	Particular object	World as a whole
Feeling	Specific feeling states	Diffused feeling states
Impact	Behaviours and thoughts	Global, pervasive influence on perception and motivation

As Table 1 shows, the focus of Emoti-Office lies on mood in office spaces and how this differs slightly from emotions. However, because both definitions often are used interchangeably and both concepts are this closely related, this paper will still refer to emotions as a key term.

3   Design Process

With a focus on using emotions in office situations, possibilities and design needs were explored together with potential users. The focused user group is office workers ranging from 18–40 years old. For this reason, the exploration sessions with users were held in real office situations to provide context. This research was conducted with approval from the ERB board of the Eindhoven University of Technology, Industrial Design.

3.1   Exploration Sessions

To gain a deeper understanding and get additional perspectives, participants were invited for design ideation sessions [14]. These were structured sessions for co-constructing stories [5] of what the solution could behave like, set in a focus group format. Following this methodology [5], participants were first introduced into the topic and asked for current experiences (sensitization phase). After this phase, the concept was introduced and participants were asked to write ideal scenarios where emotions were used in an office context (envisioning phase). From here, dialogue with the researcher and the participants in a focus group setup was had on these concepts to come to rich stories, design suggestions etc. with the group. After a pilot test, the choice was made for sessions with two participants to allow for more time per participant for in-depth explanations.

From two sessions with participants, the following results were generated during the discussion of the stimulation phase. Currently participants from both groups confirmed that (open) spaces were not good locations to allow office workers to work focused. Next to that, it was found that open office setups do not allow for having extreme emotions. For instance, participants indicated that feeling sad or happy could not be openly expressed in such a setting.

From discussing the envisioning phase, several key points for designs were generated. Firstly, participants stated that the design should help people process how they feel and support them in their working activities, instead of trying to change their emotions. From here, the idea arises from participants to focus on routines that people having in their working days, which could be combined with the idea of using Outlook calendars. Next to that, participants felt that the system should be transparent on how your data is used to generate results and that they would like control over the final decision.

4   Design: Emoti-Office

To understand the working needs of employees in different situations using existing technology, there are many variables that change an employee's desired response. To give a basis for understanding needs, Emoti-Office uses contextual and emotional data. Below, the functioning of the design will be explained in different sections.

4.1   Emotions

As discussed in the related work, various models on emotions have been proposed. This research uses the emotional model from Ekman [8] which has six basic emotions. This model was chosen over other work for its large testing in other fields. Next to the selection of an emotion, intensity of this emotion can also be selected.

To gather the emotion and intensity from employees, self-reporting was chosen as the preferred methodology. This is motivated from an ethical standpoint for two reasons. Firstly, the user of the system is aware that the emotion is being input and thus has more control over this personal data. Secondly, from a larger societal perspective humans can express their emotions differently based on culture [19]. The usage of self-reporting also can have the benefits of being portable, less intrusive, simple to implement and more accurate [9].

4.2   Context

Dependent on the situation of the employee, different needs might arrive. For instance, at your desk you have different needs compared to sitting in a meeting room or joining for a digital meeting. To understand the context, a company agenda solution such as Outlook could be used. Using the Outlook calendar event functions[1] data such as meeting location, participant amount etc. can be retrieved. For managing resources such as meeting rooms, desks or company equipment, communication with outlook can also be used. Here, room groups with labels could be introduced such as 'silence desks', 'talking desks' and 'meeting rooms'. These labels could differ per company and it's needs. This way, different room types for different activities could be booked using existing software infrastructure. By communicating with existing technology, adoption threshold of this new system is very low, because of low changes that need to be made in infrastructure, education and employee time investment.

4.3   Application Design

To combine the elements of self-reporting data, importing context and translating these into adaptations, an application can be used. This allows for entering of emotions regardless of an employee being close to a computer. From exploration sessions, users' preference towards a personalized and transparently functioning system were made clear. To do achieve this, users can set personal 'Routines' that are based on rules from variables. For instance, employees who like to sit at a certain desk on Mondays, or who want to sit in a 'quiet space' when answering emails. Whilst certain routines can most likely be applied for multiple people, many routines will

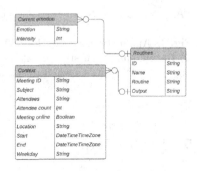

Fig. 1. Entity Relationship Diagram showing how rules and context determine routine activation.

be inherently personal and could depend on professional needs and an employee. Processing and storage of emotional and routine data, could be done locally to give employees more safety and security over their data, and to lower chances of employers viewing or deriving emotional data. A visualisation of data flow

---

[1] Microsoft documentation, last accessed 28-05-2022: https://docs.microsoft.com/en-us/graph/api/resources/event?view=graph-rest-1.0.

for this system is presented using an Entity Relationship Diagram which can be seen in Fig. 1.

Employees could set these routines up in the application. When the system creates a suggestion, it will show the respective suggestion for each routine. Users can then accept or deny these suggestions. Denying gives the options of allowing for one-time deviations, changing the routine outcome or making the routine more specific. This way, users are aware of how data is used, and have full influence over the system.

The application interface can be seen below in Fig. 2. A so-called 'Digital Twin' asks for current emotion, and duplicates the user's emotion in the application. Sketches for different emotions were designed specifically for this prototype for copyright reasons, but a platform such as Bitmoji[2] might be integrated to show customized digital twins.

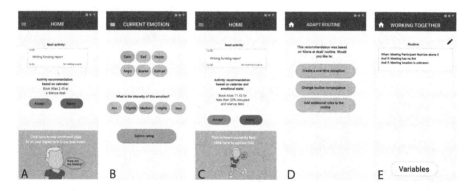

Fig. 2. Application screens for: A) Home screen with suggestion based on context B) Rating emotional state C) Digital Twin reflecting current emotion and improved suggestion D) Options when rejecting routine outcome E) Routine setting screen.

5   Evaluation

To evaluate the initial design, an remote online evaluation was performed by 46 participants (all above 18 years, 25 male, 18 female, 2 prefer not to say, 1 non-binary). Participants had experience in office situations. Online scenario testing was done for its feasibility and ability to test with a large and diverse group of participants.

Three scenarios with the designed system were created, which can be seen in Fig. 3. Each scenario showed a different element of the system: (A) changing an existing routine (B) using Outlook meetings to give spatial advice for working locations and (C) measuring emotion and executing a linked routine.

---

[2] Bitmoji platform, last accessed 28-05-2022: https://www.bitmoji.com/.

Scenario order was randomized to avoid sequencing effects. After each scenario, the After Scenario Questionnaire [17] was used to understand perceived task difficulty. After completing the three scenarios, the questionnaire combination by [28] was used to measure technology and personalization quality, empathy and behavioural intention for their fit with accessing the relevant features of the design. Here, the word 'products' was changed to 'space changes' in questions 4 and 11 to fit the research probe. Then, self-formulated questions were added to rate perceived influence on working needs, supporting emotions, and comparing situations with and without this system. Lastly, participants were asked to indicate whether they would use this system, and for reasoning on this choice.

Fig. 3. Screen captures from the three digital scenarios: A) Changing a routine B) Interaction between Outlook and system C) Rating emotional state. Images (before editing) retrieved from Pexels

5.1   Outcomes

Per scenario, after Scenario Questionnaire ratings and average rating per scenario were analyzed. Comparing the average values per scenario, no problems with perceived task difficulty were found (Scenario A: 5.14 avg, Scenario B: 5.14 avg, Scenario C: 5.34 avg).

Ratings on the combination scales [28] can be seen in

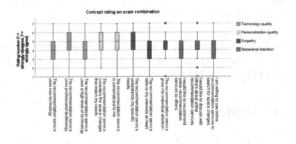

Fig. 4. Boxplots of ratings, color sorted on question category

Fig. 4. Averages were all in the mid-range of the 7 point scale and showed overall rather positive appreciation for the statements.

The final questions on the influence of this design on the working environment, support of needs in current work environment and the preference towards using this system were also analysed. The influence of the system leans towards positive in terms of supporting needs and giving space for emotions. Making negative -1, neutral 0 and positive 1, gives support in working needs an average of 0.43 and space for emotions an average of 0.36. Most respondents (65.2%)

indicate how working needs are already supported in their current working environment. 63% states to prefer having this design in their working environment. The evaluation thus shows no major usability problems and indicate that the proposed design is welcome by users.

6   Conclusion and Future Work

Emotions can be an important aspect in a work environment. Emoti-Office explores the possibility to integrate emotions in a calendar planning system and was perceived as a welcome addition.

First findings show how this system is perceived to improve working needs and space for emotions in the office on average. As future work, next to the contextual elements from Outlook, other data sets (such as weather) and sensors (such as personal smart devices, connected cars) could potentially be investigated as data input for such scenarios. Next to that, the addition of more prominently introducing emotions into the office could have (unforeseen) consequences, and thus deserves further research.

Next to that, further development and more implemented testing should be done. A possible limitation is the self-reporting of emotions. On the one side, users might not be truthful about them [9], however, as long as the emotional input is enhancing the system, we argue for using emotions to improve the user experience.

Emoti-Office contributes to the field of smart offices with design space exploration, a design, validation and future work recommendations. This work has significance in how it could yield existing technologies to further improve the needs of office workers.

Acknowledgement. The authors of this paper want to thank all participants of the evaluation study for contributing to this research and would like to thank Bas Goossen and Günter Wallner for their input.

References

1. Ashton, K., et al.: That 'Internet of Things' thing. RFID J. **22**(7), 97–114 (2009)
2. Bauer, J.A., Spector, P.E.: Discrete negative emotions and counterproductive work behavior. Hum. Perform. **28**(4), 307–331 (2015)
3. Bellet, C., De Neve, J.E., Ward, G.: Does employee happiness have an impact on productivity? Saïd Bus. Sch. WP **13** (2019)
4. Bernhaupt, R., Boldt, A., Mirlacher, T., Wilfinger, D., Tscheligi, M.: Using emotion in games: emotional flowers. In: Proceedings of the International Conference on Advances in Computer Entertainment Technology, ACE 2007, pp. 41–48. Association for Computing Machinery, New York (2007). https://doi.org/10.1145/1255047.1255056
5. Buskermolen, D.O., Terken, J.: Co-constructing stories: a participatory design technique to elicit in-depth user feedback and suggestions about design concepts. In: Proceedings of the 12th Participatory Design Conference: Exploratory Papers, Workshop Descriptions, Industry Cases-Volume 2, pp. 33–36 (2012)

6. Davenport, T.H., Thomas, R.J., Cantrell, S.: The mysterious art and science of knowledge-worker performance. MIT Sloan Manag. Rev. **44**(1), 23 (2002)
7. Desmet, P.M., Vastenburg, M.H., Romero, N.: Mood measurement with Pick-A-Mood: review of current methods and design of a pictorial self-report scale. J. Des. Res. **14**(3), 241–279 (2016)
8. Ekman, P.: An argument for basic emotions. Cogn. Emot. **6**(3–4), 169–200 (1992). https://doi.org/10.1080/02699939208411068
9. Fuentes, C., Herskovic, V., Rodríguez, I., Gerea, C., Marques, M., Rossel, P.O.: A systematic literature review about technologies for self-reporting emotional information. J. Ambient. Intell. Humaniz. Comput. **8**(4), 593–606 (2016). https://doi.org/10.1007/s12652-016-0430-z
10. Gallacher, S., et al.: Mood squeezer: lightening up the workplace through playful and lightweight interactions. In: Proceedings of the 18th ACM Conference on Computer Supported Cooperative Work & Social Computing, pp. 891–902 (2015)
11. Gross, T.: Towards a new human-centred computing methodology for cooperative ambient intelligence. J. Ambient. Intell. Humaniz. Comput. **1**(1), 31–42 (2010)
12. Izard, C.E., Libero, D.Z., Putnam, P., Haynes, O.M.: Stability of emotion experiences and their relations to traits of personality. J. Pers. Soc. Psychol. **64**(5), 847 (1993)
13. Jack, R.E., Garrod, O.G., Schyns, P.G.: Dynamic facial expressions of emotion transmit an evolving hierarchy of signals over time. Curr. Biol. **24**(2), 187–192 (2014)
14. Jonson, B.: Design ideation: the conceptual sketch in the digital age. Des. Stud. **26**(6), 613–624 (2005)
15. Kadoya, Y., Khan, M.S.R., Watanapongvanich, S., Binnagan, P.: Emotional status and productivity: evidence from the special economic zone in LaoS. Sustainability **12**(4), 1544 (2020)
16. Khezri, M., Firoozabadi, M., Sharafat, A.R.: Reliable emotion recognition system based on dynamic adaptive fusion of forehead biopotentials and physiological signals. Comput. Methods Programs Biomed. **122**(2), 149–164 (2015)
17. Lewis, J.R.: Psychometric evaluation of an after-scenario questionnaire for computer usability studies: the ASQ. SIGCHI Bull. **23**(1), 78–81 (1991). https://doi.org/10.1145/122672.122692
18. Liu, J., et al.: EEG-based emotion classification using a deep neural network and sparse autoencoder. Front. Syst. Neurosci. **14**, 43 (2020)
19. Marsh, A.A., Elfenbein, H.A., Ambady, N.: Nonverbal "accents": cultural differences in facial expressions of emotion. Psycholog. Sci. **14**(4), 373–376 (2003)
20. Mauss, I.B., Robinson, M.D.: Measures of emotion: a review. Cogn. Emot. **23**(2), 209–237 (2009)
21. Mower, E., Matarić, M.J., Narayanan, S.: A framework for automatic human emotion classification using emotion profiles. IEEE Trans. Audio Speech Lang. Process. **19**(5), 1057–1070 (2010)
22. Munoz, S., Araque, O., Sánchez-Rada, J.F., Iglesias, C.A.: An emotion aware task automation architecture based on semantic technologies for smart offices. Sensors **18**(5), 1499 (2018)
23. Oswald, A.J., Proto, E., Sgroi, D.: Happiness and productivity. J. Law Econ. **33**(4), 789–822 (2015)
24. Picard, R.W.: Affective computing for HCI. In: HCI (1), pp. 829–833. Citeseer (1999)
25. Picard, R.W.: Affective Computing. MIT Press, Cambridge (2000)

26. Picard, R.W.: Affective computing: challenges. Int. J. Hum. Comput. Stud. **59**(1–2), 55–64 (2003)
27. Quintana, D.S., Guastella, A.J., Outhred, T., Hickie, I.B., Kemp, A.H.: Heart rate variability is associated with emotion recognition: direct evidence for a relationship between the autonomic nervous system and social cognition. Int. J. Psychophysiol. **86**(2), 168–172 (2012)
28. Yoon, N., Lee, H.K.: AI recommendation service acceptance: assessing the effects of perceived empathy and need for cognition. J. Theor. Appl. Electron. Commer. Res. **16**(5), 1912–1928 (2021)
29. Zhao, Y., Wang, X., Goubran, M., Whalen, T., Petriu, E.M.: Human emotion and cognition recognition from body language of the head using soft computing techniques. J. Ambient. Intell. Humaniz. Comput. **4**(1), 121–140 (2013)

Correction to: Considering Users' Personal Values in User-Centered Design Processes for Media and Entertainment Services

Melanie Berger⬤, Guillaume Pottier, Bastian Pfleging⬤, and Regina Bernhaupt⬤

Correction to:
**Chapter "Considering Users' Personal Values
in User-Centered Design Processes for Media
and Entertainment Services" in: R. Bernhaupt et al. (Eds.):**
Human-Centered Software Engineering, **LNCS 13482,**
https://doi.org/10.1007/978-3-031-14785-2_8

In an older version of this paper, the first author's second affiliation was missing and Fig. 3 and Table 1 required changes. The paper has been corrected.

The updated original version of this chapter can be found at
https://doi.org/10.1007/978-3-031-14785-2_8

Author Index

Printed in the United States
by Baker & Taylor Publisher Services